FINDING HOPE

IN THE

AGE OF MELANCHOLY

FINDING HOPE
IN THE
AGE OF MELANCHOLY

David S. Awbrey

LITTLE, BROWN AND COMPANY

Boston New York London

First Edition

The author is grateful for permission to include the following previously
copyrighted material:
Excerpt from "Vacillation" reprinted with the permission of Simon and Schuster
from *The Collected Works of W. B. Yeats, Volume 1: The Poems,* revised and edited
by Richard J. Finneran. Copyright 1933 by Macmillan Publishing Company;
copyright renewed © 1961 by Bertha Georgia Yeats.
Excerpt from *Four Quartets,* copyright 1943 by T. S. Eliot and renewed by Esme
Valerie Eliot, reprinted by permission of Harcourt Brace & Company.

LIBRARY OF CONGRESS CATALOGING-IN-PUBLICATION DATA

Awbrey, David S.
    Finding hope in the age of melancholy / by David S. Awbrey — 1st
ed.
        p.   cm.
    ISBN 0-316-03811-3
    1. Hope — Psychological aspects.   I. Title.
BF575.H56A96   1999
128 — dc21   98-6267

10 9 8 7 6 5 4 3 2 1

MV-NY

Book design by Julia Sedykh

Printed in the United States of America

To my sister Marilyn,

who also has crossed the abyss

I have always thought
that this experience of melancholia of mine
had a religious bearing. . . .
The fear was so invasive and powerful
that if I had not clung to scripture-texts like
"The eternal God is my refuge," etc.
"Come unto me, all ye
that labor and are heavy-laden," etc.
I think I should have grown really insane.

WILLIAM JAMES

CONTENTS

ACKNOWLEDGMENTS

I would like to thank my agent, Suzanne Gluck, whose confidence in this project made it possible. The book could not have been done without the support and wise counsel of Bill Phillips, my editor at Little, Brown and Company.

I am also grateful to Dale Goter, whose friendship kept me reading the newspapers.

Special appreciation goes to Susan Awbrey, for reasons only the two of us know.

For her encouragement, guidance, and love, I am deeply indebted to my wife, Diane.

FINDING HOPE

IN THE

AGE OF MELANCHOLY

1

"THE AILMENT OF OUR AGE"

Into the Flames

Imagine being stripped of all hopeful emotion. Imagine all your aspirations suddenly going limp. Imagine everything that inspired you becoming trite. Imagine losing all positive thoughts. Imagine a complete deadness within yourself. Imagine life without flavor. Imagine a shapeless void where self-absorption had filled every nook an instant earlier. Imagine thinking that nothing has value, that life is a cruel hoax, that your personal character is based on self-deception. Imagine a bright red, yellow, and blue fire turning corpselike gray.

I don't have to imagine. It all happened to me.

It began in September 1991, the month I turned forty-three years old and reached my career pinnacle.

I wanted to be the complete journalist. I was born to it. My father was a great journalist. "Don't let the bastards get you down" was his primary career advice. My mother was a junior-high English teacher; my childhood dinner-table conversations often became corrective lessons in grammar and syntax. Education, political activism, Christian compassion, and public service were central family values. The New Testament verse "Every one to whom much is given, of him will much be required" was drilled into me from infancy.

I was the kid who delighted in telling the emperor he had no clothes; most of my career was as a newspaper editorial writer. A colleague gave me a button that she said captured my personality: 95 PERCENT OF EVERYTHING IS CRAP. I had a touch of the Puritan, a Cotton Mather tendency toward judgment and moralism. Twice, in different parts of the country, readers described me as a "self-righteous asshole." I took it as the ultimate professional compliment.

I got my first journalism job the old-fashioned way—through nepotism. My father asked a friend at a small newspaper in Iowa to give me a chance. Almost from the first day, my ambition was to become the editorial page editor of a major metropolitan newspaper, which in the journalism industry is defined as a paper with more than 100,000 daily subscribers. In September 1991 I would reach that goal.

It was even better that I would be the chief opinion writer for *The Wichita Eagle*, the largest newspaper in Kansas, my native state.

My family has been in Kansas since the wagon-train and cattle-drive days of the early 1880s. My great-grandmother, my grandmother, and my mother taught in Kansas schools. My great-grandfather had been a county judge, a city mayor, and a state legislator and in the 1920s had run unsuccessfully for governor of Kansas and for the U.S. Congress. My grandfather was a respected attorney in our family's hometown of Hutchinson.

My father began his journalistic career in the late 1930s, with famed Kansas editor William Allen White, "the sage of Emporia," and had worked as a reporter, editor, and publisher for the largest newspaper chain in the state for almost fifty years.

I graduated from Hutchinson High School and received a bachelor's degree in history and a master's degree in religious studies from the University of Kansas.

Whatever else Kansas is, it is home. It is where I belong.

I spent the first fourteen years of my career in journalism outside of Kansas — in Iowa, Maryland, Pennsylvania, Illinois, California, Nebraska — because I wanted to prove myself professionally away from my father. Indeed, when I worked the graveyard shift for United Press International in Maryland, my editor in Baltimore did not care that my father was one of the best-known journalists in the Midwest. All he wanted was the state news update for morning drive-time radio.

My father's death of cancer in 1985 prompted me to write George Neavoll, editorial page editor of the *Eagle*, about a job on his staff. By a coincidence that I interpreted as fate, an *Eagle* editorial writer resigned the day Neavoll received my inquiry, opening a position that I took in April 1986.

Five years later Neavoll was leaving Wichita to become editorial page editor of the newspaper in Portland, Maine. I was promoted at the *Eagle*, and on September 14, 1991, my wife and I were hosting George's going-away party at our house.

Many of the city's prominent citizens turned out to honor Neavoll: the mayor and members of the city council, the bishop of the Roman Catholic diocese and other clerics, respected professors from Wichita State University, numerous newspaper colleagues, the local member of Congress and a smattering of state legislators, a federal judge, and the leaders of several civic and charitable organizations.

In the summer before the party, Wichita had been in the

national news spotlight for the activities of Operation Rescue, a militant pro-life group that tried to close abortion facilities. Operation Rescue sent thousands of pro-life activists into the streets, many of whom were arrested for blockading clinics. A pleasant Midwestern city was torn apart by the most divisive issue of contemporary U.S. politics. Neighbor stopped speaking to neighbor; arguments broke out at workplaces; Christian charity was in short supply among the churches embroiled in the abortion dispute.

By mid-September the abortion protests had slackened, and the community was struggling to recover. By attracting people on both sides of the abortion debate, Neavoll's party represented a community healing, a chance for civic leaders to reconcile, or at least to reestablish civil relations among one another.

The harmonious mood was heightened by the coolness of a late summer's evening that drew the guests into the backyard garden.

Feeling good about the party's progress and smug about my career prospects, I wandered into the living room. I stood before the fire, the first of the season, confident that I was up to the challenges before me. I had been a well-regarded journalist on both coasts and several stops in between. I had won several professional awards. I appeared regularly on a statewide public television program to analyze and comment on the issues of the day. Now, I was to cap my career on a big-time newspaper — part of the Knight-Ridder chain, one of the nation's premier media corporations — located in a city fifty miles from my birthplace. I thought my father would have been proud that I was continuing his half-century legacy in Kansas journalism.

A bemused smile of self-satisfaction crossed my face. *So this is success,* I thought to myself, nodding my head in agreement. It certainly seemed so, judging by what I saw as I glanced around the living room. I definitely liked what the place said about me.

On the walls were fine-art prints and oil paintings, purchased in galleries from SoHo to Santa Fe that showed my quirky but discerning aesthetic taste. Crammed into a large curio cabinet was a collection of small statues of local deities brought back from Asia, Europe, and Latin America that symbolized my cultural sophistication. The well-crafted, Frank Lloyd Wright–influenced furniture, set atop a large Oriental carpet, combined my appreciation for fine styling and daily practicality.

I turned back to look into the fire, my glowing ego as warm as the blazing logs. Then it happened. My body started to shudder. I moved closer and stretched out my hands to the heat. My face felt ashen. My breathing quickened. My chest muscles tightened. A chill began in my lower back and spread to my gut and up through my lungs. I couldn't swallow. My essence emptied into a hellish fury of flames.

"Gross hypocrite," my inner voice said. "You'd better be happy, because you've got to live with what you have done."

It was the first time I had admitted the truth. George Neavoll, my mentor, the person who made me his assistant editor three months after I joined his staff and allowed me alone among his editorial writers to have a personal column, was partly a victim of my treachery. Like Jacob stealing Esau's birthright, I had helped shove George out of his job to take it myself. I now faced the personal consequences of my betrayal, of my rabid ambition that left no mercy for anyone who dared frustrate my aspirations for political and corporate power.

Business-management texts might cite it as a case study of tough-minded but necessary office politics, a Darwinian struggle for power that produces the strongest, most determined, and most savvy leaders for the corporation. George lost and left; I won and stayed.

George is an almost saintly man, a person who adopted stray dogs and always had a kind word for the lonely, often confused people who gravitate toward newspaper offices. Once while walking back to the *Eagle* after lunch, he picked a dead bird from the gutter and put it in his office refrigerator until a county wildlife officer could determine what it died from and, perhaps, warn of an impending avian epidemic. He was active in human-rights issues, conducting numerous letter-writing campaigns in the *Eagle* editorial pages on behalf of dissidents from Turkey to Taiwan. He was a borderline mystic and believed that an appeal for prayers he put in his Sunday column helped save his wife's life during a stroke. *Dignified, sincere, compassionate*—words seldom applied to journalists—described George.

But I was not content to be his lieutenant, his loyal subordinate. During the past year I had plotted his overthrow and my accession to the editorial page editor slot. I was a masterful guerrilla warrior, the Che Guevara of the opinion pages. I sensed severe tension between George and his boss, *Eagle* editor Buzz Merritt, and skillfully exploited that personality clash. A hard-nosed news veteran, the chief of the Knight-Ridder Washington bureau during the Watergate scandal, the editor who oversaw the Pulitzer Prize–winning story of Senator Thomas Eagleton's mental problems that knocked the Missourian off the 1972 Democratic presidential ticket, Buzz had little in common with George. I hitched myself to Buzz. I conspired in the gradual, drip-by-drip humiliation of the man who trusted me, a water torture of diminished prestige, perks, and authority. George's expense account was cut; he no longer could take trips to the conferences and seminars that kept him highly visible within the news profession and allowed him to bring his human-rights crusades to a broader audience. I replaced George in conducting the morning editorial staff meetings that set the paper's agenda. George's favorite issues—international human rights, the environment, a trolley system for Wichita—became lower profile. Editorial staff members got the unwritten message to take management matters to me, and they started treating George like a beloved but eccentric uncle—humor him, don't take him seriously. The word was subtly spread to the local leadership community that I was the key player in editorial decisions. I put on my most trustworthy face and in my most concerned, empathetic voice told George how sorry I was, and though I couldn't understand why, Buzz wanted him gone.

After thirteen years in Wichita, George took the first opportunity out.

And as I stared into the fire, I tumbled from the mountaintop of prideful self-satisfaction and landed on a vast psychic terrain flattened by despair, a frontierless geography of shame over my own disloyalty.

At first I denied that anything was wrong. Over the next few weeks, I poured myself into my new job. I wrote the kind of editorials I wanted to, the way I wanted to, on the subjects I cared about. I was shaping opinions, afflicting those who transgressed my moral and political visions, pontificating ideas I thought should be universally accepted. I lost myself in the daily swirl of meetings, deadlines, writing, and telephone calls. I pushed aside the memory of my dishonesty toward George and didn't allow it to enter my daily routine. I wanted to move on, suppress any incipient guilt, and fabricate an even stronger self-image to project my elevated professional status.

But at night, a time of reckoning. I usually got to sleep easily. Then, about 2 A.M., I had my regular bathroom run. Back in bed, I was joined by what I called the demons, sadistic inquisitors demanding responses to impossible questions: "Why me?" "Why is this happening?" "And just what is happening?" And while those interrogations hung in the air, a sphinxlike riddle filled my consciousness: "I've got what I wanted, why am I getting this?"

Dozing fitfully, I passed the next couple of hours with no

physical sensations, no palpable impulses, my life-spirit seemingly abducted by a sallow-complexioned pod person who strongly resembled me, but with none of the spark of my former self.

Finally exhausted, I would fall asleep about 4 A.M., and out of the deeply submerged, watery recesses of childhood terror an old nightmare arose.

When I was in the third grade, an amateur paleontologist came to our classroom to talk about dinosaurs, always a fascinating subject with kids. He said that 100 million years ago what is now Kansas was the center of a great inland ocean. The waters teemed with primitive fish, huge leatherback sea turtles, and giant swimming lizards called mosasaurs. Remains of those creatures are abundant in the chalk beds of western Kansas, which is a major source of fossilized marine vertebrates for museums around the world.

My eight-year-old mind was astonished by the mosasaur, which has been called the *Tyrannosaurus rex* of the primeval ocean. At a length of between thirty and fifty feet, the mosasaur was a voracious killer. With its gaping jaws and insatiable appetite, it would eat anything that got in its way and swallow its prey whole. During his lecture our classroom visitor displayed a fossilized mosasaur jawbone, its rapier-sharp teeth still capable of tearing through skin or scale, that was found just a few dozen miles from our school building. He also showed us an artist's rendering of a mosasaur vaulting out of the water to snag a flying pterodactyl with the grace of a largemouth bass taking a dragonfly.

For weeks I dreamed of the mosasaur. I would be swimming in the ocean and the beast would emerge from the depths and attack me. I would be sitting on the shore and the leviathan would rise up from the waves and drag me into the water. I would be jumping off a diving board and the reptile would leap to grab me in midair. Ever since, I have spastic shivers—unrepressed mosasaur memories?—whenever I am in an ocean or lake; I much prefer to swim in chlorinated pools.

Almost thirty-five years later the mosasaur reappeared in my dreams. In those blackest moments before dawn, I left late-twentieth-century America and found myself in the oceans of the Cretaceous period. *Chomp!* I disappeared headfirst into the guts of an eating machine. My body was merely a morsel, a tasty tidbit for one of the hungriest creatures ever to appear on earth. I could swim like an Olympic freestyle sprinter, yet with one flip of his massive tail the mosasaur would overtake me.

In his classic study, *The Understanding of Dreams and Their Influence on the History of Man,* French scholar Raymond de Becker says that fish or whales in dreams signify contact with deep psychic layers inaccessible to awakened consciousness. When they appear, Becker says, the dreamer can expect that formidable, if not fearsome, archaic forces are rising in the soul. In the Bible, for example, Jonah must live in the belly of a great fish—a profound regression into the soul—before recognizing divine truth. In *Moby Dick* Captain Ahab chases the white whale with a mystical love that is consummated only in death.

From Becker's insights I interpreted the nightmarish mosasaur as the symbol of my deceit toward George Neavoll. My career ambition had triumphed over basic human decency. But the moral crime wasn't just against George; it bludgeoned my personal self-respect, any claim I had to honor, fealty, and true friendship.

And what did I receive for my thirty pieces of silver?

I was devoured by the media mosasaur. Plunging to self-loathing, I was no longer in full control at work. Horrified by my capacity for villainy, distrustful of my motives, I lacked the inner confidence to stand apart from the incessant images and verbiage of the daily newspaper and television. I lived in the churning stomach of bold headlines, glib analysis, derivative opinion, chatter, titillation, and trifles that often substitute for informed wisdom in the modern media.

It is a despair that goes by many names—the blues, depression, melancholy, a Great Sadness—because no single term captures the lack of personal meaning and life purpose, whose absence makes sufferers feel that their world is in a state of constant collapse and fragmentation. And language, which tries to categorize and thus rationalize, adds to the pain. No description, no metaphor, no synonym, can provide the sanctuary of comprehension for ineffable feelings that defy definition.

The immediate cause of this darkness could be the death of a friend or family member, a lost job, a ruined love affair—any disappointment or difficult life transition. It could be a late-arriving inheritance from a troubled, abusive family life in which positive childhood emotions were blunted. It might be caused by an inability to cope with cultural upheaval. It might result from spiritual desolation among people who no longer feel accepted by a transcendent power.

It could also come at the height of personal success, turning the pleasure of accomplishment into self-revulsion from the shock of recognizing the shallowness of our own aspirations and the sheer vanity of a life of frenetic but totally self-centered activity.

But is melancholy only a private affliction?

A Social Epidemic

It's hard for journalists to see the connections, the intersections between a breaking news story and the deeper cultural movements that influence daily events. The first draft of history that appears in the morning newspaper is usually a rough outline that won't be filled in for years, and then probably by scholars rather than news-hounds. The larger context of American life is often obscured as each news cycle brings demands for fresh information; the news is chopped up to feed the yawning maw of the mass media and digested before the next day's offerings. Also, reporters tend to move from story to story—from beat to beat—and aren't able to pursue a long-term trend to its conclusion.

In more than two decades in journalism, I covered numerous stories tracing how fretful life has become for some Americans in the late twentieth century. Yet, because those stories centered on specific places and a limited number of individuals, I had no wide perspective on the pervasive changes hitting U.S. society. I saw people's lives fractured and their communities' hearts torn out by corporate and political actions made thousands of miles away, but the whole picture was disjointed; I noticed the small pieces, not the social mosaic.

While working for the Associated Press during the late 1970s, I was sent to the small town of Watsontown, Pennsylvania, where the local Zenith plant was closing. The factory was one of the last places in the United States that built television sets, and it was being shuttered because the manufacturing could be done more cheaply in Mexico or Asia. The story I wrote accentuated how the shutdown affected individual workers, many of whom had fol-lowed their parents into the plant and expected to be there the rest of their working lives; I met one young couple who had courted on the assembly line and now were left with no paychecks, a mort-gage, and two school-age kids. The loss of Zenith, the largest em-ployer in the region, also devastated the surrounding community by removing its economic lifeline.

A few years later I worked on a newspaper in southern Illinois and monitored the virtual collapse of the Midwestern coal indus-try. Federal environmental laws had made it uneconomical to burn high-sulfur Illinois coal, so the jobs of thousands of miners — and patterns of life that had existed for generations — were eliminated. My stories dealt primarily with the immediate political situation, the problems of air pollution and the impact that acid rain and other environmental issues had on coal miners, their families, and their communities. I will never forget the vacant stares of miners who had been buddies since grade school. With the closing of the mines, they could no longer afford the fees for their summer slo-pitch softball team that had kept alive their memories of boyhood, one of the few consolations in their payday-to-payday lives. A future programming computers? No, boozing and wife beating.

In the early 1990s the economics I had observed earlier in my career arrived down the hall from my office. Pushed for greater profits by Knight-Ridder executives in Miami eager to impress Wall Street money managers, *The Wichita Eagle* began to shed dozens of jobs. Many veteran employees were pressured to take early-retirement packages; some younger workers were put on the street with only a few weeks of severance pay.

But my job was safe, and I chalked up the layoffs to doing business today. A Knight-Ridder stockholder through the corporate 401(k) plan, I even admired my employer's cold-bloodedness.

Meanwhile, I read books, and reviewed some of them in the *Eagle,* by contemporary Cassandras warning of dire consequences facing the United States. Black intellectual Cornel West, in his book *Race Matters,* describes Americans as "rootless, dangling people" who suffer a "silent depression" because of the loss of industrial jobs and declining incomes. In *Head to Head,* economist Lester Thurow predicts that Europe will soon overtake the United States economically. Historian Paul Kennedy, in *Preparing for the Twenty-First Century*, forecasts worldwide environmental disaster. Former *New York Times* reporter Hedrick Smith cautions in his book *Rethinking America* that American society could crumble unless it adapts to new economic realities.

I lived in parallel worlds. I sympathetically bid colleagues farewell as I watched them clean out their desks and enter an uncertain job market. I then returned to my word processor to write editorials and columns on the need for U.S. corporations to restructure their operations and upgrade technology to compete in the global economy.

How myopic, how dimsighted I was. That's why it took an intense personal crisis to impel me to ask the serious questions about a late-twentieth-century American society that is mired in despondency.

Foremost, I realized that—like the job losses in Pennsylvania and Illinois and at the *Eagle*—my depression was not an isolated incident. The problems precipitating depression came in all sizes and from all directions, but I had lots of company. By all indications depression is epidemic in the late twentieth century: "Major depression is the most common problem a primary-care physician treats," said Dr. Wayne Katon of the University of Washington.

Evidence of the plague also is found in the large number of books published in the 1990s on the subject.

Beginning in 1990 with novelist William Styron's surprise bestseller, *Darkness Visible,* the list of widely read and critically acclaimed memoirs of depression includes Martha Manning's *Undercurrents,* Wilfrid Sheed's *In Love with Daylight,* Kay Redfield Jamison's *An Unquiet Mind,* Tracy Thompson's *The Beast,* and Elizabeth Wurtzel's *Prozac Nation.* Psychiatrist Peter D. Kramer's *Listening to Prozac,* which rings alarms about the effects of antidepressant drugs on personality and character development, has been one of the most controversial books of the decade.

Furthermore, stories about depression are a staple of television talk shows and newspaper feature sections; such well-known

Americans as journalist Mike Wallace, humorist Art Buchwald, and entertainer Dick Cavett have publicly discussed their depression; trend-hopping comedians always get an insider's laugh of recognition from their hip audiences merely by mentioning Prozac.

Although age-hobbled seniors and angst-ridden teenagers seem especially vulnerable to depression, the disorder is increasingly common among middle-aged Americans, many of whom are financially affluent, high-achieving, and otherwise successful individuals. Depression was cited by 66 percent of the physicians responding to a 1996 Gallup survey as the most common emotional health problem among men at midlife. A study of the Harvard University class of 1971, whose members include some of the nation's most privileged and wealthy individuals, found that almost one-third had experienced a difficult midlife crisis. In the March 1995 issue of the *Florida Bar News,* Benjamin Sells, a psychotherapist and former practicing attorney in Chicago, reported that in a survey of 105 occupations, lawyers ranked first in experiencing depression.

Depression also has received wide notice in the scholarly and popular press. During a search in December 1997 at the Wichita State University library, I found 3,273 entries on depression in the periodical index and another 557 listings in the book catalog.

Although the studies, monographs, dissertations, research reports, memoirs, and other writings often disagree over the exact causes of depression, the current medical consensus holds that it is mainly a physical ailment connected to brain chemistry or genetics. "The outlook for the patient suffering from depression is bright, for he or she is experiencing a treatable biochemical imbalance," says psychiatrist Ronald Fieve in his book *Moodswing.*

While not disputing the medical analysis that some people are biologically prone to depression, many social scientists think that the illness could be ignited by a patient's unique personal factors: gender, childhood difficulties, divorce, age, ethnicity, race, economic status.

Given America's legacy of Puritan piety, self-reliance, and rugged individualism, categorizing depression as a personal problem—linked to the individual's biological makeup and, perhaps, life condition—is understandable. Although some people in recent years have been quick to castigate society for their hardships, Americans don't typically define their personal troubles by their historical situation or make public issues of private stresses. Even during the economic downfall of the 1930s, for example, middle-class Americans often blamed themselves for their failure to prosper.

Considering depression as an autonomous entity and treating it with clinical detachment—as a medically curable condition regardless of cause—means that few Americans see melancholy as a spiritual or moral crisis, an outgrowth of contemporary culture that cuts across biological or sociological determinants. This medicalization of melancholy allows physicians and psychologists to avoid examining an American society that produces large numbers of depressives. Yet if a disease indicates that something is wrong with an individual, epidemics suggest that something is wrong with U.S. culture beyond the personal demographics and biochemistry of some of its melancholic members.

And that epidemic is growing as the century closes.

A study of depression published in the *Archives of General Psychiatry* in 1985 found that successive generations of Americans in the twentieth century have suffered higher rates of the ailment. In his book *Speaking of Sadness*, Boston College sociologist David A. Karp notes several studies showing that baby boomers have a higher incidence of depression than earlier generations. Adds Martin E. P. Seligman, a psychology professor at the University of

Pennsylvania who has written extensively on depression: "Every large-scale study of mental illness across the 20th century finds that contemporary Americans are more than 10 times as likely to have a major bout of depression as were their grandparents." Since human genetics and bodily chemistry haven't changed for millennia, the documented increase in depression over the past few decades can't be explained solely by biology.

Moreover, since human physical makeup is universal, the biological diagnosis fails to account for the wide disparity in depression among nationalities. As reported in the *Journal of the American Medical Association,* a study led by Myrna M. Weissman, a psychologist at Columbia University, found that depressive episodes in different countries varied by a factor of more than 10, with the United States and other Western nations having the highest rates.

For me, the best analysis comes from researchers who attribute much of the rise in depression to the drastic social shifts of the twentieth century—a period that saw the United States go from a primarily rural nation to an urban one; that witnessed sweeping political, economic, and technological change; that experienced a wholesale reordering in relations between the sexes; that, in summary, has been one of the most tumultuous epochs in history.

According to Dr. Frederick Goodwin, former director of the National Institute of Mental Health, the erosion of traditional moral restraints and the breakdown of cultural coherence have left many Americans without firm social mainstays.

"In the same era that we have seen, essentially, a doubling of depression among the young," he said, "we've seen a doubling of divorce rates, a sharp decline in net parenting time and a tripling of the mobility rate"—all of which weaken the bonds of authority and set people loose to grapple with society as best they can.

"We live in a society that places less and less emphasis on getting along with others," said Barry Schlenker, psychology professor at the University of Florida. "The world is a place where people are on their own."

Alienated. Burned out. Despairing. Strung out. From "depresso-rock" singers and "junkie chic" fashion models, from church pulpits and pop psychology, from self-help manuals and scholarly tomes, those words describe millions of Americans in the 1990s.

And the problem is not just in their head.

Angels of Melancholy

One of the most telltale indicators of the cultural anxiety of the late twentieth century is the arrival of thousands of angels—on bedspreads, wallpaper, earrings, night-lights, ceramic doodads, and almost anything else that can fit a heavenly host. Seraphim, cherubim, thrones, dominations, virtues, powers, principalities, archangels, and angels: the entire celestial hierarchy has swarmed over the United States; polls show that 69 percent of Americans believe in angels and that 46 percent of the respondents think they have a personal guardian angel.

Not since John Milton wrote *Paradise Lost* in the seventeenth century have angels been as prominent as they are in the 1990s. And because popular culture reflects social mood, the flocks of angelic beings indicate that millions of Americans feel that life has become so chaotic that they need supernatural help.

Part of it is superstitious jitters at the end of the millennium, a quiver both meaningless and portentous—like watching a car odometer turning from 99,999 miles to 00,000, suggesting both a new beginning and a loss of the familiar. Although scholars argue that calendar makers centuries ago miscalculated Christian chronology, and the new millennium actually started uneventfully sometime in 1997, apocalyptic angst goes unrelieved.

Eschatological tremors, however, are predictable for the dying moments of the 1990s. The fin de siècle often produces convulsive cultural dynamics. The late eighteenth century, for example, saw the French Revolution and the Industrial Revolution that set the European political and economic framework for decades to come. It also witnessed provocative literary ideas—from Goethe, Blake, Rousseau, Coleridge, and others—that led to the Romantic era and still affect us today. Likewise, the late nineteenth century was a tempestuous period in the arts, politics, and philosophy—Nietszche, Freud, the Impressionist painters, Oscar Wilde—that swept away long-accepted habits of mind and behavior.

As the twentieth century expires, people and society are on the edge. The decade of the 1990s is characterized by political acrimony, economic insecurity, artistic anarchy, intellectual confusion, religious uncertainty, a fear of the future, and a loss of permanence. People lack psychological moorings. They feel victimized by uncontrollable historical forces. Personal relationships are unstable. Morals are fluid. And social foundations are shaky.

Are those factors causes or symptoms of a deeper cultural eruption? Is the loss of nerve simply a personal failure? Is the crisis of self-confidence the death rattle of a decadent civilization? Could the words that poet T. S. Eliot wrote in 1925 be a prophetic vision of Americans in the 1990s? "We are the hollow men / We are the stuffed men. . . . Shape without form, shade without color."

According to one of the decade's important plays, the spiritual vacuum of contemporary America also affects the company of heaven.

Tony Kushner's epic two-part drama, *Angels in America,* winner of the Pulitzer Prize and several Tony awards in the early 1990s, centers on Prior Walter, a gay character and AIDS victim.

Prior's visiting angel is the Continental Principality of America, who claims to be the same angel who appeared in the early nineteenth century to Joseph Smith, the founder of the Mormon religion. In a climactic scene the angel complains to Prior that God—"Bored with His Angels, Bewitched by Humanity"—has deserted paradise because he is fascinated by earthly activities.

In words that also could depict contemporary America, the angel describes a God-forsaken heaven:

> *And bitter, cast-off, We wait, bewildered;*
> *Our finest houses, our sweetest vineyards,*
> *Made drear and barren, missing Him.*

The terminally ill Prior, however, resists replacing the angel as the voice of prophecy, the herald of miraculous events, the trumpeter of a new millennium. Instead, in Kushner's play, America in the late twentieth century is beyond redemption, wasting away from diseases of the flesh and the spirit, of interest to God only as a diverting amusement.

Americans in the 1990s have more sources of stress than any generation in recent memory. No single clear and present danger, as in the Great Depression or World War II, but a constellation of worries test the nation's energy, unity, and good humor. The United States has met the physical needs for most of its citizens, but it confronts a psychological and cultural crisis of a magnitude rarely experienced in its history. It is a social illness with many symptoms but no accepted diagnosis, no precise definition that could aid in treatment.

My description for the late twentieth century is the "Age of

Melancholy," a phrase taken from Søren Kierkegaard, one of the most influential philosophers of the modern era, who said that "melancholia is the ailment of our age." The term captures something of the gray, brooding cloud covering the current American psychic horizon.

The trajectory that Western society has followed since the Renaissance is sputtering downward. Over the past half millennium, Western civilization could be read as a progressively upward story of the liberation of the individual. Human reason and scientific inquiry became the primary standards for truth. God was dethroned as the ultimate authority, leaving humanity with no challenger to earthly or cosmic supremacy. It was a magnificent effort, one that produced incredible wealth, technological innovation, philosophical insight, and political freedom. All that has been for the good—up to a point.

That point has been reached in the late twentieth century. Although benefiting from the struggles and living the fulfilled visions—political liberty, material comfort, high levels of education—of their ancestors, few contemporary Americans are content with their lives. Part of that stems from humanity's innate restlessness, but something deeper is happening. Things no longer seem guaranteed to get better and better.

American society appears trapped in a cultural cul-de-sac. Hopes that social discontent could be stifled by economic prosperity haven't panned out. Similarly, hopes that mental-health therapies could alleviate emotional misery have not been totally realized. Yes, both financial security and personal stability are highly desirable, but millions of well-educated, affluent Americans with money and access to the best psychological treatment feel that their lives are less interesting, less purposeful, and less meaningful than they should be. Instead, they feel victimized by a powerful economy of distraction that grows rich by producing ever newer

ways to divert them from boredom, anxiety, and spiritual emptiness. Many people lack an organizing mission in life; they feel a
void where there should be a core of values.

That's why when angels come to America in the 1990s, they
bring tidings of melancholy.

Downsized, Disengaged, and Demoralized

After some of the most extensive polling of the 1990s, Daniel
Yankelovich concluded that "the American public is in a foul
mood. People are frustrated and angry. They are anxious and off
balance. They are pessimistic about the future and cynical about all
forms of leadership and government."

A respected public opinion analyst, Yankelovich added, "The
levels of American cynicism, resignation, and shoulder-shrugging
equal or even surpass those of world-weary Europeans."

Certainly the current generation could be knocked as ungrate-
ful, tantrum-throwing pouters. Americans today live in bigger
houses, drive better cars, have longer life expectancies, hold more
college degrees, play with a greater variety of electronic gadgets,
and take more exotic vacations than did their parents.

Moreover, the country is not at war and faces no mortal foreign
threat. It is not engulfed in domestic unrest or violent political
conflict. It is not on the brink of economic depression. National
crime rates are dropping. Unemployment is at a record low. Welfare rolls are decreasing. Even the much-chafed-over federal bud-
get deficit is declining, and inflation in the late 1990s is barely
a blip.

Nevertheless, millions of Americans feel a nagging unease
about the future and their place in it, a dissonance between what

they read in the economic statistics and their personal well-being. Americans are doing better but feeling worse. "When people talk of the economy being strong, they don't seem to feel that they too are better off," said Daniel Kahneman, a psychologist at Princeton University who studies social and labor issues.

Although help-wanted classifieds are chock-full of ads, many Americans feel vulnerable in their own jobs and fear they couldn't find other work that pays as well. They have a vague sense that although they earn good wages, the nation's growing economic inequality can't be good for themselves or the country. And while family income has inched up in the past few years, most of the new money comes not from raises but from people working longer hours. To boost their international competitiveness, many U.S. corporations have cut jobs and benefits and sent work overseas, further undermining financial security among millions of Americans. Meanwhile, even as they risk their children's college tuition and their own retirement funds on a continued boom in the stock market, many Americans are frazzled by economic volatility and feel little control over their lives.

This is not what I and most other college-educated baby boomers bargained for at the launch of our professional careers. When we joined the workforce, most of us now middle-aged, middle-class, middle-management Americans accepted the implied corporate promise that loyalty and job proficiency would bring a lifetime of regular promotions, heftier paychecks, and a retirement of travel, golf, and sunshine. Today, at a time when many of us corporate warriors have spent twenty or more years in frontline trenches and anticipated settling into a deeply grooved pattern of life, the old business order has melted and we are seeing rewards we sought for a lifetime evaporate.

Once perched comfortably in vice-presidential or regional-sales executive suites, collecting frequent-flier miles as medals of corporate valor, identities embossed on business cards, millions of hard-charging, follow-the-rules baby-boom Americans have found ourselves as nothing more than dispensable overhead to boards of directors obsessed with meeting the covetous demands of Wall Street speculators. Rather than as members of a corporate family, we are treated as assorted "skills packages" valuable only for our profit-generating potential. Yet, for many Americans, personal lifestyle expectations have not been downsized to match precarious careers.

The United States in the 1990s suffers from what sociologist Daniel Bell called the "cultural contradictions of capitalism"—the traditional Protestant ethic that encouraged Americans to deny themselves and sacrifice for the future has been shunned in favor of an ethic of consumption, a rampant consumerism based on immediate gratification, an insatiable appetite for material goods, power, pleasure, and a "he who dies with the most toys, wins" mentality.

Few win that game, but it's the middle class's favorite sport.

The belief that more stuff would appease Americans has been dispelled in the late twentieth century. In 1957, when economist John Kenneth Galbraith published *The Affluent Society*, which scrutinizes the rising consumer culture, the average American's annual income was less than $8,000 in inflation-adjusted dollars. Today, the per capita income is more than $16,000, and Americans enjoy a much more materially luxuriant lifestyle than forty years ago. Yet, according to the University of Chicago's National Opinion Research Center, the number of Americans describing themselves as "very happy" with their lives dropped from 35 percent in the late 1950s to 29 percent in the 1990s.

What's notable about the 1990s is that Americans increasingly worry about the nation's core values, which in previous eras had provided a durable cultural foundation regardless of political discord or economic disquiet. For example, a Gallup poll taken shortly before the 1996 presidential election found that 78 percent of Americans thought the nation's moral values were weak. By a 53 percent to 38 percent margin, they put morality above economics as the nation's primary problem. While corporate earnings and the stock market soared in the 1990s, so did illegitimacy, illegal drug use, and reports of spouse abuse.

The erosion of individual and national confidence caused partly by economic insecurity and moral ambiguity has isolated Americans just when they need connections and attachments. The fear, anger, and grief that have devastated families also have turned many communities into social ghost towns.

One of the great concerns of the 1990s is the loss of the "civic virtues" that once glued society together. Observers since Alexis de Tocqueville, author of the classic nineteenth-century study *Democracy in America,* have noted the central role that voluntary, religious, and charitable associations play in America. But in the past few years, many Americans have turned inward and withdrawn from churches, YMCAs, Elks Clubs, the Red Cross, and similar groups that give society equilibrium, enable people to engage one another as neighbors, and provide a focus for life other than narrow personal interests.

The same estrangement occurs within the family. According to Laurence Steinberg, a psychology professor at Temple University, many parents have become "seriously disengaged" from their children's lives. A Steinberg study found that at least 25 percent of parents were passive or negligent toward their children. Only one in three children reported daily conversations with their parents, and half of the parents said they did not know their kids' friends or where their children went after school. Similarly, the *Journal of the American Medical Association* reported that mothers and fathers now spend an average of ten to twelve hours less with their children than in the 1960s.

In the 1990s the traditional social cement—economic stability, community institutions, strong families, a common values system—has crumbled. Many Americans who were once community-spirited activists are huddling inside their individual shells, hoping to avoid the social storms swirling around them and to protect what they have.

And, sapped by melancholy, Americans in the late twentieth century don't seem to have the boldness and courage earlier generations summoned in their times of national difficulty.

Change Agents

In a pivotal scene in David Hare's play *Racing Demon,* the Reverend Lionel Espy is being rebuked by his bishop. It seems that Espy has neglected the sacraments and is burned out by the religious life.

"I would even say the church was a joke," Espy tells his superior. "In our area it's an irrelevance. It has no connection to most people's lives."

Although Hare's play, first produced in 1990, centers on the contemporary Church of England, it also applies to other major social and political institutions in the late twentieth century.

In a 1995 interview with *The New Yorker,* Hare said that he encountered chronic disenchantment within the Anglican Church while researching his drama. "Many of the clergy I've met have a pervasive melancholy—a sadness," he said.

The ennui Hare detected is significant because tap-root institutions such as the Church of England nurture Western civilization's most hallowed traditions. It's a critical historical sign if they become extraneous to the lives of average people, as Hare implies is the case with the Anglican Church that has fostered English cultural and social life since the reign of Queen Elizabeth I in the sixteenth century.

When long-established institutions no longer elicit people's trust or confidence, people lose an element of stability in their lives. In Western history, churches, universities, legislative bodies, families, and communities have helped create a cultural matrix that offered security, a feeling of belonging, and a comprehensive worldview. In the late twentieth century the institutional web that defined culture, set customs, and put private concerns into a wider social network has been ripped apart.

The dissolution of moral and intellectual principle is especially noticeable at the highest level of learning in America. Once the guardians and transmitters of traditional Western values, major U.S. universities, primarily in the social sciences and humanities, are places of distraction and bewilderment in the 1990s—even to the point of dismissing the pursuit of absolute truth as a worthless endeavor.

Under such labels as deconstruction, postmodernism, and critical theory, intellectual thought in the 1990s is characterized by randomness, relativism, nihilism, marginality, and other terms that suggest an end to the historic Western search for a common wisdom.

Although universities once incubated intellectual thought that often grew into social action, academic journals today are so packed with specialized verbiage that they are impossible for the educated layperson to comprehend. Each discipline has carved out a pedantic ghetto and barred outsiders from entry with a wall of polysyllabic blabber. The ivory tower has never been more remote from the concerns of general society, meaning that some of the nation's sharpest brains have deserted the less-degreed American citizenry.

Fortunately, whenever people become morally befuddled, politically disillusioned, and spiritually despondent, Western civilization has a record—perhaps a latent survival instinct—of thrusting certain individuals forward to redefine society. Many of these individuals suffer from melancholy and match British philosopher Bertrand Russell's description that "those with any imagination and understanding are filled with doubt and indecision." These people are attuned to society's underlying tensions, and their frustration and discontent help generate new artistic perceptions, political goals, or philosophical concepts that rejuvenate society.

In his book *Man's Search for Himself,* psychologist Rollo May portrays these people as follows: "By and large they are the ones for whom the conventional pretenses and defenses of society no longer work. Very often they are the more sensitive and gifted members of society."

May's observation dovetails with the research previously cited that many of today's melancholics come from society's top strata —doctors, lawyers, corporate executives, and other individuals who have achieved great professional and social stature. Despite their accomplishments, many of these people are intensely sad; their psychic antennae have picked up deep disturbances in themselves and society.

In an egalitarian democracy like the United States it may be politically incorrect to say such things, but the cosmopolitan upper echelon is usually the avant-garde of Western civilization. By virtue of their education, natural abilities, and often vibrant personalities, members of the cultural and economic elite can reshape culture.

This argument is expanded upon later, but in retrospect, culturally sophisticated melancholics can be seen as both the morticians of an old consciousness and the midwives of a cultural and spiritual rebirth. The remarkable transformations of the Renaissance and Reformation, for example, were accompanied by widespread complaints of melancholy among artists and religious visionaries. The Romantic poets and painters of the early nineteenth century expressed a nostalgic melancholy for the past and looked with foreboding upon the nature-destroying Industrial Revolution. The late nineteenth century was not only the belle epoque that reimagined art, fashion, and literature but a time of physical and mental exhaustion and moral apathy among much of the West's cultural elite.

To me, the melancholy of the late twentieth century might be a harbinger of change comparable to those previous eras. I resurrect an idea from earlier generations that melancholy can be a means to acquire greater truth about life—that depression can be a sublime discontent. Through despair, people can clarify what is important in life, connect themselves to timeless reality, and create a cherishing society. Out of the current cultural malaise could come the reaffirmation of the religious, moral, and political heritage that constitutes Western civilization's best contribution to humanity.

My premises are controversial. They question the prevailing opinion among many professionals that depression is merely another disease that can be treated as the mental equivalent of a broken leg. My arguments go beyond the accepted practices—as effective as those therapies might be to relieve depressive symptoms—of anesthetizing melancholics with psychoactive drugs and persuading them that most of their emotional complaints could be cognitively rearranged.

This book is not a confessional of depression or a testimonial of recovery. That's been done by people much more skilled than me in the literary arts. I have neither the novelist's talent nor the poet's gift to capture the hellish emotions and disabling fears that accompany depression. Public self-disclosure is not my natural instinct.

In my self-perception I am a meet-the-deadline journalist, lacking only the pulled-brim hat, coffee-stained trench coat, ash-dropping cigarette, and direct phone line from the police station to the rewrite desk to match the Hollywood stereotype. In my newspaper career, facts and events, rather than personal feelings or artistic impulses, dictated what I wrote.

Depression, however, sent me toward self-discovery — to a quest for what novelist William Faulkner called the "eternal verities." This book is my account of my search for significance.

The Suffering Self

As outlined by Erik Erikson, the famous psychoanalyst and a specialist in human development, a healthy personality is formed from the proper balance between inner stability and social solidarity. People want to see themselves as unique, but they also want a nourishing social environment. Rapid change, however, makes individuals and societies grope for coherence. That is what is happening in the late twentieth century: people are jury-rigging their own identities to help them cope with a stressed-out culture.

Without sound social architecture, people are poor craftsmen of their own characters. "If the social context is unreliable, it follows that he (the individual) cannot say anything legitimately and reliably about himself," Erikson says. Yet rather than concentrate on personal integrity and moral consistency, American society has surrendered to what sociologist Philip Rieff called "the triumph of the therapeutic," in which psychology, medicine, and bureaucracy have largely replaced the spiritual teachings, ethical values, and historical awareness that once gave Western civilization its special vitality.

I emphasize cultural and religious history to explain the current wave of melancholy. Could it be—is it possible?—that depression is God's way of breaking down human arrogance and renewing the traditional bonds between the divine and its creation?

The relentless secularism of the late twentieth century, when not ridiculing claims of God's direct participation in human undertakings, dismisses perceptions of spiritual causation as superstition or interprets them as literary metaphors. History, however, can be conceived as something other than humanity's ongoing evolution from the primitive mists of religious mythology to the supposedly clear light of human reason, logic, and science. Indeed, for most of Western history, people assumed God's handiwork in their affairs.

The most riveting instances of God's intervening in history are such miracles as the parting of the Red Sea or an unexpected victory in a great military battle. Yet, as impressive as those events are, the most powerful evidence of God's activity comes from human suffering.

For example, Jesus Christ endured incredible humiliation on the cross to redeem human sin. Saint Francis abandoned his privileged life to preach to the wretched poor. Inspired reformers like Jane Addams practiced a social gospel in the most miserable neighborhoods of urban America. The Reverend Martin Luther King, Jr., expanded justice through the liberation struggle of America's oppressed. And one of the true saints of the twentieth century, Mother Teresa, found God through her painstaking work in the fetid slums of Calcutta.

An exceptionally powerful account of God's acting through

human pain is the biblical book of Isaiah, which discusses the figure of the Suffering Servant. Written during the Babylonian Captivity, when the Hebrews were in exile and the future of their nation was at stake, the prophetic Songs of the Servant center on God's working in human history. God uses the Servant, described by Isaiah as "a bruised reed" and "the man of sorrows," to introduce the new era of history that would begin with the return of the Hebrew community to Jerusalem following its imminent emancipation by the Persian king Cyrus. Enduring grief laid on by God, the Servant suffers severely, but he is finally exalted as an instrument of the divine historical plan.

Suffering humbles human pride, which rages in the late twentieth century. Despair often induces people to ask fundamental questions about existence, especially when it is experienced during times of economic prosperity and technological ingenuity that heighten human power. Depression can teach people that they can't rely on themselves to solve the problems of life and exposes them to their own weaknesses. The cure is to turn to the ultimate source of strength, God, who uses suffering to compel people to confront the inescapable human condition of flawed, finite beings who seek infinite meaning.

Any lasting significance and purpose in life must arise from the belief that history is not an accidental series of haphazard events, that there is a coherent plot to the human story that eventually makes sense. Faith requires people to acknowledge that human reason alone can't explain all things. It is what the melancholic Hamlet means when he tells his rationalist friend Horatio: "There are more things in heaven and earth . . . than are dreamt of in your philosophy."

Burdened by melancholy, I sought a religious faith that would be viable for myself and other temperamentally skeptical Americans in the late twentieth century. As explained later, it is not a brain-dead faith in a grandfatherly deity who ensures our worldly prosperity and quickly forgives our misdeeds, but a connection to what theologian Paul Tillich called "the ground of being." It is the doubt-tinged faith of "Pascal's wager," which asks people to bet whether they would be better off believing in God or not. It is the courage to take Kierkegaard's "leap of faith," which dares humanity to discard vanity in a desperate jump toward divine truth. It is a faith that finds joy in searching for the Holy Grail with no expectation of holding it in our hands—a faith that is truthful according to its practical results in easing what philosopher William James labeled "the sick soul."

Although prompted by my personal trauma, this book isn't an idiosyncratic analysis, a fanciful conceit that the Age of Melancholy of the late twentieth century could open a new chapter in the human story. My mentors include some of the best minds of Western civilization.

Especially influential for me has been British historian Arnold Toynbee, whose massive *A Study of History* is a landmark of twentieth-century scholarship. In a lecture given at Oxford University in 1940, Toynbee asserted that a spiritual interpretation might be the only way to make sense of history.

"If religion is a chariot, it looks as if the wheels on which it moves towards Heaven may be the periodic downfalls of civilizations on Earth. It looks as if the movement of civilizations may be cyclic and recurrent, while the movement of religion may be on a single continuous upward line," Toynbee said.

Toynbee argues that the higher religions—Christianity, Islam, Judaism, Buddhism—are convergent paths leading to the same spiritual truths. Although the post–Cold War world has been afflicted by religious strife and close-minded fundamentalism, the global society also has exposed many people to other spiritual traditions. Buddhism and Islam, for instance, are among the fastest-growing religions in the United States, and Christianity has found millions of converts in such non-Western countries as South Korea and Nigeria. As the world becomes more interdependent, humanity's understanding of itself and God could deepen. "In this matter of increasing spiritual opportunity for souls in their passages through life on Earth, there is assuredly an inexhaustible possibility of progress in this world," Toynbee wrote.

From Toynbee and other writers, artists, and philosophers mentioned in this book, I'm convinced that the most potent figures in Western history aren't princes, presidents, or generals, but spirit-starved, anxiety-wracked individuals seeking meaning in life. That description fits millions of Americans at the end of the twentieth century. And that's why, although it presents some dire observations about the current situation, *Finding Hope in the Age of Melancholy* is an optimistic book. Melancholy could be the divine voice that compels Americans to discover themselves, build their communities, and explore their soul.

2

MIDDLE OF THE STORM

Bright Futures in the Past

Until the time I stood blank-eyed, ashen-faced, and soul-depleted before the fires of melancholy, all I knew about the midlife crisis came from such movie comedies as *Middle Age Crazy* and *Carnal Knowledge,* in which guys risk their careers and long-standing re-lationships to try to capture the fervor and sexual vitality of their youth. Prior to George Neavoll's party, midlife complaints were laughable to me—self-pity by men who poured Rogaine on their balding heads, liposuctioned their middle-aged guts, and sought a hot young "trophy wife" because they couldn't face the harshness of aging or let go of the "glory days" of high school sports, college fraternities, or early career triumphs.

Understanding of my melancholic crash began in the psychol-ogy section of the Wichita Public Library, where I found a small book that validated my misery. In 1975 Sam Keen, a psychologist and bestselling author, published *Beginnings Without End,* a jour-nal he kept during a time of profound personal trouble.

As he neared age forty, Keen fell in love with a younger woman and divorced his wife, the mother of his children. "Beyond question I found myself at mid-life in a radical crisis; like a plant whose roots had been torn from accustomed soil," Keen wrote.

One morning Keen realized the toll his crisis had taken. His ex-wife had remarried. His lover had left him. His academic career was in shambles. "Depression lurked and easily invaded any empty moment," Keen says.

My emotional pain and instincts as a professional journalist said that Keen and I had been thrown into something more than a personal crisis—something pivotal to America in the late twentieth century and even to the human condition. Although I had covered presidential election campaigns, interviewed Nobel Prize winners, reported natural disasters, and analyzed historic political developments, I was now both subject and chronicler of the biggest story of my journalistic career.

I listened to doctors at the Menninger Foundation in Topeka, Kansas, one of the nation's leading psychiatric institutions: "The midlife crisis is real. Depression often comes in the forties, fifties, or sixties, when life really does change," said Dr. Kathryn Zerbe. "We know we have reached the peak of our career, we are not as sexy, and our kids are growing up and having lives of their own."

I read books: Howell Raines's poignant memoir, *Fly Fishing Through the Midlife Crisis,* in which the editorial page editor of the *New York Times,* an influential figure in U.S. politics, finds that power and status offer no exemption from middle-age distress; psychologist Ross Goldstein's *Fortysomething,* which tries to help baby boomers navigate the shoals of middle age; and clinical psychologist James W. Jones's *In the Middle of This Road We Call Our Life,* which says that relief from the midlife crisis comes through finding a "connection to a greater reality that gives us meaning and purpose."

Each of them was valuable, but the most important book for

me was British writer C. S. Lewis's *The Screwtape Letters,* which contains the advice an old devil, Screwtape, gives his nephew and apprentice devil, Wormwood, on how to lure people to damnation.

For a soul-snatching devil, the best prospects include middle-aged men and women who are set in their ways and have grown used to their situation in life. "The long, dull monotonous years of middle-aged prosperity or adversity are excellent campaigning weather," Screwtape observes.

The senior devil notes that people who have not fulfilled their personal goals are good candidates for hell. The loss of youthful loves and hopes, the drabness in their lives, and the resentments they feel provide "admirable opportunities of wearing out a soul by attrition."

The easiest pickings, however, are middle-aged people whose lives have been gratifying, Screwtape says, because happiness "knits a man to the World. . . ."

"His increasing reputation, his widening circle of acquaintances, his sense of importance, the growing pressure of absorbing and agreeable work, build up in him a sense of being really at home on Earth, which is just what we want," Screwtape notes.

Screwtape's diabolical observations of middle-aged conceit have been expressed in many ways through Western history:

- Aesop, the ancient Greek writer of fables: "We would often be sorry if our wishes were gratified."
- Oscar Wilde, the late-nineteenth-century British wit: "When the gods wish to punish us, they answer our prayers."
- Joseph Campbell, an anthropologist and scholar of mythology: "People are often climbing the ladder of success, they get to the top and they realize they're climbing against the wrong wall."

- Sigmund Freud, the famed psychiatrist, who discovered what he called the "wrecked by success" syndrome, which brings people to ruin because they can't cope with their own achievements.

Most mental-health professionals and other experts on depression and the midlife crisis focus narrowly on the personal impact. Yet, coupled with—and aggravated by—the social woes outlined in Chapter 1, the emotional turmoil that often comes with middle age could drastically affect American society as millions of baby boomers enter their forties and fifties. Like poodle skirts and butchwax in the 1950s, Vietnam protests and the sexual revolution in the 1960s, career pathing in the 1970s, and designer-label consumption in the 1980s, the midlife crisis could be the baby boom's central experience of the 1990s. And as they have throughout their lives, the baby boomers are certain to bring American culture along with them—intensifying the melancholy of the late twentieth century.

When the deep secrets within us connect to the world outside us, social consciousness is formed. In the last decade of the century, that process has been set off anew by the epidemic of depression and the desperate search for meaning in life by millions of middle-agers. That many of these baby boomers are among the nation's most financially and professionally successful individuals shows that wealth, status, and power don't ensure happiness. Ultimately, society must change when a critical mass of its talented members are disenchanted with prevailing cultural values and feel that something vital is missing from their lives.

The most astute guide to what is in store for millions of middle-aged Americans and, by extension, U.S. society is Swiss psychiatrist Carl Jung, one of the seminal thinkers of the twentieth century.

Between 1914 and 1918, when he was thirty-eight to forty-three years old, Jung suffered a midlife crisis. Exploring his pain through what he called an "experiment with the unconscious," Jung learned that for a middle-aged person "what originally meant advancement and satisfaction has now become a boring mistake, part of the illusion of youth, upon which he looks back with mingled regret and envy, because nothing now awaits him but old age and the end of all illusions."

To comprehend his own predicament—and apply his experience to all humanity—Jung developed his theory that individuals go through different stages and that each season in life has a unique function.

According to Jung, the first thirty-five or forty years of life are when people mature physically, establish themselves in society, and get some impression of what life is about. The primary concerns at this stage of life revolve around sex, power, and financial well-being. The second half of life is reserved for cultural and spiritual matters—contributing to the community, developing a personal philosophy.

Essential to a fulfilling life is a successful transition between ages. Attitudes typical at age twenty-five—a reluctance to make long-term commitments, for example—can make people neurotic if dominant at age forty-five. They are the middle-aged crazies, perpetually trapped in an endless adolescence—like unrepentant Clark Griswolds lusting after Christie Brinkley in the Chevy Chase movie *Vacation*.

Midlife is the most important crossroads of adulthood because it determines the direction of the final decades of life. The challenge of the middle years is to undergo a personal renewal that leads to greater compassion for others and to a spiritual rebirth.

While treating his mostly affluent, cosmopolitan, and well-educated patients, Jung noticed that despite their privileged position, they were profoundly morose. "There has not been one whose problem in the last resort was not that of finding a religious outlook on life," Jung concluded.

To describe what his middle-aged patients needed to do, Jung coined the term *individuation,* which is the integration of the unconscious, timeless self with the finite, temporal personality. The point is that each person has a distinct self that is hidden beneath the superficialities and worldly demands of society. The task at midlife is to breach the cultural barriers, rescue the self, and liberate the soul.

Those who find their true self have a new agenda in life. They can put their failures and accomplishments into perspective. They can abandon their youthful pride and obsessions. They become more interested in being a collaborator—rather than a star player—in society's political and cultural games. And they have a strong life mission: to expand human wisdom and pass it to the next generation.

"A human being would certainly not grow to be 70 or 80 years old if this longevity had no meaning for the species," Jung wrote. "The afternoon of life must have a significance of its own and cannot be merely a pitiful appendage of morning."

Negotiated well, the midlife crisis can be a great opportunity. Youthful enthusiasms have cooled. The soul, instead of the ego, is being tended. Humility is recognized as a desirable trait; arrogance is evidence of immaturity. Spirituality is seen as participating in community, as well as nourishing the psyche and seeking the divine. Pragmatic wisdom is found in the regret-tinged remark of Henry David Thoreau: "The youth gets together his materials to build a bridge to the moon, or perchance a palace or temple on the earth, and at length the middle-aged man concludes to build a woodshed with them."

A big part of midlife agony is the begrudging surrender of the childish illusion that life should be painless. Birthdays measure what is lost rather than what is being gained. Maturity now means decay. The mirror doesn't lie. Bodies tire easily. Career opportunities disappear. We realize that our bright futures are behind us, and that even the most satisfying lives carry disappointed reminders of what might have been.

Most important for American baby boomers who thought that eternal youth was their birthright, middle age presents a younger generation that looks upon them as old and in the way.

And it is the shock of mortality—the impersonal inevitability of our own demise—that must be confronted first if the second act of life's drama is to have a happy ending.

Mortal Fears

Two months after the initial onset of my midlife depression, I was having Thanksgiving dinner with my mother and several of her friends at the Town Club, a white-tablecloth restaurant that for decades has served lunch and dinner to Hutchinson's bankers, lawyers, and Main Street businessmen and has provided a place for afternoon gossip and bridge games for their wives and widows.

I was the youngest of half a dozen people at the table. The others were well into their seventies or early eighties. At age forty-three, I was the kid.

During dessert Peg Casey, one of my mother's dearest friends, remarked that she had been at the Town Club a few weeks earlier and had looked around the main dining room and wondered, "Where are all the old people—my parents' crowd—who are usually here?"

In telling that anecdote, she became wistful. Her parents' generation had long since died. She, my mother, and their friends were now the "old people."

And if they are the old people, I thought to myself, *I am the middle generation.* I was at the time of life that Mrs. Casey had momentarily placed herself in, thinking that the "old people" were someone else.

As both the twentieth century and the second millennium near an end and the baby-boom generation reaches middle age, millions of Americans perceive that their time is running out.

Middle age is a period of loss. Parents die. A close friend might suffer a heart attack before age fifty. Children enter college, a hard jolt to those baby boomers whose self-image retains a bit of that idealistic undergraduate eager to remake the world. But now paying hefty tuition bills, those middle-aged Americans must admit that, instead of radically changing society, they only adapted to it.

Part of middle-age melancholy is the stark realization of how flimsy so much of life is—how fragile the pillars of our self-esteem are. Careers can be smashed in a corporate merger. An illness or accident can suddenly alter life's plans. A touch of arthritis or a wrenched back can mean the end of noontime YMCA basketball games, and we fear that we will never again feel the innocent joy of purely physical energy. Divorce happens because we stop noticing each other—and decades of memories no longer enrich life but torture us with reminders of pleasures never to be repeated. The accumulated tokens of middle-class success—titanium golf clubs, NBA tickets, our 401(k) mutual fund portfolios—seem small compensation for failing to read Shakespeare, for missing our kids' soccer games, for not chucking it all and starting that small business and becoming our own boss.

And all the while the constant reminder: tick . . . tick . . . tick . . .

"Each passing instant snatches from you the cake-crumb of

happiness meant to last the year," wrote nineteenth-century French poet Charles Baudelaire.

The life-wrenching crisis comes after we recognize that hours, minutes, and seconds are all that stand between us and death. And this is not death in the abstract, but our own, individual, unique death. Yet how are we using this increasingly scarce commodity? Does time still have something to offer? Or are we just trying to negotiate our own inevitable decay at minimal personal cost—to just get life done?

Clock-time-death anxiety further heightens the apprehensions we already have about our life. We can't deny the truth of these lines by eighteenth-century English poet Thomas Gray in his "Elegy Written in a Country Churchyard":

> *The boast of heraldry, the pomp of pow'r,*
> *And all that beauty, all that wealth e'er gave,*
> *Awaits alike th' inevitable hour.*
> *The paths of glory lead but to the grave.*

American philosopher William James called death "the worm at the core" of humanity's pretensions for happiness. It is the only fear that has no antidote, the only terror that can't be laid to some psychological maladjustment, the only truth that can't be disputed by philosophical theories, the only fact that can't be denied.

The problem is that many middle-class, middle-aged Americans have internalized society's definitions of happiness. Painful, discomforting thoughts—especially our own death—frighten us because we lack the inner resources to develop new options to revive zest for life. Abandoning familiar routines would throw us into a psychic wilderness, forcing us to grapple alone with our own inner torments. So we try to repress the fear of death. Like backsliding dope addicts, we numb ourselves again on the old narcotics of money, career titles, status, and pleasure to blot out the penetrating dread of extinction.

And rather than listen to the wisdom of our aging bodies telling us to move beyond youth, many of us try to deceive nature.

During the 1990s a multibillion-dollar market—tummy tucks, hair transplants, face-lifts, anti-aging creams, treadmills, Stair-Masters, health-food concoctions—has grown rapidly to cater to wrinkling baby boomers seeking to prolong adolescence. For example, a survey by the Clairol company found that 10 percent of the 45 million American men in their forties and fifties color their hair. According to the American Academy of Cosmetic Surgery, men accounted for 10 percent of all plastic-surgery patients in 1980; by 1994 they were 26 percent of a much higher number of procedures. Another study found that sales of facial-treatment products like wrinkle creams and mud masks increased about 5 percent a year in the mid-1990s, after years of flat or declining sales through the late 1980s. Also, the number of women joining gyms and health clubs rose 108 percent between 1987 and 1995.

In their huffing and puffing on the exercise bike, their slicing and rearranging of body parts, some people are merely seeking greater self-confidence or a visual-image edge in a highly competitive corporate world. But in their obsession with hips and hair, people can condemn themselves to spiritual euthanasia long before physical death.

A good cautionary tale for today's middle-aged mutineers against mortality is Leo Tolstoy's novel *The Death of Ivan Ilyich.*

A wealthy, career-centered lawyer who had never bothered himself about the larger questions of life, Ilyich is moved to reflection after a fall leaves him with a severe bruise that turns into a fatal cancer.

"His mental sufferings were due to the fact that in the night . . . the thought had suddenly come into his head: 'What if in reality my whole life had been wrong?' It occurred to him that what had appeared utterly impossible before—that he had not lived his life as he should have done—might be true after all," wrote Tolstoy, the nineteenth-century Russian novelist who created Ivan Ilyich out of his own midlife crisis.

For the first time in his life, Ivan is thrown back nakedly on himself; all his outside defenses lie impotent before the presence of death. It is he—not some anonymous other person—who is going to die. Toward the end Ivan passes beyond his own ego by finding love for a peasant servant boy who visits his bedside. From there Ivan reconciles with his wife and son. The pain of death then lifts. The confrontation with death binds Ivan to humanity through love.

Ivan's story warns us middle-aged Americans to stop massaging our egos and to focus on what we want to do with the remaining years of life. The midlife crisis helps identify what is important by drawing us toward the ideals that hold the most positive potential to guide us toward the grave. It's the same point made by the ancient Greek philosopher Socrates, who says that all philosophy is a meditation upon death, and by the sixteenth-century French essayist Michel de Montaigne, who observed that "to philosophize is to learn how to die."

Ivan Ilyich finally accepted death as real and part of the natural order. That was the most he could hope for, because he had no time to make major changes in his life. But today's middle-aged Americans can anticipate as many as four more decades of life. The chances that those years will be productive and enlightened hinge largely on attitudes adopted at midlife.

As Ivan Ilyich learned to his dismay, we seldom get a second chance to acquire wisdom. That is especially true as the years harden our habits and we shy from the risks necessary to find new roles in life. Once squandered, time can never be recovered. As the years mount, not only is the loss personal, but the entire society is deprived of whatever awareness we might have offered.

Ironically, a deeper engagement with life might lie through a serious consideration of death. As William James said, "No man is educated who has never dallied with the thought of suicide."

The possibility of suicide consumed my mind in the weeks following the Thanksgiving dinner at the Town Club. I never tried it, though I did get a morbid thrill debating the most efficient means of extermination: gunshot; but a cocktail of sleeping pills and vodka gimlets might be the smoothest exit and not mess up my corpse. I was struck by how dispassionate and analytical I became in thinking about my death. Suicide often results from mental derangement, yet I had never felt more rational than when deliberating whether to do myself in.

My tendency to intellectualize self-annihilation was reinforced by reading twentieth-century German philosopher Walter Benjamin, who said that the modern era exists "under the sign of suicide" because this century—which sits at the summit of human knowledge—has committed some of the most horrid acts of human history. To Benjamin, who took his own life, suicide is a deed of "heroic passion" because killing oneself is an irrevocable protest against modern life. It is the final assertion of human integrity and decency in a despicable world.

This romantic revolt against evil appealed to me. Defy convention! Seize your own dignity! Scorn to anyone satisfied with the trivialities that society offers! Resist the agony that is too much for such a sensitive soul to bear!

I spared my life because I recognized that suicide is the climactic ego trip, a self-congratulatory compliment that the victim has suffered too much to even hope that things will get better. By putting their pain foremost, suicides selfishly dismiss the heartbreak they cause family and friends. What is so damnable about suicide is that it mocks all reason to live. Although often thinking themselves unworthy and deserving punishment for real or imagined sins, suicide victims send the message that the world is too imperfect, too ambiguous to tolerate and that people who continue struggling to find meaning in life are delusional suckers who can't accept the cold logic of self-destruction.

Fortunately, most depressives come to the same realization I did and don't fall to fatal temptation. But to gain the wisdom that despair can lead to, they must commit something of a psychological suicide.

Like an ancient forest that is choking itself to death, they have to tear the underbrush from their psyches to give room for new growth. Suicidal-prone depression can serve as the harrowing tool that rips through old attitudes and roots out the decayed mental stumps that clutter our paths to the future. Through the clear-cut perspective that reveals melancholic pain as potentially life-affirming, depressives can make freely chosen commitments to accept personal responsibility for themselves and the world.

A Hermit's Solitude

In the spring of 1993, a year and a half after my midlife crisis began, I was at a dead end. I had been on Prozac for a year. The antidepressant drug helped me function smoothly, though mainly by dulling rather than relieving my inner psychic tensions. Idling in neutral wasn't enough for me. Additionally, I didn't want my personality and mental stability to depend on a pharmaceutical company.

I talked to mental-health professionals about my condition. They gave me a textbook overview of depression and offered useful strategies—stay active, get exercise, try to clarify what's bothering me. All that helped. For example, I went on a rigorous swimming program at the Wichita YMCA: thousands of yards up and down the pool, four or five days a week; I set goals I could measure —"Gotta do five miles this week" or "Great, I lost another two pounds"—to gain self-confidence. The enveloping sensation of the water offered womblike security. My mind might be in torment, but depression-inspired fitness meant my body never felt better.

My job became my refuge. The moment I entered the door of *The Wichita Eagle* building and convened our 9 A.M. editorial board meeting to discuss the topics of the day, I melded my personality into the production of news and opinion. My role as editorial page editor set my hourly schedule and organized my thoughts. That's the thing about newspapers: they are daily; so was my life—reacting to a governor's press conference, a new legislative tax plan, or a silly remark by a school board member held any stalking emotional monsters at bay.

But something had to be done. The expectation that the depression was a temporary setback that would lift after a few months—a year or so at the most—was obviously wrong. The demonic mosasaurs still made their regular 4 A.M. visits. My marriage was disintegrating. My self-contempt and unresolved guilt had not abated.

Questions kept arising: questions about the purpose of life, about the existence of God, about the meaning of death. Big questions. Fundamental questions. Gnawing questions. Questions that I had toyed with as a graduate student in religious studies twenty years earlier, although at that time I used them primarily as an intellectual pose—along with the meerschaum pipe and the Simon and Garfunkel albums—to prove that I was a person of spiritual depth and philosophical substance. Only now, I felt an urgency to those questions. The answers weren't merely academic point-scoring, but intensely personal.

I hit upon the idea of a retreat. Maybe I could spend a few months at the University of Kansas, where I first pondered those questions and where I might pursue them with a middle-aged journalist's desperate need to know rather than as a know-it-all twenty-three-year-old graduate student.

Fortunately, my boss, *Eagle* editor Buzz Merritt, was sympathetic. Knowing that some readers might doubt the credibility of a newspaper whose editorial page editor was perceived to be wacko, we labeled my June–August stay at the university a working sabbatical. To maintain a presence in print, I would send my weekly column and a regular quota of editorials to the *Eagle* via laptop computer while also pursuing my personal project.

I had not spent much time at the university in Lawrence since receiving my master's degree in 1972. Just as my mental geography had shifted in the previous two decades, the campus had undergone major physical change, reflecting its growth from an 18,000-student university during my years to an enrollment of almost 30,000. New buildings had mushroomed, old ones had expanded. Yet enough remained the same that I felt home again.

I rented an apartment within walking distance of the campus. The university gave me a library card and access to the swimming pool and other facilities. My schedule was set. Mornings writing for the *Eagle*. Early afternoons in the library searching for whatever looked interesting. Late afternoons doing laps in the pool or lifting weights. Evenings reading or mulling over life's perplexities.

I also tried to recapture some of the intellectual curiosity of my undergraduate days by auditing a course in Asian art history, a subject I knew nothing about.

After the initial euphoria of being back on campus, my first task was to measure what I had lost over the past twenty years. Youth was gone; that was evident when a Kappa sorority woman in my art history class asked if I were a retiree just taking courses for entertainment. More painful, I found little in common with old friends who had remained in Lawrence; the passions of our student activism during the 1960s had turned from youthful fervor to middle-aged reminiscence.

Walking on campus those first summer weeks, I realized how dead the past was. In the student union, the humanities building, the off-campus bars—all my old haunts—I continually encountered ghosts of my undergraduate self. But the specters were more reminders of what I had become over the past twenty years than spirits that could infuse me with new enthusiasm for life.

I was student body president at the University of Kansas during the 1969–70 academic year. Elected as head of a dissident, activist ticket, I denounced the university as a handmaiden to the military-industrial complex and insisted that the academic curriculum be more "relevant" to students rather than serve the interests of corporate society. I battled the Lawrence police in the streets to resist the Vietnam War and earned my New Left credentials by spending several summer weeks in the unair-conditioned city jail. I attended national conventions of the Students for a Democratic Society. I traveled cross-country to Black Panther headquarters in Oakland, California, to try to forge an alliance between black-power militants and white student radicals. I also was a for-the-duration recruit in the sexual revolution. And I turned on and tuned in with psychedelic drugs.

But in the 1980s and 1990s I was a Reagan Republican writing editorials that often sought to reverse the excesses of my earlier collegiate political and countercultural beliefs. I advocated a tougher academic curriculum. I demanded hard action against the

drug scourge that was destroying the nation's poorest neighborhoods. I urged sexual restraint to limit the tragic death toll from
AIDS and the social debacle of unwed teen pregnancy. And I criticized the anti–nuclear weapons movement for what I saw as a
naive view of Soviet communism.

Although my changes of heart and mind could be interpreted
as a pragmatic maturing, or seen as evidence that age, government
reporting, and regular exposure to politicians are the mortal enemies of youthful idealism, I viewed myself cynically as I reflected
on my life during my return to campus. Maybe I was guilty of unconscious opportunism — blowing with the popular political
winds to advance my career. Or perhaps my powers of persuasion
were most effective when I cared nothing about contradiction.
Regardless, the best spin I could put on it was that I personified
Ralph Waldo Emerson's comment that a foolish consistency is the
hobgoblin of little minds; if so, I had a genius for philosophical
flexibility and complexity.

What was indisputable is that moral and intellectual permanence is not found in politics. I had built a career on political reporting and opinion writing, but the sweeping ideological swings
of the past few decades made it all seem ridiculously ephemeral.
Something — an idea, a principle, a system — might eventually
make sense of it all. But that coherence surely isn't crafted in legislatures or newsrooms.

So there I was at midlife. Disenchanted with my career. Distrustful of my personal motives. Disillusioned by my political
ideals. Separated from my wife. In contact with my newspaper colleagues only through a modem and telephone line. Living in familiar surroundings that were inhabited by total strangers.
Struggling with doubts that seemed to multiply the more I con-
templated them.

Alone, exiled, I was an outcast never to return to my former life.

In the Bible when God wants to test people or move them to change their lives, he condemns them to loneliness. "Young children despise me; when I rise they talk against me," laments Job when God torments him. "All my intimate friends abhor me, and those whom I loved have turned against me."

Gradually and hesitantly, slowly and skeptically, I used the loneliness to restart my life. I learned that loneliness, perhaps the most widespread complaint of the late twentieth century, contains—like a homeopathic medicine—the germ of its own cure: solitude.

Common to every great religion is the spirit-moved individual who rejects the values of the world and seeks truth in a desert, on a mountaintop, or in any remote place where silence lets God be heard. Moses learned of his life mission from the burning bush while living with nomadic shepherds after his exile from Pharaoh's court. Jesus endured forty days of temptation by Satan in the wilderness. Buddha withdrew from his aristocratic life and found enlightenment during a lengthy meditation under the Bodhi tree. Muhammad received a divine vision while holed up in a cave near Mount Hira.

Each of these spiritual guides had to distance himself from society to experience, in the words of nineteenth-century English cleric John Henry Newman, "the soul alone, face to face with God alone."

An awakening came to me several weeks into my Asian art history course when the instructor mentioned the Japanese religious concept of the *kami*. It proved to be my epiphany, my cosmic click.

A brief explanation: In Japanese Shintoism, a *kami* is a spiritual force of creativity, growth, or fertility. It can be found in nature (wind and lightning), in natural objects (the sun, mountains, trees, rivers), in some animals, and in ancestral spirits. Because Shintoism has no absolute deity, *kami* are the organizing principles of the universe, and the world functions through their harmonious relationships.

While returning to my apartment after that art history class, I noticed a tree on the hill overlooking the university's football stadium. It was a six-foot-tall pine tree with branches stretching out octopuslike to a diameter of about fifteen feet. It was surrounded by a small stone berm. The overall impression was of a giant Japanese bonsai tree. Out of need for a personal spiritual symbol, this, I decided, was a *kami*.

Over the next several weeks I sat alone for at least an hour a day on the stone ledge that buttressed the tree, just thinking about things. I imagined myself a hermit-scholar in a Chinese landscape painting, unfairly banished from the emperor's palace, transcribing classical poems through brush-and-ink calligraphy, brooding over life's injustices while resting in a small arbor beneath a towering mountain.

My initial problem was that I had no legitimate complaints. I had a happy childhood. My parents had been supportive and devoted. My father had died, but we achieved closure in the last days before his death. I had a beautiful, caring wife. I was well educated. I had a satisfying career. I had job security. I was financially comfortable. I was in good health. I had accepted the rules for success, and they worked for me. In short, I had no socially correct excuse for unhappiness. I would find no compassion on afternoon television talk shows, no therapy as a societal victim. I was an unsympathetic white guy. I should "just snap out" of my funk, as many people suggested.

Philosophers call it "existential dread." It is the feeling of insignificance in an infinite universe. It is the misery of being only a momentary blip on a timeline that stretches from the pre-Genesis void to the postapocalyptic eternity. The only thing I truly know is that I will die, and that either death will leave me as rotting compost or I will fall on the mercy of a God who is probably none too pleased with me.

Perhaps that's why many people shy away from solitude. It's easier to get caught up in socially sanctioned, time-devouring activities, as I had done with my newspaper job. There is always a new must-see movie, a job promotion to pump up the résumé, another high-tech gimmick to play with. They might be mere vanities, but, hey, they are better than being bummed out by that muck about wretchedness and nothingness.

Or you can take the impassive approach and decide that the fates rule the world and there is nothing you can do except adapt and flow with the prevailing tide. Why resist? Settle for a life of predictable normality, undisturbed by either the mania of extreme pleasure or the paralysis of radical doubt. The future will take care of itself. An attitude of detached dignity takes care of most of life's misfortunes.

For me, neither hedonism nor stoicism was a viable choice. One ends in a pitiless morning-after hangover; the other results in a weary boredom toward the mysteries of life.

As a journalist, I lived in the concrete world of legal records and eyewitness accounts, and I tried to be an honest broker of factual information. But now I sought immaterial truths. I needed to feel life deeply; I yearned for moral resonance to give life a coherent structure. Anything less would condemn me to an incomprehensible universe.

And all I had was melancholy.

Melancholy became the emotional and intellectual catalyst that caused me to ransack my consciousness. Crucially, I realized that I was not exempt from the human condition. From the spiritual essence and the physical presence of the *kami* tree, I recognized that the anxiety of existence is that we humans participate in both the sacred and the profane. Were we merely biological creatures of bone, brain, and muscle, we could not hurt so much, we would not be so frustrated by the limits of our own knowledge, we would not have the capacity to believe in a transcendent reality. For those reasons, I embraced depression; the terrifying fear that my life had no meaning became a desperate search for a meaningful life.

August arrived and my summer sabbatical was ending. I decided to perform a personal ritual to seal a passage in my life that was at least as significant as the first time I left college two decades earlier.

During spring graduation ceremonies at the University of Kansas, amid the medieval panoply of black robes, brightly colored graduate-school hoods, and youthful exuberance, students walk "down the Hill" from the summit of the campus to the football stadium, where they receive their diplomas in front of parents and friends. As I had done years earlier, the new graduates pass by the *kami* tree, which perhaps gives them an additional blessing from an Asian culture far different from Western collegiate traditions.

On my final day in Lawrence, solemnly, reverently, I staged a personal ceremony by retracing that graduation path down the Hill. Inside the stadium I walked across the field on the 50-yard line from the student side on the east to the alumni section on the west, to symbolically acknowledge my middle-aged reality. Just as a college commencement marks a new beginning after adolescence, my ritual meant my summer at the university was a second start in adulthood.

I left my campus hermitage and returned to the "real world" with a greater sense that I was truly maturing, by opening myself to the paramount life experiences that occur after age forty. I decided to write this book, partly because no journalist feels that an event actually happened unless it is down on paper, and partly to give other people caught in an emotional midlife whirlpool confidence that their melancholy can swirl into a positive outlook for the second half of life.

Everyone grows older, but not everyone grows up. The solitude brought on by midlife melancholy made me sadder but wiser. I was sad because I lost my youthful enthusiasm that treated the world as my toy. I was wiser because I realized that the world was not conceived to meet my infantile whims or respond to my childish conniptions.

Maturity is not always greeted eagerly. The midlife crisis can leave people in limbo. They refuse to leap into their depression for fear of confronting the shadows lurking in their darkened consciousness. Instead, they spend their days in whimpering self-reproach and bitter narcissism, moping over mortality, popping antidepressant pills, and moaning that life is a conspiracy against their personal happiness.

Yet the reluctance of some middle-aged melancholics to explore their psyche is understandable. As I learned in my initial steps out of my midlife crisis, hope and redemption lie on the far side of hell.

Entering the Depths

The fourteenth-century Italian poet Dante begins his epic poem *Divine Comedy* with a self-description that would resonate with many middle-aged, melancholic Americans in the last decade of the twentieth century: "In the middle of the journey of life I came to myself in a dark wood, where the straight way was lost."

To get through his dark wood, Dante has to descend through

all the circles of hell, climb the mountain of purgatory, and finally arrive in paradise. Although few of them share Dante's medieval Christian theology, many Americans today can identify with his midlife distress.

After I returned to Wichita following my summer sabbatical at the University of Kansas, the metaphor of midlife as a voyage of self-discovery and renewal held great meaning. It led me to a diligent study of history, religion, and literature. Rather than concentrate on modern psychological and medical theories of depression, with their clinical-talk therapies and biotechnical treatments for the affliction, I explored the great thoughts and words of the past as the best way to explain the human condition and how my current crisis fit into a life pattern. I was constantly amazed how classical myths, scriptural writings, and centuries-old legends and stories applied directly to the personal traumas of millions of Americans in the 1990s.

Confidence that I was on the right road toward the second half of life continually rose as I followed in the well-worn steps of some of the formative writers and personalities of human civilization. Especially important for me were the myths of premodern societies that found despair embedded deeply in the archaeology of the psyche.

According to Carl Jung, every individual participates in a collective unconsciousness that molds the psychic core of humanity. Each culture has its unique mythological images and motifs, but most stories can be broken down into what Jung called "elementary ideas" — the universal, archetypal experiences of being human. Thus, decoding myths can reveal some remarkable insights about human nature—its fears and hopes—that have not fundamentally changed since our Paleolithic ancestors drew sacramental beasts on cave walls.

One of the most familiar stories in the library of humanity's psychic heritage is the wayfarer who suffers severe hardship to gain wisdom. While physical trials are often part of the ordeal, spiritual and mental torment usually carry the primary plot of the story.

The biblical tale of Jonah, for example, warns what happens to people who refuse to obey a spiritual call—a call perhaps similar to that brought on by the midlife crisis.

A Hebrew prophet, Jonah is ordered by God to travel to the city of Ninevah and preach repentance to its sinful inhabitants. Jonah shirks the command and embarks on a ship traveling in the opposite direction from Ninevah. While he's at sea, a violent storm arises. The crew suspects that the tempest is caused by an angry God. Jonah admits that he is fleeing God, so the crew tosses him overboard to calm the waters. A huge fish swallows Jonah, who remains alive in the animal's stomach for three days and is vomited onto the shore. God reiterates his call for Jonah to go to Ninevah. This time he complies. After hearing Jonah's warnings of imminent destruction, the people of Ninevah repent and are spared God's wrath.

Jonah, however, feels deceived by God's pardoning of Ninevah. While Jonah pouts on the outskirts of town, God arranges for a plant to grow next to him for shade. But the plant quickly withers, which saddens Jonah. God then reveals his message: if Jonah could mourn a single plant that he had no part in creating, couldn't God show mercy to thousands of his own children?

Jonah's adventure has special meaning today as a spiritual sojourn. He rejects God's decree, preferring instead to enjoy his own comforts. The result is a severe psychological storm that throws the sinner into the belly of the beast. Rebirth begins when the traveler accepts God's summons. Enlightenment comes when Jonah apprehends God's intentions and acquires compassion for others.

Numerous other Western literary masterpieces depict life as a series of personal and spiritual missions. The ten-year voyage of Odysseus to reach home after the Trojan War can be read as an extended midlife crisis of a king who wants to remain a warrior-hero rather than accept his responsibilities to his subjects and family. Medieval legends demand that any knight seeking truth has to overcome physical hardship and spiritual agony to find the Holy Grail. In Edmund Spenser's sixteenth-century poem *The Faerie Queene,* the Redcrosse Knight enters the cave of Despair where Una, the symbol of true faith, blocks his attempted suicide. Similarly, John Bunyan's seventeenth-century Puritan classic, *Pilgrim's Progress,* forces the hero, Christian, to slog through the Slough of Despond and travel through Vanity Fair before reaching the Celestial City.

But the deepest ruts on the road to self-consciousness lead through hell. It seems that only by facing damnation can individuals fulfill themselves. From the dawn of history in the ancient Near East, humans have believed that torments of body and soul are necessary to burn away the evils that hinder self-understanding.

In an ancient Sumerian legend, Inanna, queen of heaven, visits the netherworld, which is ruled by the dark side of her own self, in the form of her sister. On her journey below, Inanna has to discard her earthly powers and material adornments, which symbolize worldly pride, beauty, and wealth. Inanna is killed by her evil sister and her corpse hangs on a stake for three days and nights. But Inanna is resurrected with the help of two angels, and she takes the dead back to earth with her, apparently wiser for the experience.

The Greek myth of Persephone has similar elements of death and revival. The daughter of Demeter, the goddess of the harvest and fertility, Persephone is kidnapped by Hades, who takes her to his kingdom. Enraged over the loss of her child, Demeter causes a massive famine. Zeus finally orders Hades to return Persephone to earth. But because she has eaten a pomegranate seed (the food of the dead), Persephone is sentenced to live in Hades half the year. In Persephone's absence during the cold months, Demeter allows nothing to bloom or grow on earth.

The lesson is that Demeter's heartbreak over losing her daughter causes great suffering that leaves the earth barren, but the pain gives way with Persephone's return in the spring, a time of nurturing and creativity. Despair and love turn the cycle of death and regeneration.

The most dramatic hell visitation is Dante's descent to the underworld, which begins on Good Friday in the year 1300. Led by the ancient Roman poet Virgil, who represents human knowledge, the middle-aged Dante spirals down the nine circles of hell. On each ring, the damned are punished in a manner appropriate to their sin—illicit lovers are blown about by furious winds that represent their carnal lusts; gluttons are torn apart by Cerberus, the ravenous three-headed dog of hell; murderers and other violent criminals nearly drown in a roaring river of blood while centaurs shoot them with arrows when their heads bob up. On the lowest circle, at the center of the earth, Dante finds Lucifer buried up to his waist in ice, chewing on the heads of the great betrayers of antiquity, Cassius, Brutus, and Judas.

The gruesome horrors of hell having broken the attractions of sin, Dante crawls out of the inferno on Easter morning and begins to climb upward to purgatory and his eventual destination, paradise.

Although vastly different in time, culture, and religious outlook, these mythological, scriptural, and poetic plunges into the lowest depths usually compel their characters to come to grips with their own malevolence. But it is almost always a reluctant passage through psychic hell; sometimes forced, as with Dante, by midlife turmoil.

"The dread and resistance which every natural human being experiences when it comes to delving too deeply into himself is, at bottom, the fear of the journey to Hades," wrote Jung.

The common plotline in these hellish journeys is that people must sacrifice themselves, especially their pride and temporal attachments, to experience spiritual renewal. That's because hell is not so much a subterranean torture chamber as a psychological dungeon. To be truly free, people first must undergo a symbolic death—abandon their egos at the bottom of the fiery abyss. From those ashes a purified self emerges, one capable of transcendence.

According to seventeenth-century English poet John Milton and other writers, the original road to hell was paved by prideful egos. Medieval legend and *Paradise Lost* have it that the first occupants of hell were Satan and his angelic allies who revolted against God because they wanted divine powers for themselves. God and his loyal angels hurled the rebels into hell, where they have reigned ever since.

Satan's sin was the capital crime of pride. Satan insolently tried to seize God's ultimate moral authority to define good and evil and to render justice and judgment.

It's hard for many Americans in the late twentieth century to think in terms of sin. The word reeks of guilt, fire and brimstone, something from the days of dunking stools and scarlet letters, something Western civilization outgrew when it discovered syndromes, personality disorders, neuroses, psychoses, manias, abnormalities, paranoias, hysterias, and other psychic pathologies.

But my melancholy wasn't wholly amenable to mental tinkering or medicinal readjustment. As effective as they often can be, modern therapies couldn't reach the terrors within my inner core. For me, the best explanation of my guilt-induced depression sounded medieval: hubris, vainglory, *superbia,* moral corruption —all of which come under the rubric of pride, which theologians list as the first of the deadly sins.

By magnifying my own ego, by placing the highest value on career and power, by deceiving my friend and mentor George Neavoll, by ignoring the spiritual dimension of life, and by relying on my own intellect to arbitrate truth, I followed Satan in taking a godlike role for myself. As I learned in my selfish pursuits, pride tells us that we are masters of our own universe, that other people are pawns or obstacles to be subjected to our will. I proved Dante's fundamental point—seconded by C. S. Lewis's devilish Screwtape —that the worst sinners aren't weak people who succumb to lures of the flesh, but strong individuals who see themselves as God. Augustine, a skilled diagnostician of sin, put it well: Every "proud man heeds himself, and he who pleases himself seems great to himself. But he who pleases himself pleases a fool."

Ironically, a shortage of pride is a major complaint today. Not sneering self-confidence, but self-doubt, low self-esteem, and a surfeit of self-loathing are the psychic ailments especially familiar to our age.

Yet those self-demeaning traits also can reflect the sin of pride because they center entirely on the individual, absent any reference to others—God or community—that could sustain us. Like self-defensive hedgehogs tightly rolled up in themselves, depressives often feel that the world has targeted them specifically for unhappiness, and they flaunt a sort of snobbishness in the severity of their torments.

Joel P. Smith, formerly vice president of Stanford University and president of Denison University, illustrates this perverse strain of melancholic pride in his essay "Darker than Darkness," published in the autumn 1997 issue of *The American Scholar.* To help a fellow depressed patient named Clare, Smith gave her a copy of

William Styron's memoir *Darkness Visible*. Clare hated it, calling it a "crock" and saying that Styron had a "candy-ass" depression that didn't force the novelist to rely heavily on drugs, much less electroconvulsive therapy. Smith understood the woman's reaction: "Styron's book will almost certainly offend a veteran like Clare or me. . . . It rankles us, no matter what the virtues of Styron's book may be, to feel he speaks for us."

Likewise, I silently boasted that no one else could suffer such emotional flagellation as I did and remain a major player at the newspaper and in state politics. Depression became a mental hair shirt that I wore in self-mortifying exaltation. I now wonder whether I loved my pride so much that I wanted to confess it fervently and not let it go.

I don't mean to be cruel or seem to be shooting the mentally wounded, but pride not only comes before a fall, it can keep us down.

An old Christian verse describes this vanity:

> *And the devil did grin*
> *For his darling sin*
> *Is the pride that apes humility.*

That's the insidious nature of sin: in excess, it turns a good (self-worth) into an evil (self-absorption). People who don't respect limits find that healthy self-respect becomes utter selfishness and that reasonable self-concern deteriorates into untrammeled arrogance. Freed from the reins of moral accountability to others, self-love degenerates into narcissism and rejects any virtue—compassion, charity, faith—that demands self-denial, restrains the gratification of our desires, or suggests that we are not the hub of creation.

As taught by ancient Greek mythologists and great Christian theologians, salvation lies over the dead body of our own ego. Surrendering conceit allows the true self to find lasting peace. Looking back, I was so hardened by the pursuit of my own ambitions and self-glorification that, for me, the only thing worse than a life-changing depression would have been no life-changing depression.

I endured the psychic death that Inanna, Persephone, and Dante show is necessary for the birth of a new self; in my case, a self released from pretense and prepared to learn from the misery of melancholy and alienation. As Orestes tells Zeus in Jean-Paul Sartre's play *The Flies,* "Human life begins on the far side of despair."

This book's credibility rests on my middle-age struggle with depression and the charting of a purposeful direction for my life that came out of it. Each person's life, however, is a continual search, to be concluded only in an eternal destiny that none of us in our brief span of earthly time can totally ascertain. So, I can't offer readers a clear Mercator projection, with precise longitude and latitude, of the moral universe, only honest reflections on lessons that I have acquired.

As a journalist, I appreciate that the words *communication* and *communion* stem from the same linguistic root. The communicator needs a community to speak fully—the reader is always in my mind as I attempt to comprehend and bring some coherence to the story of my life.

Through the half decade I spent on this project, I was motivated by the words of Thomas Merton, a Trappist monk and a great spiritual leader of the twentieth century: "A man cannot enter into the deepest center of himself and pass through that center to God, unless he is about to pass entirely out of himself and give to other people in the purity of selfless love."

The rest of this book is intended to serve that goal: to give others optimism that winter will become spring, that we can find our true selves by losing our overweening egos, that midlife is a time to break our plummet into nothingness and begin anew, that we have to cross the frozen ice of the deepest circle of hell to get to heaven.

3

A MELANCHOLY
CIVILIZATION

~

The Dark Side of History

The first melancholic in Greek mythology was Bellerophon, a character in the *Iliad*.

According to Homer, Bellerophon was a native of Corinth and without fault. "The gods gave him beauty and the fine, gallant traits that go with men," Homer says in his epic poem about the Trojan War.

Unfortunately for Bellerophon, Anteia, the wife of Proetus, the king of Argos, falls in love with him. But he would not be seduced. In retaliation, the scorned Anteia lies to her husband that Bellerophon lusted after her and demands his death to preserve her honor.

Proetus, however, would not do the dirty work himself. Instead, he gives Bellerophon some tokens that have a hidden meaning and sends him to Lycia, where Anteia's father is king. Once he sees the tokens and understands the fatal message they contain, the king orders Bellerophon to undertake several life-threatening tasks, including fighting the Amazons, a tribe of female warriors.

Impressed by his visitor's courage and success in his difficult missions, the king gives one of his daughters to Bellerophon in marriage. The couple has three children and live in great splendor.

"But the day soon came when even Bellerophon was hated by all the gods," Homer wrote. "Across the Alean plain he wandered, all alone, eating his heart out, a fugitive on the run from the beaten tracks of men."

Abandoned by the gods, Bellerophon feels melancholy as a state of emptiness, as a spiritual crisis because he has lost divine favor. It's a blankness remarkably similar to the Age of Melancholy of the late twentieth century, also an era when people search for a larger context for life.

The comparison between Homeric Greece and high-tech America is not far-fetched. Both eras experienced fundamental cultural change: one from the Bronze Age to a literary culture, the other from iron and industry to silicon and information. Individuals in both ages feel vulnerable to impersonal forces—Olympian gods, free-market economics—that care little for humane values. And in each period, melancholy is a powerful undercurrent of historical transition.

But Bellerophon is more than a mythological figure or a case study in literary sociology; he was my psychotherapist. He helped me see melancholy as a symptom of a deeply disturbed society. He confirmed my growing belief that depression not only is an individual complaint but might also be an important cultural indicator.

For me, Bellerophon corroborates Carl Jung's use of mythology as a sourcebook for psychological analysis. Jung perceived a collective human consciousness and common mental habits that extend through history and "preform and continually influence our thoughts and feelings and actions." Perhaps, I thought, human consciousness uses melancholy as a warning that something is disastrously wrong in society. Perhaps depression shouldn't be approached mainly in an isolated, subjective context. Perhaps medical and mental-health experts are not the only physicians for melancholy. Perhaps religious figures, philosophers, novelists, poets, and historians who have poured their life energy into fundamental questions of existence can offer insights to counter the disillusionment and doubt of the 1990s.

This approach toward depression has a distinguished pedigree. In his book *Four Hasidic Masters and Their Struggle Against Melancholy*, Nobel Prize winner Elie Wiesel tells of a man who sought assistance from Rebbe Pinhas of Koretz, the leader of an eighteenth-century Jewish community in Poland.

"Help me, Master," the man pleaded. "I need your advice, I need your support. My distress is unbearable, make it disappear. The world around me, the world inside me, is filled with turmoil and sadness. Men are not human, life is not sacred. Words are empty—empty of truth, empty of faith. So strong are my doubts that I no longer know who I am—nor do I care to know. What am I to do, Rebbe? Tell me, what am I to do?"

"Go and study," the Rebbe replied. "It's the only remedy I know. Torah contains all the answers. Torah is the answer."

Focusing on several distinct eras, from classical Greece to Gilded Age America, I have found that melancholy is usually part of the leitmotiv, an aspect of what in German is called *Zeitgeist,* the "spirit of the age," whenever Western civilization undergoes a wrenching transformation. French psychoanalyst Julia Kristeva sums up the point in her book *Black Sun,* a scholarly examination of the impact of depression on art and philosophy: "The periods that witness the downfall of political and religious idols, periods of crisis, are particularly favorable to black moods."

Knowing that Western civilization has been in the dregs before and went on to great political, artistic, and intellectual achievements, late-twentieth-century Americans should take heart that they are not historically isolated, and confidently take risks to transcend despair—to brave hell—and move boldly into the third millennium. Out of our era's struggle with melancholy could come a deeper appreciation for the human condition that generates a new burst of creativity.

Western civilization has a different perspective when viewed through the lens of melancholy. Instead of an always upward journey toward more efficient technology, greater material wealth, rational thought, scientific fact, power over nature, and global domination, Western history can be interpreted as a melancholy-induced narrative. It is the story of emotional stress and mental strife among Europeans and Americans to find a spiritual dimension within themselves and to establish moral coherence within Western society.

Melancholy appears to be a special discontent that holds a unique place in American and European culture. Anthony J. Marsella, in his study *Depressive Experience and Disorder Across Cultures,* says that "many non-Western cultures do not even have a concept of depression that is conceptually equivalent to that held by Western mental health professionals."

Marsella adds: "Oftentimes, it is only when individuals in non-Western societies become Westernized that we find similarities to the pattern of depression found in the Western world."

Since antiquity, as expressed in Job's bitterness toward God and the eye-gouging tragedy of Sophocles' Oedipus, despair has helped form the Western mind-set and introduced new perceptions on life.

The ancient Greeks recognized melancholy's cultural dynamic. In the book *Problemata Physica,* often attributed to Aristotle, the author wonders, "Why is it that all those who have become eminent in philosophy or politics or poetry or the arts are clearly melancholics?"

Diagnosed as a "philosopher's disease," melancholy reduced people to relentless bleakness, but it also revealed eternal truths about human existence. Feeling that their lives had lost meaning, depressed individuals suffered severely—especially in their separation from society—but their estrangement also heightened spiritual awareness.

In Greek, *melancholia* means "black fluid." The Greeks thought that the body is governed by four basic "humors" that correspond to various organs and to the four elements—blood to fire, phlegm to water, black bile to earth, and yellow bile to air. Good health requires harmony among internal bodily humors and external conditions.

Under this theory, melancholy is caused by a glut of black bile, which is produced by the spleen. Its symptoms, said Hippocrates, include an "aversion to food, despondency, sleeplessness, irritability, restlessness" and "fear and depression which are prolonged."

A certain level of "black bile" is vital to good health. Aristotle compared it to wine, which in the right amounts can induce such positive effects as congeniality. Likewise, the right balance of black bile can give a person deeper sympathy toward the human condition and greater resiliency to life's unavoidable setbacks.

In excess, however, wine causes drunkenness and a loss of control. Too much black bile can lead to a ruinous alienation from society and a careworn personality.

The trick for Aristotle was to find the "golden mean," the right level of black bile to generate constructive energy without throwing the individual into depressive paralysis.

Realizing that melancholics customarily withdraw from society, the ancient Greeks prescribed companionship for treatment and asked the sufferer to remain active to counter the tendency toward inertia.

Yet the Greeks also understood that solitude gives melancholics enough distance to see society and humanity in a critical light. The gap between the depressive and society creates the imaginative tension that enables the melancholic, as the *Problemata Physica* observes, to produce great art or to propose fresh philosophical insights.

Therefore, to the Greeks, melancholics were social rebels and agents of social realignment. They were the artists who unveiled new visions of truth while also removing themselves from normal human society. Theirs were lives of deep sorrow, but of immense compassion. They were often geniuses, yet they could not enjoy ordinary pleasures.

During the second century two of the ancient world's greatest physicians, Rufus of Ephesus and Galen, described melancholics as misanthropic and sad individuals who suffered from mental delusions and gastrointestinal distress. Accepting the Hippocratic "humor" theory, Rufus and Galen prescribed bloodletting to remove the black bile in extreme cases. For less severe cases, they recommended mild herbal purgatives, including aloe and thyme, which were thought to dilute black bile and to aid in its elimination from the body. Sexual intercourse was also suggested to flush out black bile.

Melancholy was an everyday disorder at the end of the classical era. Late in the fourth century the Roman Empire fell into decadence, and barbarian hordes threatened the city of the Caesars. The looming disaster spawned bizarre and desperate behavior. Some people sank into debauchery. Others held themselves aloof in stoic fatalism. And many people explored the new mystery religions from the East or tried to resurrect the forlorn pagan gods of Rome's glorious past.

Amid the disarray of the impending collapse of Rome, a man from North Africa wrestled with an inner conflict between his carnal desires and his spiritual needs. "With what lashes of words did I not scourge my own soul," Augustine wrote in his *Confessions,* thought to be the first true autobiography in Western literature.

Describing one of the most famous scenes in early Christian history, Augustine wrote of his final conversion to the new faith. Sitting in a garden in Milan, Augustine heard a voice saying, "Take and read." He opened the Bible, and his eyes landed on the passage "not in chambering and wantonness," which persuaded him to leave his profligate lifestyle and accept Christianity.

Written when Augustine was in his mid-forties, *Confessions* is packed with such phrases as the "region of destitution" and "the region of death" referring to a perverse society and the saint's inner discord.

After his conversion Augustine became a bishop of the young church and one of its formative theologians. His writings, which stress humanity's sinful nature and the impossibility of attaining salvation through politics or other earthly efforts, helped frame the emerging medieval worldview. Augustine's melancholy-clouded doubt and its resolution through faith ushered in a social consciousness, and a religion-dominated society, that lasted almost a thousand years.

To the medieval mind, Christianity was the antidote to depression. The New Testament offered the hope that the pagan Homeric melancholic lacked. Christ's sacrifice on the cross, atonement, and divine redemption gave purpose to human life.

In medieval Christian doctrine, melancholy was worse than any of the seven deadly sins—pride, anger, sloth, lust, gluttony, envy, and avarice. Depression was closely associated with sloth because the melancholic's isolation, loss of enthusiasm, physical lethargy, and spiritual fatigue indicated a lack of faith in God's revelation.

Despair was an unforgivable sin. The other sins are primarily offenses of the body or signs of surrender to earthly or licentious temptations. Despair, however, denies God because it deflates the soul and divorces the individual from God's grace.

Worse, despair often leads to suicide, which is a mortal sin in Roman Catholic theology. Suicide is the final rejection of God because it destroys human life, which was formed in the divine image and is God's greatest creation. Suicide is also the abandonment of society and a crime against community, so it is an offense against all humanity.

In the twelfth century Saint Hildegard of Bingen tied melancholy to humanity's first sinful act in the Garden of Eden. According to the saint, after defying God by eating the apple, Adam felt a melancholy humor "curdling in his blood. . . . As when a lamp is quenched, the smoldering and smoking wick remains reeking behind . . . the sparkle of innocence was dulled in him, and his eyes, which had formerly beheld heaven, were blinded, and his gall was changed to bitterness, and his melancholy to blackness."

Noting Satan's role in the drama in Eden, medieval Europe often saw melancholics as possessed by the devil. The Catholic Church's sacrament of confession and assignment of penance were part of the therapy for melancholy. In difficult instances, exorcism was a way to break the devil's hold on the depressive.

As it was at the close of the classical era, melancholy was pervasive when the medieval world succumbed to the Renaissance.

Central to the Renaissance was the self-glorifying, nonconformist individual who mapped his own path in life. That inevitably led to a plague of loneliness as people relied on themselves, rather than on the church, to define meaning. The new attitude was expressed by Petrarch, named poet laureate in Rome in 1341, who was miserably unhappy despite great personal success. In his book *The Secret Conflict of My Cares,* Petrarch complains that he was the victim of a "terrible plague of the soul, melancholy," that caused him to "feed upon my tears and sufferings with a morbid attraction."

Melancholy even had its own Renaissance scholar. In his huge book *De Vita Triplici,* Marsilio Ficino, a fifteenth-century Florentine priest and physician, says that people born under the astrological sign of Saturn were prone to melancholy. He also revived the ancient Greek concept of melancholy as an illness of intellectuals, whose studiousness produced a surfeit of black bile. Because Saturn, in the astronomy of the day, was the highest planet and black bile was the base humor of Earth, the melancholic—combining the loftiest and the lowest—was uniquely suited for "a life of creative contemplation," Ficino wrote.

With its rediscovery of classical learning, global explorations, new literary forms, and magnificent art, the Renaissance is usually seen as an era of reawakened optimism. But at the time many people thought they were enduring one of history's most dismal periods.

A powerful image of this feeling is German artist Albrecht Dürer's *Melancholia I,* an engraving produced in 1514. In the picture, the winged figure of Melancholia sits in the midst of a saw, a plane, scales, a hammer, and other instruments of the arts and sciences, which are strewn about a study. In a direct rebuke to the humanism of the Renaissance, Melancholia broods over the futility of human knowledge and the vanity of education void of divine inspiration.

Three years after Dürer's masterpiece, Martin Luther launched the Protestant Reformation, shattering Western Christianity's already strained unity and worsening Western Europe's already melancholic temperament. As British historian John Hale wrote in his book *The Civilization of Europe in the Renaissance:* "Psychological depression, characterized as 'melancholy,' was a condition that medical literature had discussed since antiquity. But never before had so much attention been paid to this expression of hopelessness, undealable-with inner confusion and the suicides that have been attributed to it as in the generations that followed the introduction of the [Protestant] reforms."

Protestants had their own theories on melancholy. Timothy Bright, a sixteenth-century Englishman, devotes much of his *A Treatise on Melancholie* to differences between garden-variety melancholy and "the conscience oppressed with sense of sin." In the centuries since Bright, the damnation-fearing depressive has been a stock Protestant type.

Unlike the Roman Catholic faith, which lets the institutional church share the burden of human depravity, Protestantism puts the entire weight of human sinfulness on the individual. Among salvation-obsessed Reformers, such guilt-laden pressure caused considerable anxiety while also unleashing amazing energies—the Protestant work ethic—as people tried desperately to convince themselves of their own worthiness in God's eyes.

In *The Anatomy of Melancholy,* written in 1621, Robert Burton, an English clergyman, notes this religious grade of depression. Out of "fear of God's judgment and hell fire," he wrote, some people are driven to despair: "The last and greatest cause of this malady is our own consciences, sense of our sins, and God's anger, justly deserved, a guilty conscience for some foul offense formerly committed."

To treat this form of melancholy, Burton recommends gentle persuasion and—for hard cases—excommunication from the church. Although endorsing "diet, air, exercise" as therapies, Bur-

74

ton insists that "faith, hope, repentance are the sovereign cures and remedies."

Melancholy was so widespread in the sixteenth and seventeenth centuries that it was embedded in the most famous character in English theater.

"How weary, stale, flat and unprofitable / seem to me all the uses of this world," sighs William Shakespeare's Hamlet, who also complains that all "goes heavily with my disposition" and refers to "my weakness and my melancholy." With his indecision, pessimism, self-pity, disgust with other people, obsessive introspection, irritability, and intense mood swings, Hamlet is a textbook example of the depressive of his day.

John Donne, a clergyman, poet, and younger contemporary of Shakespeare, also saw depression as part of his era's temperament. "God hath accompanied, and complicated almost all of our bodily diseases of these times, with an extraordinary sadness, a predominant melancholy, a faintness of heart, a cheerlessness, a joylesnesse of spirit," he wrote.

By the end of the seventeenth century, the scientific revolution, led by Galileo and Isaac Newton, had taken hold. Rationalism, partly a response to the brutal wars between Catholics and Protestants, weakened the hold of religion on Western Europe. William Harvey's idea on the circulation of the blood yielded new biological theories on melancholy. Rather than linking melancholy to a religious cause, some physicians attributed it to sluggish blood flow to the brain, which meant that less nerve energy went to the body, leaving the patient slow and sad.

By despiritualizing melancholy and giving it a biological explanation, physicians helped lay the groundwork for the eighteenth-century Enlightenment's confidence in science and reason. Also during much of the eighteenth century, the influence of such empirical thinkers as John Locke in England and David Hume in

Scotland and the often antireligious *philosophes* in France made belief in human progress and knowledge the dominant faith among the educated classes in Europe.

Yet even at the height of the Enlightenment, melancholy was a strong undertow against the prevailing cultural tide. In a nod to Augustine, French philosopher Jean-Jacques Rousseau titled his autobiography *Confessions,* in which he lists endless complaints about life's woes and held up his raw feelings and emotions, instead of logic or scientific inquiry, as the most reliable tests of truth. Despair permeated the work of British poet William Cowper, whose despondency and religious mania left him to conclude that "God moves in a mysterious way." Also in England, poet Thomas Chatterton became an icon for generations of frustrated, unappreciated artists after he poisoned himself in 1770 at age seventeen in a fit of grief. In Germany Johann Wolfgang von Goethe's *The Sorrows of Young Werther*, published in 1774, further etched the pose of tragic, gifted youth through the melodramatic story of a man who can't find happiness because of his acute sensitivity. Werther finally commits suicide.

The connection between melancholy and sweeping change was apparent in the aftermath of the two great upheavals of the late eighteenth century, the French Revolution and the Industrial Revolution. The hopes for justice and equality raised by the storming of the Bastille in 1789 were cut short by the terror of the guillotine and the imperialism of Napoleon's armies. The "satanic mills," in English poet William Blake's description of the new economy of steam engines and power looms, destroyed a simpler way of life and set highly regimented, production-driven capitalism on its unstoppable course.

In response, many European artists pined for the Middle Ages and other earlier periods of history or ventured off into realms of fantasy. That disenchantment found popular expression in the novels of Sir Walter Scott and Victor Hugo and the poetry of William Wordsworth, Samuel Coleridge, and Lord Byron. Those writers share a melancholic rejection of their own times, and several of them turned inward or submersed themselves in nature to quench their spiritual thirst. But they could not find contentment even in love and beauty. "Ay, in the very temple of delight / Veil'd Melancholy has her sovran shrine," wrote John Keats in his "Ode on Melancholy."

And at the apex of Victorian optimism, literary critic Matthew Arnold eulogized the loss of traditional religion. "The Sea of Faith / Was once, too, at the full, and round earth's shore. . . . / But now I only hear / Its melancholy, long, withdrawing roar," Arnold wrote in his poem "Dover Beach."

In nineteenth-century America, melancholy adapted to a rapidly changing country and its aggressively expanding population. On his visit to the United States in the early 1830s, French aristocrat Alexis de Tocqueville found a country that sounds strikingly familiar today.

"In America," Tocqueville wrote in *Democracy in America*, "I have seen the freest and best educated of men in circumstances the happiest to be found in the world; yet it seemed to me that a cloud habitually hung on their brow, and they seemed serious and almost sad even in their pleasures." This uneasiness, he concluded, was because Americans "never stop thinking of the good things they have not got."

The anxiety amid material abundance that Tocqueville noticed in the Jacksonian era had become a common observation by the end of the nineteenth century.

The term was *neurasthenia*—also called "American nervousness" after an 1881 book of the same name by Dr. George Beard—

which was defined as the sickness of modern civilization. Its symptoms included physical and mental lassitude, physical list-lessness, and emotional fatigue. It especially affected young, well-educated, socially privileged individuals. Among its victims were Woodrow Wilson, Henry Adams, Eugene Debs, Jane Addams, and William James—all of whom made major contributions to American society despite their psychic debilities.

The complaint was that new technologies (telephone, electric lights, nationwide rail system), urbanization, the modern corporation, mass production, a mass consumer market and mass media, the rise of organized labor, the changing role of women, political corruption, the destruction of nature, the closing of the Western frontier, immigration, Populist agitation, and the questioning of biblical religion by Darwinian science had set Americans adrift from their traditional harbors. A speeded-up, citified, racially mixed, intellectually confused society proved too much for some tender minds accustomed to the respect, stability, and deference of an earlier America.

Physicians categorized this melancholy as *tedium vitae,* a torpid "tiredness of life." Philosopher William James, who wrote extensively on the subject, said the ailment sapped the vigor for life among many of the most talented members of his generation, partly because the ruthless determinism of evolution-based theories undermined their religious faith and weakened confidence in their own free will.

To James and other patrician members of the educated, upper middle class, a self-referential sentimentality, a depressive weariness, and even repeated nervous breakdowns indicated an emotional depth of soul that countered the blustering, boosting, and hustling of the rampaging capitalist economy of the Gilded Age.

At the highest levels of American society, melancholy even became a fashion statement. The languid, invalid woman who suffered mightily for her mordant sensibility to the stresses of the period was a romantic ideal. Effete, upper-middle-class men found such vapid and fragile women particularly desirable because they displayed a feminine delicacy that sharply contrasted with the proletarian rudeness and nouveau riche boorishness of the larger society.

Meanwhile, in Europe *le mal du siècle*—the sickness of the age—had become a plague. Through the 1870s, 1880s, and 1890s, Europe trembled with social and political disintegration. Drastic change occurred in almost every area of life. Daring new ventures appeared in literature, music, architecture, painting, and sculpture. Inspired and embittered by the ill-fated Paris Commune of the early 1870s, political revolution filled the air through the rising anarchist, syndicalist, Marxist, and socialist movements. German philosopher Friedrich Nietzsche and his amoral superman challenged the rational, liberal, and idealistic assumptions that had dominated philosophy for most of the century. And in Vienna, psychiatrist Sigmund Freud plumbed the depths of the human subconscious, churning up fears, sexual drives, and neuroses that many people wished he had left submerged.

From the vantage point of the late twentieth century, those developments are seen as cornerstones of the modern era. But at the time, they made many people feel that the world was coming unglued. Revered traditions, long-accepted ethical principles, ancient religious concepts, established political systems, and familiar artistic forms were being subverted by the forces of moral decay and social chaos.

Predictably, in a society that saw itself degenerating, melancholy wafted through the cultural air. Some of the most powerful images of the late nineteenth century were from a group of writers and artists known as the symbolists. Such painters as Gustave Moreau and Odilon Redon and poets Stéphane Mallarmé and

Arthur Rimbaud often dealt in melancholy motifs. The favored season is autumn; the preferred time of day is dusk; the atmosphere is rainy and watery; the moon hovers above; the mood is anomie, solitude, and anticipation of death; sexuality is ambiguous, if not impotent.

"Ennui descends on me like the autumn mist," swooned Ephraim Mikhael. "The flesh, alas! is sorrowful and I have read every book," groaned Mallarmé. "Springtime lasted but a day / One by one the flowers died," moaned Grégoire Le Roy.

With their mystical incantations and rejection of realism, the symbolists helped create the cultural space for people to contact a hidden reality "beyond" things that could be seen, felt, or smelled.

To Freud, the psychic disturbances and cultural cracking-up of the late nineteenth and early twentieth centuries revealed often-hidden aspects of human nature. In his essay "Mourning and Melancholia," Freud says that the depressive "has a keener eye for the truth than other people who are not melancholic. When in his heightened self-criticism he describes himself as petty, egoistic, dishonest, lacking in independence . . . it may be, so far as we know, that he has come pretty close to understanding himself; we only wonder why a man has to be ill before he can be accessible to a truth of this kind."

As Freud notes, melancholy can expose some of the deepest realities of the conscious and unconscious human mind. As we have seen, several of the major transformations in Western civilization—the end of antiquity, the Renaissance, the Reformation, the Romantic era, and the Mauve Decade of the 1890s—included outbreaks of melancholy. Each of those ages experienced sweeping cultural and spiritual discontent along with remarkable artistic and philosophical achievements that have become centerpieces of Western society.

Furthermore, aside from the late classical era, each of those periods—like the late twentieth century—was a time of major improvement in the material standing of most Western nations. Nascent capitalism helped finance the Renaissance and sent European ships to explore the world. The Industrial Revolution brought the steam engine, the railroad, and an agricultural bounty that eventually enhanced the quality of life for the vast majority of people. The late nineteenth century in the United States incubated the Progressive Era that fought a variety of social and political evils. And the 1990s has seen a skyrocketing stock market, low unemployment, and astounding technological invention.

But living in a melancholic age puts a heavy burden on the human psyche. Everything is up for grabs. The journey to the future requires a tightrope walk across the abyss. The instinct for survival screams for escape, for a hiding place from despair. That's why the melancholic soul from Homeric Greece to late-twentieth-century America can identify with Bellerophon—"a fugitive on the run."

Creative Gloom

A historical survey of melancholy helps measure the social impact of the ailment, but it is also important to understand how individuals were affected. Biographies of noted melancholics, both actual persons and literary characters, show that the West would lose much of its intellectual complexity, artistic dynamism, and spiritual depth without these tormented people—people who set off cultural tides that swamped their age and rippled through later generations.

Before the suicidal Kurt Cobain, before the self-destructive Jim Morrison, before the tormented Sylvia Plath, before the moody

Marlon Brando, and before the surly James Dean, there was Young Werther.

The main character in an eighteenth-century novel by Johann von Goethe, Werther is the prototype of the alienated, misunderstood youths who have drifted sullenly through American movie theaters, rock concert halls, and college campuses in the post–World War II era.

Werther also is a dramatic example of how melancholy has affected Western culture over the past two hundred years. Indeed, Werther would find kindred souls traipsing around Italy with Lord Byron, discussing literary style with Virginia Woolf, or sipping midnight coffee with the brooding, underemployed teens and twentysomethings of late-twentieth-century America.

Told in a series of letters, Werther's story is of a highly intelligent, artistically inclined young man who falls in love with a woman. She rejects him for a more emotionally and financially stable suitor. Torn by hopeless passion, Werther immerses himself in poetry and philosophy and reflects despairingly on life. A world once filled with sunlight and possibility now appears dark and cruel, leading Werther to kill himself with a pistol shot to the head.

Werther's story, written in 1774 and based partly on Goethe's own life, struck a deep chord among Europeans disillusioned with the dry, sterile culture and orderly philosophy of the Enlightenment. It set off a wave of suicides, especially among young men who felt that their emotions were stunted by an unsympathetic society. Even Napoleon Bonaparte, then a young recruit in the French army, caught the Werther fever and wrote how he submitted "to the liveliness of my own melancholy: what turn will it take today? towards Death."

History had other plans for Napoleon, and he did not end as an obscure suicide. But his reaction to Werther is an example of the hold that melancholy has had on the Western imagination. A short list of famous depressives forms a cultural honor roll: Vincent van Gogh, Leo Tolstoy, Edgar Degas, Jack London, Gustav Mahler, Diane Arbus, Ernest Hemingway, William Faulkner, George Orwell, William Inge, Anne Sexton, Jackson Pollock—the names could go on.

Melancholy influenced those people in different ways, but academic research has found a strong connection between depression and creativity. The May 1996 issue of the *British Journal of Psychiatry* published a two-year study of one hundred British and American writers that noted high rates of mental torment among the group. "It's simply a confirmation of what other people also suspected, which is that writers are prone to depressive bouts," concluded Dr. Felix Post, a British psychiatrist who conducted the survey.

The lonely, morose painter or novelist shivering in an unheated garret is something of a romantic caricature, but the prevalence of melancholy among artistic individuals suggests that depression can be a powerful stimulant of the imagination. And in the direction that creative consciousness changes, the rest of society inevitably follows.

Using biography as therapy for melancholy, I have selected three writers from three different eras: French essayist Michel de Montaigne, Danish theologian Søren Kierkegaard, and American philosopher William James. Each man is a persuasive writer. Each played a pivotal role in the West's cultural history. And each was a melancholic who sought a new relationship between God and humanity.

Montaigne was born in 1533 at his father's chateau near Bordeaux in southwestern France. It was a time when Erasmus and other humanist reformers were pushing for moderate change in church and state. The comic genius Rabelais was mocking the arid scholasticism of the still-medieval Sorbonne in his satire *Pantagruel*. Many French leaders were sponsoring the new learning of the Renaissance. King Francis I was a strong patron of the arts and literature, and his court drew such luminaries as Leonardo da Vinci and Benvenuto Cellini. Tolerance was an admired virtue.

But when Montaigne reached adulthood, a more coarse age had begun. Savage wars between Catholics and Protestants divided France and many of its families; three of Montaigne's seven siblings became Protestant while the others stayed Catholic.

Educated in the classics, a moderate Catholic, and a member of the minor nobility, Montaigne served as a local official during part of this violent period. He didn't enjoy the largely legalistic work, but one good thing came of it—his friendship with Etienne de La Boétie, a fellow public servant who had written a treatise against tyranny.

After La Boétie's early death, Montaigne tried to relieve his depressive grief through amorous affairs. At his father's urging, he married the daughter of a colleague and sired six children, only one of whom survived infancy.

On his thirty-eighth birthday in February 1571, Montaigne, dispirited by society and generally despondent, announced his retirement to "the bosom of the learned virgins, where in calm and freedom from all cares he will spend what little remains of his life, now more than half run out."

From this midlife crisis emerged one of the great books of Western civilization, a new literary form and a new view of humanity.

Montaigne's *Essays* is the first example in Western literature of a person's critically examining himself, a self-portrait by a man scrutinizing his attitudes on subjects ranging from friendship to dietary habits. Montaigne outlines his mission by saying, "The greatest thing in the world is to know how to belong to yourself."

That level of self-dissection had not happened before. Such previous autobiographical works as Augustine's *Confessions* and Boethius's *The Consolation of Philosophy* are primarily descriptive accounts of religious awakening or coping with adversity, not personal introspection and soul-searching to reveal God and human nature.

As explained by Montaigne, the *Essays* resulted from "a melancholy humor . . . born of the solitude in which I had taken refuge, that first put into my head this notion of writing."

Montaigne's testimonial approach is so familiar today that it is hard to imagine how novel his self-analysis was to his contemporaries. Rather than blame the devil or divine retribution for his despair, he looks inside to find the cause of his horrible thoughts and temptations. His soul gave birth "to so many chimeras, so many fantastical monsters, one after the other, without order, without sense, that, so as to contemplate their ineptitude and strangeness," he had to record them.

This "melancholic in his lonely tower," as English poet John Milton described Montaigne a century later, thought that people needed to be alone to truly know themselves. For the wise person touched by melancholy, learning the lessons of the soul consumes a lifetime. "Let us not fear that, in a solitude like this, we shall be crouching in boring idleness," Montaigne wrote.

Like sixteenth-century mariners, his contemporaries who were exploring new lands across the seas, Montaigne helped set Western civilization on a comparable voyage of personal and spiritual discovery. Self-knowledge, not religious dogma, and self-awareness, not philosophical tenets, were the best ways for Montaigne to examine himself and to feel God's presence.

For Montaigne, the self is never static but always seeking. Life is marked by contradictions that, paradoxically, give harmony to this world "of different tones, sweet and harsh, sharp and flat, soft and loud. If a musician liked only one kind, what would he have to say? He must know how to use them together and blend them. And so must we with good and evil, which are consubstantial, with our life."

Montaigne's writing, begun as a therapeutic exercise to help him withstand melancholy and recover from the death of his closest friend, helped mold the modern personality of the self-made individual. Although he always acknowledges God, by delving into himself and confronting his own terrors, Montaigne helped make self-revelation a defining characteristic of Western society.

The severe inner analysis pioneered by Montaigne was deepened several centuries later by my second example of the depressive as a cultural revolutionary. Søren Kierkegaard, the "melancholy Dane" who was often ignored or ridiculed during his lifetime in the early nineteenth century, has had an enormous influence on twentieth-century philosophy and literature. American theologian Reinhold Niebuhr called him "the profoundest interpreter of the psychology of the religious life . . . since St. Augustine."

Born in Copenhagen in 1813, Kierkegaard is the modern world's prophet of despair. His biography is brief. The son of a wealthy merchant, he had no real job and lived off his inheritance. His one love affair failed because of his depression and indecision. A recluse, he shunned outside society but was obsessed by reviews of his work in the popular press. He wrote prolifically, often under pseudonyms, but few of his books sold well in his lifetime.

But Kierkegaard's internal life was as fertile as his public life was barren. Highly sensitive and tormented, Kierkegaard anguished over the uncertainty of humanity's place in the universe and the discrepancy between our ideals and actions. A shattered man living in a shattered world, Kierkegaard devoted much of his time to his *Journals,* which he described as a "cabin of melancholy" and are noted for their poetic expressions of his fear of being forsaken by God. But that pain was the central element of Kierkegaard's life. "From my early childhood," he wrote, "the arrow of suffering has been planted in my heart. So long as it is there I am ironical—pull it out and I will die."

For us living in the Age of Melancholy of the late twentieth century, Kierkegaard's most powerful work is *The Sickness Unto Death,* the most penetrating psychological study of despair ever written.

Kierkegaard saw despair as humanity's greatest terror. People do everything possible to avoid or deny despair or to minimize its impact, but such attempts are in vain because despair is an indelible part of the human condition. By cutting off all avenues of escape—wealth, status, sexuality—despair forces humanity to stand naked before its horror of meaninglessness and mortality. For Kierkegaard, melancholy is a spiritual sickness caused by humanity's sinful alienation from God, not just a mental, emotional, or medical disorder.

Largely forgotten in the decades immediately following his death, Kierkegaard emerged in the mid-twentieth century as an intellectual grandfather of existentialism, probably the most powerful set of philosophical ideas in the West since World War II. One of existentialism's primary concerns—that reason and logic can't account for the dread, guilt, anxiety, and the incompleteness of human life—has its roots in Kierkegaard's writings. From Kierkegaard's perception that life is inherently ambiguous, if not downright absurd, have flowed many of the central cultural themes of the postwar era.

Kierkegaard alone would be ample evidence of the heavy influence of melancholy on twentieth-century European and American thought. But when William James is also taken into account, melancholy is indisputably a distinct cultural force in the current century. Based partly on his struggle with depression, James's books *The Varieties of Religious Experience* and *The Will to Believe* are among the most respected works ever written by an American.

As a personal aside, I strongly identify with James, certainly not because of any comparable intellectual acumen but because his lifelong struggle to justify religious faith to his educated but doubting contemporaries is the same task that this book undertakes. James's ideas are central to many of my arguments.

Born in 1842 into one of the most fascinating families in nineteenth-century America—his father, Henry, was an eccentric mystic; his brother was the novelist Henry James, Jr.—William James entered a society that was becoming an urbanized colossus. Trying to find a niche for himself in this new America that seemed hostile to his moral values, James searched for "a constructive passion of some kind."

Reacting to the Darwinian view of an indifferent universe that evolved without any direct, active participation by God, James felt that something essential to the human character was jeopardized if people abandoned religious belief. A professor of anatomy at Harvard and the author of a popular psychology textbook, James accepted the scientific method but rejected the materialism and emotional desolation that accompanied Charles Darwin's theories. "A terrible coldness and deadness would come over the world were we forced to believe that no informing spirit or purpose had to do with it," James wrote.

Interpreting his depression as a spiritual crisis, James says there is much to learn from the dark side. "The normal process of life contains moments as bad as any of those which insane melancholy is filled with, moments in which radical evil gets its solid turn," he wrote.

From his own experience, James concluded that a person's philosophical outlook could relieve depression. As a founder of the only American-born school of academic philosophy, Pragmatism, James argues that individuals must decide how to act in life. For James, the first pragmatic decision is to believe in free will; the possibility of choice gives humanity the power to shape a moral order.

James thought that the final test of truth isn't logical argument or laboratory experiments, but the practical consequences of an idea on individuals and society. Seeing that ethical choice and religious belief had empirically proved their value to enhance life, James says that the most reliable proof of faith lies within its ability to transform people. "God is real since he produces real effects," he wrote.

Philosopher, psychologist, political activist, public lecturer, university reformer, moralist, spiritual pilgrim, James has touched virtually every area of American culture in the twentieth century. For example, his concept of "stream of consciousness," which asks a person to carve out reality through the free flow of thoughts, was picked up by numerous writers, notably his former student Gertrude Stein, and became a key technique of modern literature. His insistence that abstract theories must yield to concrete results is such a part of the American mind that few people know that it was once—and still is in some corners—a highly controversial notion. And even the daily vocabulary of twentieth-century America is sprinkled with words that James either invented or popularized: *pragmatic, individualistic, anti-institutional, pluralistic, relativist.*

Although separated by time and place, Montaigne, Kierkegaard, and James were melancholics who rearranged social consciousness. Their psychic torment led them to reject the reigning thought patterns of their day and to open new cultural vistas for later generations.

The three men also are role models for the late twentieth century, an era of social ferment not too different from the Renaissance, the early nineteenth century, or the turn of the century. Although differing in specifics, each man worked through melancholy to realize two basic truths: that ultimate reality rests in the relationship between the individual and God, and that meaning in life is partly determined by tragedy.

As demonstrated by Montaigne, Kierkegaard, and James, historical change results less from the wars of kings than from the teachings of soul-seekers, less from the laws of legislators than from the visions of artists. Attitudes that today seem commonsensical and images that dominate the social landscape can usually be traced to troubled individuals who were dissatisfied with the conventional wisdom or aesthetic axioms of their period. Time and again, melancholic despair has stimulated new—or renewed—understandings of life that suit the emerging era.

And in the late twentieth century, that kind of massive cultural shift is rumbling through America.

Moody Paradigms

Boris Yeltsin and gay activists. Tarot card readers and computer programmers. Cocaine addicts and New Age goddesses.

At first glance those pairings seem incongruous. What would the vulgar, hard-drinking first president of post-Soviet Russia have in common with homosexuals seeking societal acceptance? What would mystical occultists have to say to Microsoft code-runners? What's the connection between strung-out dopers and tree-hugging earth mothers?

The link is that each of those individuals represents a cultural phenomenon that could grow into a new social consciousness in the next century. Indeed, studying melancholy as a historical force and feeling it as a personal trauma while also working in daily journalism, I lived in a time warp. The past, the personal, and the present coincided in philosophical texts, in my mind and on the front page.

Glance at the periods of melancholic epidemics discussed earlier—the Renaissance, the early nineteenth century, the late nineteenth century, and the late twentieth century—and the signs are the same: political dissent, economic turmoil, technological advancement, a questioning of religious orthodoxy, interest in the occult, homosexuality, greater recognition of women's roles, a wistful hope to recapture a period in the past, and a breakdown of intellectual and cultural authority.

- The Renaissance. The feudal political order collapses; the printing press and other new technologies appear; a vibrant same-sex culture emerges among Italian artists; the medieval church yields to the Protestant Reformation and the Catholic Counter-Reformation; Neoplatonic mysticism accompanies a Hellenic revival; Italian philosopher Giordano Bruno seeks spiritual truth through sex and magic and is condemned by the Inquisition; Elizabeth, the "Virgin Queen," leads England to the first rank of European powers; banker-controlled capitalism replaces the church-enforced anti-usury medieval economy.
- The early nineteenth century. The Industrial Revolution propels laissez-faire capitalism; the political order is recast through the 1830 July Revolution in France, the Jackson administration in the United States, and the Europe-wide turmoil of 1848; influenced by Mary Wollstonecraft's *A Vindication of the Rights of Woman*, published in 1792, women begin to agitate for political rights; opium-hazed hallucinations conjure otherworldly fantasies; Lord Byron, the most flamboyant poet of the Romantic

era, displays an affinity for "Greek love"; nostalgia arises for the harmony of the Middle Ages through popular fascination with King Arthur and the Anglo-Catholic Oxford Movement in England.

- The late nineteenth century. Darwinian science challenges biblical literalism; parapsychology becomes a subject of academic inquiry; theosophy attracts spiritualists in Europe and the United States; Buddhism and Hinduism become part of the Western religious scene; the prairie Populists rebel against corporate capitalism; the emancipated woman demands the vote and proclaims her sexual freedom; Oscar Wilde and other homosexual aesthetes exert enormous artistic influence; the automobile, telephone, and other machines are part of a technological boom; the Arts and Crafts movement rejects mass production in favor of medieval-guild-emulated workmanship.
- The late twentieth century. Technology explodes; global capitalism triumphs; cynicism about politics and government increases; women struggle up corporate and political ladders; alien visitations, near-death experiences, astral travel, and other reports from the beyond proliferate; New Age religions gain adherents, as do Tibetan Buddhism and other forms of Eastern thought; homosexuality and gender-bending enter mainstream culture; academic canons in literature and other humanities are deconstructed; many Americans yearn for the simplicities of the Cold War 1950s.

This brief survey reinforces for me the idea that Western civilization repeats well-trod paths. As the Roman poet Virgil says: "There will also be other wars, and great Achilles will again be sent to Troy." Although history doesn't recycle itself in every detail, it seems to fit into a predictable outline. Indeed, finding such a design has been a preoccupation for Western thinkers. And only within such a comprehensible cultural blueprint does the Age of Melancholy of the late twentieth century make sense and reassure today's Americans that we can successfully steer Western history into another, brighter phase.

Giambattista Vico, an eighteenth-century Italian philosopher often regarded as the first modern historian, said that societies initially strive for material security and, once that is achieved, then fall into moral, intellectual, and spiritual decline. "Men first feel necessity," Vico wrote in his book *The New Science,* "then look for utility, next attend to comfort, still later amuse themselves with pleasure, thence grow dissolute in luxury, and finally go mad and waste their substance."

The end of the process discerned by Vico — which sounds like an eerie prophecy for the social disconnections of the late twentieth century—is when "each man is thinking only of his own private interests."

The most famous argument against history as a series of random events is from nineteenth-century German philosopher G. W. F. Hegel, who detected systematic change in human consciousness. Hegel says that the dominant forms of government, art, and religious belief reflect what he called the spirit of a historical era. Within each spirit, however, lie tension and conflict —what Hegel labeled thesis and antithesis—that synthesize into a new era. The dialectic continues until the absolute unfolds fully, consciousness evolves completely, and history closes.

Oswald Spengler, a German historian whose major work, *The Decline of the West,* was published in two volumes in 1918–22, divides history into two alternating periods. The first is when all facets of society were in kilter, the second is when culture succumbed to division and ended in the chaos of excessive individualism. For Spengler, the twentieth-century West is in the latter stage: its suicidal death will give way to the next civilization.

A generation after Spengler, British historian Arnold Toynbee says in his twelve-volume *A Study of History* that the well-being of a society depends on its ability to adapt to new challenges, both human and environmental. He suggests that Western civilization will be doomed when it is stricken by spiritual and intellectual infirmity.

However they built their cases intellectually, all of these historians agree that civilizations start, flourish, decline, and disappear. History moves in forseeable waves, peaking and dipping. A culture's survival hinges on whether it can respond effectively to hostile situations—either from the outside or of its own making—or fall victim to its own inertia, skepticism, hedonism, and lack of creativity.

The disintegration of the old order—which once was the new establishment—is inevitable, as are the melancholic epidemics that accompany the convulsive uprooting of old structures. Yet since the ancient Greeks, Western civilization has escaped the destiny of cultures that now exist only in nostalgia or libraries. In Western history the thread of melancholy stitches the cultural patchwork.

In the late twentieth century the jargon for historical movement—supplanting Hegel's dialectic and Toynbee's challenge and response—is "paradigm shift." Although the term has become a cliché to describe everything from new styles in women's shoes to the latest research in astrophysics, the idea helps explain how society changes.

As discussed by Thomas Kuhn in his 1962 book, *The Structure of Scientific Revolutions,* a paradigm is a conceptual model of how the world works. It puts facts, data, and experiences into a coherent system. Paradigms shift, according to Kuhn, in response to new scientific discoveries or similar intellectual breakthroughs. An example is the switch from Ptolemaic to Copernican cosmology during the Renaissance that put the sun, not Earth, at the center of the universe.

Initially, the new paradigm incites a wholesale social and intellectual reordering as people apply the new insights to all aspects of life. Learning expands and people develop more complicated and sophisticated social behaviors and technologies. Eventually, however, the new paradigm is depleted. It becomes an ossified orthodoxy unable to inspire new perspectives or to resolve its own inherent contradictions. Its mission complete, the paradigm implodes.

Sudden change, as occurred in the melancholic eras sketched previously, liquidates social systems, personal identities, and accepted rules of conduct. In effect, society has a wholesale emotional vaporization that clears the cultural psyche for new attitudes and actions. When long-standing social codes lose validity, people are free to experiment with everything from sexual relationships to political ideologies. That's why historical paradigm shifts are usually periods of creativity and anxiety. The emerging society has not yet decided what it expects from its members, so everything is possible because nothing has universal sanction. Gender roles are in flux. Magic and superstition offer esoteric answers to help people cope with cultural disarray. Long-term class and political arrangements are disrupted.

Western civilization's last great paradigm shift before the present Age of Melancholy was in the late nineteenth century, a period that erected much of the framework for the twentieth century. As mentioned, the Gilded Age experienced both melancholy among society's most sensitive minds and massive cultural change. It also exhibited many of the social and political paroxysms noted by the philosophers of history.

Let's join Henry Adams, the scion of the presidential family, a noted historian and a melancholic, as he visits the Paris Exposition of 1900. Touring the displays of America's industrial prowess—the hissing steam, the gears and levers, the noisy engines of progress— Adams falls into a deep funk. He is especially awed by the Dynamo, the electricity generator that powers the new machine age.

In the Dynamo, Adams finds the modern age's new symbol of devotion, a new divinity for the new century. Adams contrasts the Dynamo to the Middle Ages, when adoration of the Virgin gave Western society an inner harmony and unity that linked human- ity to divine authority. Modern society, however, worships pure power, especially the highly organized technological power that Adams says could never satisfy the deep human need for meaning in life. With power an end in itself, individuals feel alienated—a "certain cerebral restlessness," in Adams's phrase—because his- tory has no purpose other than to consume energy, and society eventually exhausts itself in an irrational, entropic burst of "cos- mic violence."

Like his friend William James, Adams never reconciled him- self to the new technological order. But his metaphor of the Dynamo and the Virgin captures the drastic cultural change that overwhelmed America at the turn of the century. Man-made in- dustrial power, not God, would henceforth govern the human imagination.

The same point was made by German sociologist Max Weber, a contemporary of Adams who shared the American's worry about the displacement of religion in modern society. The loss of rever- ence for the divine, Weber says, means that the "ethic" of material wealth would dominate Western civilization. Abandoning the cul- tural richness of traditional religion, modern people have submit- ted to a faceless, merciless industrial system—what Weber called "an iron cage"—that offers individuals financial prosperity in ex- change for mind-numbing routine. Enhancing organization and efficiency, not serving spiritual values or human feelings, had become society's central operating principle.

The issues raised by Adams and Weber are exponentially more serious at the end of the twentieth century than they were at its beginning. We Americans are wired so tightly into our modems and fax machines that many of us have lost the capacity to think for ourselves. Instead, we continually feed more information into our brains and are deaf to the voices deep within ourselves that ask whether any of it has any meaning. Rather than contributing to knowledge and wisdom, information is processed simply to be launched into cyberspace.

The late twentieth century is a dialectical struggle, a Richter-scale shift of cultural tectonics, in America's social psyche. The Dynamo has proved a false God. The twentieth century has not brought peace and social harmony through science and technology, but massive destruction, bloodshed, and millions of atomized, disinherited individuals who deny any allegiance to universal moral ideals or spiritual beliefs.

Much of the psychological depression of the 1990s is due to a personal disconnection from a larger vision of life. There is no consensus, no clear direction to the future. The culture no longer inspires society, and the bonds of shared experience that once held people together are reduced to TV, pro sports, and plotless but visually spectacular computer-enhanced movies. Unless Americans regain a broad purpose in life, they will remain secluded within their corporate cubicles, sending binary bytes into a cybernetic mist, or sequestered in their living rooms, watching moronic sitcoms in the dark.

The end of the twentieth century is the Age of Melancholy partly because many people are like me in rejecting the materialistic, soul-denying, and morally indifferent culture that has broken

Western civilization's once-intimate relationship with nature, community, and divinity. We want to return to the Virgin. The next two chapters show how this is possible—how paradigms can shift backward, see how we got here in the first place, and then move history forward.

4

THE POSTMODERN EGO

The End of the Orgy

The party is over, says Jean Baudrillard.

And anyone who has lived through the postwar half century in America or Europe would understand what party the respected French sociologist is talking about:

"If I were asked to describe the present state of affairs, I would describe it as 'after the orgy.' The orgy in question was the moment when modernity exploded upon us, the moment of liberation in every sphere. Political liberation, sexual liberation, liberation of the forces of production, liberation of the forces of destruction, women's liberation, children's liberation, liberation of unconscious drives, liberation of art. The assumption of all models of representation, as of all models of anti-representation.

"This was a total orgy—an orgy of the real, the rational, the sexual, of criticism as of anti-criticism, of development as of the crisis of development. We have pursued every avenue in the production and effective overproduction of objects, signs, messages, ideologies and satisfactions. Now everything has been liberated, the chips are down, and we find ourselves faced collectively with the big question: What do we do now that the orgy is over?" Baudrillard wrote in his 1993 book *The Transparency of Evil.*

Baudrillard's orgy is a metaphor for modernism, the cultural mind-set that has presided over American and European artistic and intellectual life for most of the twentieth century. The breakdown of modernism—its failed ambitions, its murderous political heritage, its aborted philosophical conceptions—is a central element in the Age of Melancholy of the late twentieth century.

The cultural framework erected by Western civilization over the past five hundred years has splintered. The fragmentation in contemporary arts, the dearth of compelling projects, the lack of an overarching vision, the vulgarity and crass commercialism of many artistic productions, warn us that the great creative moments of Western culture might lie only in the past. Intuition tells us that we will not see another Pound, Cézanne, or Beckett in our lifetime, much less another Sophocles, Michelangelo, or Milton. The current generation lives within the cultural gulf that opens at the close of an era. We are astonished by many of the achievements of twentieth-century modernism, yet we are embarrassed by its excesses while also wondering whether anything of comparable significance will take its place in the foreseeable future.

Just as modernism arose during a time of historical transition that recast cultural models, its decay marks another climactic turn in Western civilization—into the Age of Melancholy.

In a declarative remark, British novelist Virginia Woolf said that "on or about December 1910, human nature changed."

Although Mrs. Woolf exaggerated the malleability of basic human nature, almost everything else was in turmoil at the time of her proclamation. Modernist thought had captured the artistic and literary elites, such as Mrs. Woolf's Bloomsbury Group, and its influence would pervade twentieth-century European and American society.

The cultural argument was that the nineteenth-century certainties no longer applied and that dominant art forms—academic realism in painting, straight narrative in fiction—could not capture the complexity of the new era. Modernism would reorganize Western civilization's perceptions and reinterpret history to match the momentous changes of the turn of the century. To do so required artistic styles and ideas that would upset tradition and often offend established sensibilities.

But I found that modernism was more than an artists' rebellion against nineteenth-century stuffiness and smugness; it was a revolt of biblical proportions by humanity against God. And, like the first defiance to divine authority, it began with the devil.

Before Mrs. Woolf and her friends bickered, swapped mates, and philosophized at Bloomsbury Square in London or the "lost generation" crammed into Gertrude Stein's art-filled apartment in Paris, the devil and Faust arrived at Auerbach's Keller in Leipzig, Germany. A student beer hall, Auerbach's Keller is the site of the opening scene in Johann von Goethe's great dramatic poem *Faust*, whose title character is considered the first modernist.

Published in 1808, Goethe's story is set several centuries ago, when the devil, personified by Mephistopheles, brings the scholarly Dr. Faust to Auerbach's Keller to demonstrate his powers. While Faust and the students watch in amazement, Mephistopheles makes wine and champagne flow from the holes in a wooden table. Astounded by the devil's performance, Faust agrees to a fatal bargain—to sell his soul in exchange for unlimited learning.

Faust represents the fatal human lust—the original sin of Adam and Eve in the Garden of Eden—to attain, in Goethe's words, "god-like knowledge" and to "prove in man the stature of a god." Anticipating his modernist heirs in the twentieth century, Faust seeks to close the gap between humanity and the divine that has been maintained by Judeo-Christian religious belief. Rather than seek God's grace for salvation, the Faustian individual wants to explore the self in all its dimensions and exploit its full potential. No longer would humanity be limited by divine or traditional sanctions; instead, humanity would be restricted only by its own imagination—even if that includes, as it did for Faust, killing and sexual abuse. Humanity's destiny would be to fashion the world to suit its own purposes, not to seek eternal life by following God's plan for redemption.

Although characterized in Faust, modernism could track its intellectual origins to the remark by the ancient Greek philosopher Protagoras that "Man is the measure of all things," which means that individuals are not answerable to transcendent authority. More directly, modernism sprang from the seventeenth-century French philosopher René Descartes, whose famous statement "I think, therefore I am" is the fountainhead of the modernist claim that the self, on its own power, can detect truth. While Descartes intended to show that the thoughtful, contemplative individual could ultimately prove God's existence without miracles or other outside evidence of divine presence, his ideas led to the modernist notion that reality is verified by humanity alone.

Human autonomy was advanced further by the eighteenth-century German philosopher Immanuel Kant, who like Descartes argues that individuals unaided by divine revelation can discern truth. Making a valiant effort to give religion and morality a rational foundation in his skeptical age, Kant thought that if freed from the control of church and state, each person would discover the same moral, spiritual, and scientific truths. Kant was actually trying to preserve universal law by saying that the human mind was wired—the "categorical imperative"—to perceive what was truthful and best for all people. But by making freely thinking individuals—instead of scripture, tradition, or political hierarchy—the final arbiters of truth, he and other Enlightenment philosophers unwittingly encouraged the notion, which blossomed in the Romantic era of the early nineteenth century, that human feelings and emotions have a transcendent moral and spiritual authority equal, if not superior, to reason. Consequently, the individual, not God or society, became the primary interpreter of human experience.

No one rejected original sin and sought to expand human freedom more aggressively than the eighteenth-century French philosopher Jean-Jacques Rousseau. Dissenting from orthodox Christianity, Rousseau believed that human misfortune resulted from a repressive society rather than from a biblical fall from grace or a basic flaw in humanity's makeup. By breaking the chains of clerical and political tyranny, Rousseau argues, humanity can achieve freedom and justice. Human perfection is possible through education and progressive social institutions. Guilt, evil, and misery aren't indelible to human nature, but tools of oppression that would disappear if society put human needs above the political status quo and religious dogma.

By jettisoning God as society's primary legislator, Rousseau influenced the French revolutionaries of 1789 who decapitated the supposedly divinely anointed King Louis XVI. Whether in the form of populist democracy or Marxist despotism—both of which trace some of their fundamental ideas to Rousseau—people alone decide social structure without necessarily deferring to a divine constitution.

If Rousseau helped eject God from government, the nineteenth-century German philosopher Friedrich Nietzsche expelled him from human consciousness.

The author of *The Birth of Tragedy, Thus Spake Zarathustra,* and *Beyond Good and Evil,* Nietzsche was not a systematic philosopher but a gifted writer of immeasurable influence over twentieth-century Western culture. Pronouncing that "God is dead," Nietzsche believed that rationalism had twisted a dagger into the heart of Christianity. The discoveries of science and the demand for human liberation, Nietzsche recognized, meant that the inherited faith was no longer compelling among educated people. But the loss of traditional religion was not a source of joy for Nietzsche, because it left him with an agonizing longing for security and purpose in human life. That void, however, can't be filled by human reason, which leaves people without a source of meaning other than naked self-interest. What remains standing is Nietzsche's "last man," the culmination of middle-class morality and democratic egalitarianism that does not satisfy spiritual yearnings and strands individuals on the edge of the abyss. Once reason replaces God, humanity has no hope for supernatural salvation.

Nietzsche's solution is the superman who lives beyond the bounds of common morality, above mass culture, and is a pure embodiment of the basic human drive—the will to power. The superman dictates his own laws, establishes his own values, and practices his own virtues, living with an intensity that ignores conventional standards of right and wrong. His contempt for society—especially the "slave morality" of Christianity and "the herd" of inferior humanity—is a tribute to the honesty and integrity of his selfhood.

Stripped of illusions about God, Nietzsche says, people could face their true situation of despair and use their creative powers to remake the world. Not surprisingly, in the late nineteenth and twentieth centuries, Nietzsche's impact has been enormous on artists and writers who felt he had exempted them from bourgeois morality and entrenched aesthetic norms. He gave artists permission to explore the once forbidden, to believe in impulse, to revel in the frenzy of Dionysian ecstasy. For Nietzsche, poetry rather than philosophy, fantasy rather than science, would restore meaning to the world.

But beneath everything lies the anxiety that, for each individual, death is the end of time—everyone must face a personal apocalypse without hope of metaphysical transformation. The only justification for life is art, and the ultimate expression of imagination is to make an artwork out of your life, to defy death through total creative freedom.

Although never a formal "school" because each artist had unique methods and insights, modernism includes the drama of August Strindberg and Henrik Ibsen, the poetry of William B. Yeats and T. S. Eliot, the fiction of Marcel Proust and James Joyce, the painting of Pablo Picasso and Marcel Duchamp.

Modernism also produced a new psychology of neurotic drives and unconscious motives. It explored post-Newtonian physics, in which matter is energy, and time and space are relative. It supported a logic in which passion was more truthful than syllogisms. It believed in disbelief, and it evangelized a religion of art and myth. It propelled a movement of movements: cubism, surrealism, Dadaism, Fauvism, futurism. It was anarchist, socialist, utopian, and elitist. It saw boredom as the original sin. It questioned everything, except the terror of existence. It rejected tradition and enthroned the imagination.

"The Modernist philosopher has occupied himself with the proof that there is no authority, no source of law, no value and no meaning in the culture and institutions that we have inherited, and that the sole purpose of thought is to clear the way for 'liberation,'" wrote British philosopher Roger Scruton in his book *Modern Philosophy*.

At the end of the twentieth century, freedom-obsessed humanity has "deconstructed" itself: no secure human dignity, only blunt power relationships in a society without coherent aesthetic, ethical, or moral values; no solid criteria for truth, only transitory analyses and theories based on personal preferences. It is what Søren Kierkegaard calls "despair"—the lack of meaning in a God-abandoned culture.

As for many people of my generation, that despair was the active cancer within my melancholy. I was an unacknowledged Nietzschean—seeking substitutes for God and community in ego, career, and affluence. Most important, my pain was not a philosophical argument but convincing proof that Nietzsche had correctly identified many of the personal and social crises of the twentieth century as spiritual.

Much of the dismal history of the twentieth century has been the search for alternative gods to replace Nietzsche's dead god. Among those new gods have been the political religions of Marxism and fascism—each with its own mythology, promise of perfection, and ordained elite, and on the altars at Auschwitz and the Gulag each has sacrificed the blood of millions of innocent people.

The mass murders, spiritual anemia, and moral perversions of the twentieth century have made a travesty of the eighteenth-century Enlightenment belief that humanity could establish a reign of reason; they have done likewise for the nineteenth-century liberal ideal that education and science would lead to endless progress. Literary critic Roger Shattuck put it best in summing up the past two centuries as a period when "the West appears to consider itself capable of surviving in a condition of unrestricted knowledge and unbridled imagination. We presume to welcome Prometheus while overlooking Pandora; we do not shirk from looking on the face of God."

Much of this was foretold by nineteenth-century Russian novelist Fyodor Dostoyevsky, whose Grand Inquisitor reflects the modernist attitude toward humanity and religion.

A character in Dostoyevsky's novel *The Brothers Karamazov*, the Grand Inquisitor is a church leader in the sixteenth-century Spanish town of Seville. An elderly, scholarly man and a cardinal in the Catholic Church, the Grand Inquisitor is in charge of ridding Seville of heretics who were thought to endanger the souls of the people and the peace of society. The day before the story begins, the Grand Inquisitor had sent almost one hundred heretics to the stake—"to the greater glory of God"—in the presence of the king, the court, the knights, the church hierarchy, and the whole population of Seville.

Unexpectedly, and contrary to biblical prophecy, Jesus appears in Seville and is instantly recognized. Drawn by his radiance and compassion, the people flock to Jesus and ask his help in curing their diseases. He restores sight to an elderly man. He then stops at the steps of the Seville cathedral at the moment a funeral procession exits the building. The deceased is a young girl, the only daughter of a prominent citizen. The mother begs Jesus to raise the child from the dead. Moved by the mother's sadness, Jesus softly says, "Maiden, arise!" and the girl sits up in her coffin, holding a bouquet of white roses the mourners had put in her hand.

The Grand Inquisitor witnesses the incident and orders his guards to arrest Jesus. The crowd cowers into submission, and Jesus is led away and shut in prison. In the middle of the night, the Grand Inquisitor enters Jesus' cell alone to interrogate him. He berates Jesus for appearing in Spain at such an inopportune time—defying scripture—and threatens to burn him the next day.

During his tirade the Grand Inquisitor claims that the people can't handle the personal faith and freedom promised by Jesus. They need ironhanded political institutions, including the church, to provide them with food and other necessities and to dictate to their consciences. By returning to Earth, Jesus jeopardizes the established order and so must be eliminated.

In Dostoyevsky's parable, the Grand Inquisitor represents worldly authority and secular rationalism that see traditional spirituality as a mortal enemy. Humanity, in the Grand Inquisitor's view, must be enslaved to the things of this world and led by masters who can responsibly manage the burdens of freedom. Otherwise, people will never be content, because their undisciplined nature will cause them constant trouble and dissatisfaction. "Man was created a rebel; and how can rebels be happy?" the Grand Inquisitor asks Jesus.

At the end of the story, the Grand Inquisitor opens the cell door and orders Jesus to leave and never return. Jesus, who has remained silent throughout the interview, responds by kissing the old priest on the cheek, apparently an affirmation of his love even for the unbeliever.

The Grand Inquisitor would feel at home in late-twentieth-century America. He rejects divine authority because it restricts his personal freedom and power. He offers politics and art as spurious substitutes to satisfy people's craving for meaning in life. Humanity can forge its own happiness, although it might require a hardheaded, technically trained elite to ensure that the proper choices are made.

Dostoyevsky's tale cautions what can happen when people put selfish interests and their own powers above transcendent truth. As this century has proved disastrously, humanity alone can't construct a humane world. Unrestrained by divine morality, untouched by spiritual virtues, and undeterred by the concept of original sin, the human soul has unleashed some of its darkest impulses to horrifying results.

Within the spiritual desert of modernism, an arid, prickly philosophy has germinated—not a lush, fecund philosophy that tries to nurture the mind and ensheathe society, but an antiphilosophy that denies universal coherence to anything.

It's called postmodernism, which emerged in France in the mid-1960s as an intellectual and literary movement and hit many prestigious American universities with overwhelming force in the 1980s. For the rest of Western society, a workable date for argument's sake when modernism turned into postmodernism is November 1989, when the toppling of the Berlin Wall began a new historical era.

A brief comparison: Amid all the roiling ferment, the modern still saw design in the world and purpose in human existence. The postmodern sees chance and uncertainty as paramount. The modern sought common, lasting human values that weren't tied directly to God's revelation. The postmodern says values are transient and determined by cultural whim. The modern pursued a comprehensible truth through art, science, literature, and other endeavors. The postmodern denies the possibility of absolute knowledge and extols skepticism. The modern stressed life as intense commitment. The postmodern experiences life as ironic detachment.

For modernism, the challenge was to find a clarifying idea or unifying vision to hold the world together. For postmodernism, the human mind can't plug into objective truth, because there is no universal reality; the individual is the sovereign source of meaning. As postmodern philosopher Richard Rorty put it, "There is nothing deep down inside us except what we have put there ourselves, no criterion that we have not created in the course of creating a practice, no rigorous argumentation that is not obedience to our own conventions."

In postmodernism, Western philosophy ends in a catch-22 of its own making—there is no truth, including the statement that there is no truth. The Law of Noncontradiction—the philosophical theorem that no two opposing statements can be both true and false—is repealed. All claims to truth are fictions designed to push the program of some person or special-interest group. Any plausible truth is flexible and variable, valuable only according to its usefulness at a particular time and place. Intellectual and aesthetic standards have no objective status—Shakespeare's *Macbeth* has no more intrinsic artistic merit than a beer advertisement. The critic, rather than the author or artist, is the primary cultural player.

Honoring no religion, respecting no authority other than itself, feeling no responsibility to other people, enclosed in its own self-created reality and enveloped in cultural miasma, the postmodern ego finds itself demoralized, disillusioned, and disbelieving, but totally free from the confines of morality, history, and community. At the end of the twentieth century, the West has no source of common meaning, only scattered shards of personal autonomy— each ego its own kingdom.

In short, Western civilization at the end of the second millennium has achieved the perfection sought by Nietzsche: "Real are we entirely, and without belief or superstition."

And after the orgy? Melancholy.

The Abandoned Garden

Anglo-American poet T. S. Eliot's prophecy that the world would end with a whimper, not a bang could stand as an admonishing epitaph for Western civilization in the late twentieth century. It certainly expresses my weepy mood and that of millions of other American melancholics who fear we are wasting our lives in a twilight world, hoping desperately for, but not expecting, spiritual redemption.

The lack of coherence, meaning, and direction that characterizes the 1990s indicates that the United States and Europe have reached a critical juncture. Clearly, modernism failed to craft a cultural consensus for the twentieth century. (Eliot perhaps recognized it first; at midlife he converted to Anglo-Catholicism.) To describe the current situation, philosophers and social commentators have drafted a lexicon of prefixes that suggest something fundamental has changed, but the references point to artistic and social developments of the past.

Contemporary society is "postindustrial," "postcolonial," "posthistorical," "post-Freudian," and "post-Christian." Politics are "neoconservative," "neoliberal," "post–Cold War," and "neopopulist." Art is "neorealist," "neoconceptualist," and "neo-Expressionist." Philosophy is "poststructuralist," "neopragmatist," and "postrationalist."

Those terms are captured under the label *postmodern,* a transitory word that shows the uncertainty of this period but also carries the "after-everything," formless quality of the late twentieth century.

That mood was best expounded by novelist William S. Burroughs, a member of the Beat Generation, who could be considered the prototype of the postmodern writer. "The world cannot be expressed, it can perhaps be indicated by a mosaic of juxtaposition, like objects abandoned in a hotel room, defined by negatives and absence," Burroughs wrote in his novel *Naked Lunch.*

Not even language has independent status in the postmodern realm. "All interpretation is misinterpretation," said Jacques Derrida, a leading French postmodernist. Writer and reader bring their own baggage to literary works, making objective analysis impossible. Philosophy, religion, and art, conditioned by their social context, can be dismissed as merely a cacophony of voices or a gallery of images. The postmodern individual is a shimmering mirage because humanity can never know itself. As Argentinean novelist Jorge Luis Borges describes the protean postmodernist: "Who was I? Today's self, bewildered; yesterday's, forgotten; tomorrow's, unpredictable?"

Most important, postmodernism holds that truth is relative to an individual's perspective. For example, the creation story of a Native American tribe that believes its ancestors emerged from an underground spirit world could be as valid as anthropological research showing that the tribe entered North America from Asia thousands of years ago. To postmodernism, both claims are true based on their respective rules of evidence, and there is no objective test to measure the two claims against each other. Therefore, the Native American creation account is correct according to the truths of mythmaking; the anthropological view is accurate under the methods of social science. Facts aren't determined by independent verification but by the judgments of the individuals involved in an issue. Lacking a universal scale to weigh appeals to truth, individuals can, at best, establish only personal truths-contingent on particular assumptions.

Michael Ignatieff, a writer and literary critic, portrays the disenchantment of the late twentieth century as follows: "In the lonely garden of post-modern thought, the alleyways are littered with toppled statues. The great authorities are discredited. . . . Thinking in the 1990s means strolling through that abandoned garden. The overgrown paths are strewn with broken relics, from which only a certain departed grandeur may be inferred. And these ruins offer no inspiration, only the melancholy of vanished worlds."

Because finding meaning in life depends partly on a moral nexus that makes everything seem worthwhile, I doubt that postmodernism can provide the energy to enable Western civilization to move beyond the Age of Melancholy. In fact, postmodernist intellectuals, who control many of the nation's premier academic departments, have dismissed Western civilization's historic quest for objective truth as a voyage without a destination. That leaves millions of people to wander aimlessly in a barren, uncharted wasteland.

Without any philosophical structure or religious tradition to organize the world, postmodern individuals have total freedom to create and define themselves in the immediate present. While the Enlightenment thinkers and the modernists sought personal liberty to seek ultimate truth without hindrance and to follow that truth wherever it may lead, postmodernists want mainly to construct a personal narrative. This "scripting of the self," the phrase of French philosopher Michel Foucault, a postmodernist icon, offers the best chance for people to know themselves, even though they might never be more than a fictionalized, one-dimensional character in their own life story.

As I continued trying to work through my postmodern melancholy, I found that psychologists are among the most aggressive promoters of unfettered individuality. Indeed, while most Americans are dazed by dense postmodern prose, they respond eagerly to similar self-centered messages coming from psychology.

I started with one of the most influential figures in the twentieth century, Abraham Maslow, a founder of the humanistic psychology movement that urges individuals to choose how to behave and to fulfill themselves according to their own enthusiasms. Contrary to traditional Judeo-Christian religion, which sees the human soul as innately sinful and needing God for moral clarity, Maslow says that human nature is neutral or good. Echoing Rousseau, Maslow maintains that a repressive society, not a perverse human psyche, causes most mental problems. The goal, Maslow says, should be to release the individual's inner nature to express "itself freely, rather than being warped, suppressed, or denied." In turn, the self-fulfilled individual would help build a compassionate society in which human potential flowered.

This social-emotional liberation is the psychological equivalent of free-enterprise economics. The entrepreneurial personality, unburdened by religion or tradition, would act like an "invisible hand" leading toward a better society. The more that people loved themselves—the more they pursued their self-interest—the more they could enhance their own happiness and coincidentally improve the world.

While red or black accountant's ink gauges financial success, the self has no similar standard for how "authentic" it is. The problem is that human nature doesn't exist in a vacuum; it must act socially. That means the postmodern self is a paradox: it is complete and empty at the same time. It is a vessel overflowing with self but also an empty glass that must fill itself through choices in life that affect the larger society. However, as long as I acknowledge no social morality, except as it assists my agenda, I have no objective way to calculate my authenticity. I become trapped in a circular, egocentric logic: I have no principle to authenticate myself but my own self-interest.

Nevertheless, millions of middle-class Americans are so compulsively busy "finding themselves" and "actualizing" their existence that they never arrive at a firm identity. "Free to be me," they become psychological black holes—so self-absorbed that no light escapes, no candle illuminates society out of the Age of Melancholy.

Pollster Daniel Yankelovich estimates that as many as 80 percent of Americans have, at one time or another, actively pursued "self-fulfillment." Although the nation has a long tradition of self-improvement—from Ralph Waldo Emerson's self-reliance to Norman Vincent Peale's positive thinking to the Reverend Robert Schuller's "be happy attitudes"—at no time in history have so many Americans tried so hard to discover, realize, and develop themselves in both body and soul as in the late twentieth century.

As described by Yankelovich, for these self-seekers "self-fulfillment means having a career *and* marriage *and* children *and* sexual freedom *and* autonomy *and* being liberal *and* having money *and* choosing non-conformity *and* insisting on social justice *and* enjoying city life *and* country living *and* simplicity *and* graciousness *and* reading *and* good friends, *and* on *and* on."

The United States seems like a continent-wide self-help club, with a dog's breakfast of therapists, gurus, psychic soothsayers, motivational speakers, and outright hucksters pushing snake-oil notions and half-baked theories. In New Age worship and self-esteem workshops, encounter groups and drum circles, Eastern meditation and Western psychotherapy, many Americans try to release their "inner child," reach their "human potential," and "follow their bliss."

Curiously, this self-obsession brings little contentment. Like promiscuous teenagers, many people jump from teacher to teacher, from prophet to prophet, from self-improvement therapist to pop psychologist—never sure when they are totally "actualized." But rather than hungering for another person or pursuing truth, the main object of this flaming desire is the solipsistic self.

In Greek mythology, the gods punished the similar vanity of Narcissus by having him fall fatally in love with his own image seen in a glassy pond. He "does not fall in love with his own reflection because it is beautiful, but because it is his," wrote the poet W. H. Auden. "If it were his beauty that enthralled him, he would be set free in a few years by its fading."

While Narcissus was charmed by himself, many people today have higher aspirations—to employ their self-claimed, godlike powers to perfect themselves and the universe. According to Oprah Winfrey, whose daytime television show often features New Age celebrities, these gurus are here "not to teach us about their divinity but to teach us about our own." For example, in his bestseller *The Celestine Prophecy,* James Redfield fabricates an ancient Peruvian manuscript as a nine-step, neopagan guide for human and earthly perfection. Wayne Dyer, another popular author, urges people to practice "a veritable religion of the self in which an individual determines his own behavior" without "needing the approval of an outside force." Marianne Williamson, among the most prolific New Age writers, says in her foreword to the book *For the Love of God,* "The idea that we are separate from God is merely an illusion of consciousness."

Such comments carry the strong fragrance of serpent-excreted sulfur. Exalting themselves as divine beings who could re-create Eden, these late-twentieth-century Fausts reek of the sin of pride, which is redolent whenever people think they alone can cure existential anxieties. As British writer G. K. Chesterton put it: "That Jones shall worship the god within him turns out ultimately to mean that Jones shall worship Jones." Similarly, playwright George Bernard Shaw said, "God created us in his image, and we decided to return the favor."

What's missing in this deification of the self is a unifying structure. When people become haphazard combinations of bits of personality, they lack the gravity that comes from strong character, depth of soul, and caring community. Again, the great truth seekers of history, not the hustlers of psychic nostrums, have the most reliable answers and are the most perceptive guides to self-knowledge.

From Aristotle to Augustine, from Søren Kierkegaard to Sigmund Freud, Western civilization has linked personal identity to the larger society and to forces greater than the self. Individuality was not solitary, but mutual, arising from contact with others. The ancient Greeks, for instance, defined humans as social creatures who could flourish only in a political and communal setting. Christianity insists that humans have consciences capable of de-tecting moral laws that they didn't write but that they nonetheless willingly obey—or at least acknowledge, even in their violation.

The postmodern age not only disclaims the classical and the Judeo-Christian concepts of the self, it rejects the moral foundation laid out by Freud and refined by his erstwhile protégé, Carl Jung, to explain how human society protects itself from radical individualism.

Freud divides the human personality into three functional parts: the id, ego, and superego. The id is the reservoir of instinctual drives that are imbedded in the unconscious and are dominated by the pleasure principle. The ego is the part of the id modified by contact with the external world; it makes up most of what is commonly called consciousness. The superego contains the moral code that regulates human behavior to ensure conformity to the social contract.

Because he thought that humanity would descend into a cruel state of nature without socially sanctioned morality, Jung detected God's handiwork in the superego: "The idea of a moral order and of God belong to the ineradicable substrate of the human soul."

The postmodern self, however, has exorcised a divinely rooted morality from consciousness and recognizes no restraints on the ego.

Instead of an integrated personality molded by family, religion, and culture in sync with a coherent moral code, the postmodern self is a multiplicity of characters. Many people today juggle their various personages, trying to balance competing self-interests. One identity today, a different one tomorrow, depending on circumstances or mood.

For all its supposed sophistication and intricacy, the postmodern ego is actually what social critic Christopher Lasch called "the minimal self"—defensive, shallow, self-deluded. Postmodernism tells individuals to rely on themselves to survive life's misfortunes and disappointments. In response, some people pursue the old palliatives of material prosperity, career success, and social prestige, and model themselves after the play-all-summer grasshopper in Aesop's fable.

"To live for the moment is the prevailing passion—to live for yourself, not for your predecessors or posterity" is how Lasch described the self-adulating individualism of the late twentieth century.

The anxieties of the Age of Melancholy stem partly from the realization that the focus on the self has come at the expense of community and spirituality. Not tempered by humility toward any power greater than the self and separated from other humans to pursue personal satisfactions, compulsive egoism has ripped through faith, family, and neighborhood, which once gave people a sense of participation in a spiritual reality larger than themselves.

And in the process, the "inner child" has become a self-indulgent adolescent who wants the orgy of liberation to continue. But if the Age of Melancholy is to open a more humane, more compassionate historical era, it must include a maturing of character and a new appreciation for what it should mean to be an American citizen.

Narcissistic Loners

At a time when many Americans define themselves narrowly by race, gender, or ethnicity, it seems old-fashioned to claim an inclusive national character that encompasses all Americans regardless of background. Nonetheless, even amid the diversity, multiculturalism, and extreme individualism of postmodern society, distinctly American personality traits are detectable.

Unlike nations that trace their origins to a legendary founder or an ancestral tribe and guarantee membership to anyone who is genetically part of the national family, Americans were created by a documented historical process. From the country's beginning, Americans were seen as a new species. In his eighteenth-century essay "What Is an American?" French immigrant Michel-Guillaume-Jean de Crèvecoeur says: "He is an American who leaving behind him all his ancient prejudices and manners, receives new ones from the new mode of life he has embraced, the new government he obeys, and the new rank he holds. The American is a new man, who acts upon principles."

That means Americans have never been identified as a people of blood or mythology but as one of ideas and values, notably freedom and equality—however difficult it has been for the nation to live up to those democratic ideals.

Since the early nineteenth century, historians and social commentators have noted that the American personality tends to swing widely between excessive individualism and suffocating conformity. Historical eras are often archived by which inclination dominates; but when one becomes too strong, the American genius for social and political stability invariably kicks the other in as a counterweight.

The individualist strain has been tied to the nation's Puritan heritage, with its emphasis on personal salvation. Individualism's primary promoter was Thomas Jefferson, who believed that the nation's freedom relied on self-supporting yeoman farmers who would be steadfast defenders of independence and social equality. Jefferson feared that the nation could become an urban, commercial society that concentrated power in the hands of a few people who would form an oligarchy of wealth and privilege similar to the detested European aristocracy. Individualism was embodied in such half-legendary frontiersmen as Daniel Boone. It was reinforced by an economic system that claimed that anyone with gumption and a willingness to work hard could succeed. And it was further encouraged by the Protestant belief, preached in revivals that periodically swept across the nation, that personal experience is the truest test of faith and that individual perfection is possible even in a morally corrupt society.

Alexis de Tocqueville had a sharply contrasting impression of America. Noting that Americans were highly susceptible to public censure, Tocqueville worried that uniformity of thought threatened personal liberty. "Freedom of opinion does not exist in America," Tocqueville wrote in *Democracy in America*. Instead, Americans suspected dissent and were prone to allow the majority to impose its ideas on the minority.

Historical examples of the conformist streak that justify Tocqueville's concern include the often virulent antipathy toward immigrants, the frequent mass hysterias that "anti-American" ideas were endangering the country, and the periodic "culture wars" that pit varying lifestyles against one another.

But conformity also helped civilize the country. The instant community formed within wagon trains helped pioneers endure the hardships of westward travel. Social solidarity enabled the nation to triumph over the inhumane international tyrannies of the twentieth century. Appeals to common, if often transgressed, democratic values gave the civil rights crusade of the 1950s and 1960s much of its moral force.

Whether the individualist or conformist side of the American character is strongest depends mainly on the cultural tenor of the moment. During the nineteenth century most Americans farmed or lived in small towns and provided for themselves and their immediate neighbors. It was the era of Huckleberry Finn, who wants "to light out for the Territory ahead of the rest" when society encroaches on his freedom. It was the nation of Horatio Alger novels, which teach that by pluck and perseverance young Americans could overcome adversity and poverty to attain wealth and respect. It was the epoch of social Darwinism, which applies evolutionary biological "survival of the fittest" concepts to politics and economics.

By the early twentieth century, America was an urban society of large corporations and mass media. People worked for wages, pegged to an office clock or factory whistle. They performed specific tasks that usually required formal education and specialized talents rather than the self-taught, jack-of-all-trades skills needed by farmers and nineteenth-century artisans and mechanics. Teamwork and rule following, instead of individual initiative and a footloose mind-set, were desired disciplines. Contrary to the homespun craftsmanship of the mid-nineteenth century, the twentieth-century mass market needed mass tastes in fashions, furniture, and entertainment to feed the new consumer society.

Meanwhile, the Progressive movement encouraged unionization, restricted laissez-faire capitalism, and promoted social activism to achieve what philosopher John Dewey called a "Great Community." The Depression of the 1930s extended that agenda through such New Deal legislation as Social Security and financial regulations that expanded government's role over economic matters once reserved primarily for individuals or the free market.

Reacting to World War II and the Cold War, with the accompanying alarms about fascist and communist totalitarianism, many American social commentators worried that the country had become too conformist and was emulating the sins of its dictatorial enemies. Those fears were aggravated by attacks from Senator Joseph McCarthy and his supporters on actors, intellectuals, government officials, and others thought to be "un-American" subversives.

The main concern among many intellectuals in the 1950s

was that Americans were falling into "group-think." The titles of some of the most popular books of the period highlight the issue: William H. Whyte's *The Organization Man* warns that bureaucracy smothers individuality, especially among white-collar workers; Vance Packard's *The Hidden Persuaders* cautions that Americans have become insensate victims of advertising and other forms of psychological manipulation; John Kenneth Galbraith's *The Affluent Society* claims that a consumption-driven lifestyle distorts America's social values and diverts resources from the nation's pressing needs in education, housing, and other areas.

The America in these books is a country rich beyond belief, but its citizens lack an inner integrity able to resist government or corporate bureaucracies. Americans have surrendered their individuality and sense of national purpose for material wealth, suburban blandness, political rigidity, and the security of institutional paternalism.

The most influential critique of the 1950s is David Riesman's *The Lonely Crowd,* which argues that the American character has changed dramatically from the nineteenth century to the mid-twentieth century. Riesman says that before World War I, typical Americans were "inner-directed," which means that they were imbued by the moral canons of the Victorian era. Instilled primarily by parents and enforced by society, these standards gave Americans an internal stability — what Riesman describes as a self-contained gyroscope that might have repressed emotions but kept individuals on an even keel.

The standards, largely based on the Protestant work ethic, gave the inner-directed person the confidence to amass wealth and power. The robber barons epitomized the Gilded Age; to stride atop society was the cultural ideal, to prove your mettle in a Darwinian brawl was the highest virtue. But it was very stilted — personal ambition and emotional vacuity triumphed over reflective self-understanding.

Inner-directed personalities matched an era of capitalist expansion, which operated by what Riesman called a "psychology of scarcity." To produce the iron, extract the coal, and forge the steel of a modern industrialized economy required self-determined tycoons who thrived in brutal corporate competition with little concern for external criticism—justifying their actions on their own internal standards.

But as the nation turned in the twentieth century from a heavy-metal manufacturing and natural-resource-based economy to a consumer and installment-plan society, a new personality type emerged. This was Riesman's "other-directed" individual who would staff the modern bureaucracy and respond to an advertising-driven marketplace.

Other-directed persons don't stand above the crowd; they are part of it. They worry what their peers think of them. They have no motivations of their own and are desperately trying to conform to society's expectations. They are passive and apathetic, obsessed with maintaining appearances. They are ruled by public opinion rather than moral laws or philosophical axioms. This person is the "silent generation" collegian of the 1950s, the prefeminist, pearls and Dior-look suburban housewife, the man in the gray flannel suit.

According to Riesman, the change from the inner-directed to other-directed personality is especially noticeable in child rearing. The severe discipline and rigid structure of the inner-directed family were abandoned for warmer, child-focused parenting designed to produce children who work well with others. In the other-directed 1950s, Mom and Dad often took second place to child psychologists and educators who argued that strict parenting hindered a youngster's sociability. Ultimately, a child's sense of self-worth would be determined not by parents, religion, or moral codes but by playmates. "The peer group becomes the measure of all things; the individual has few defenses the group cannot batter down," Riesman says.

The children that Riesman and other commentators of the 1950s talk about are the baby boomers. To analyze U.S. society at the end of the twentieth century, it's necessary to follow the baby boomers from childhood to middle age because they have been the nation's most dynamic demographic group in the post–World War II period. The boomers also will lead the nation into the next millennium and will be a central part of any new consciousness that emerges from the current American melancholy. That world-view will depend partly on the boomers' generational biography.

The baby boomers have fulfilled Riesman's implied prophecy of becoming a generation with a strong group identity that holds attitudes widely divergent from its predecessors. As such, the boomers represent another drastic shift in the American character. Their personalities contain strong elements of both Jefferson's individualists and Tocqueville's conformists, and it's often impossible to tell which trait is ascendant at any particular time. Middle-class boomers prize individuality, free expression, and self-development above all else, but they pursue those goals out of a common generational mind-set.

As children in the 1950s and early 1960s, baby boomers benefited from a strong economy and coddling parents who wanted to spare their children the deprivations of the Great Depression and the horrors of World War II. But they also experienced the social restraints of the Cold War 1950s. And they were baptized in a patriotic piety that often linked Americanism to Judeo-Christian religion.

Peace of mind, however, was hard to find for many people caught up in status-seeking and nuclear-weapon phobias. And beneath the apparently placid waters of America's postwar supremacy were deep currents questioning the era's conformity and complacency.

The strongest criticism during the 1950s came from war-ravaged Europe, where novelists and philosophers viewed Western civilization much differently than did optimistic American corporate and political leaders. The most persuasive of these Europeans was Jean-Paul Sartre, a French playwright, philosopher, and, perhaps most important for the celebrity journalism of the decade, an intriguing personality. Along with companion and writer Simone de Beauvoir, novelist and sometime friend Albert Camus, and other Parisian café habitués, Sartre was a leading exponent of existentialism, one of the most influential philosophical movements of the twentieth century. Responding to the mass destruction and moral collapse of Europe during World War II, Sartre argued that God does not exist and therefore humans are totally free to do whatever they wish and are personally responsible for the consequences. Like Kierkegaard, though without his Christian faith, Sartre saw this liberty as the source of human distress and possibility. The essence of a person, Sartre thought, is determined by how individuals actively construct their lives, not by a divine sponsorship that automatically gives all humans a preset measure of integrity.

Sartre would label Riesman's "other-directed" man as "inauthentic" because, by adjusting to society, he has been alienated from himself. The inauthentic man lives a dull, routine existence in which his fantasies and personality are controlled by the mass media. For Sartre, freedom is the ability to resist the dominant society and live according to personal conscience. That may mean enduring a blank, godless nothingness — Sartre's *neant* — but it also means that individuals command their own existence and are masters of their fate.

Existentialist ideas poured into the American social mainstream largely through popular culture; Sartre himself was the subject of a cover story in *Life* magazine. But while few Americans actually read Sartre's often turgid writings, millions of them idolized James Dean, whose existentialist-dipped adolescent angst in the 1955 film *Rebel Without a Cause* discloses the flip side of the "happy days" of the Eisenhower 1950s.

The defiant attitude also resonated in one of the greatest lines of the post–World War II era.

In the 1954 movie *The Wild One,* a sneering, leather-jacketed Marlon Brando plays a motorcycle gang leader who is asked, "Hey, Johnny, what are you rebelling against?"

The response: "What've you got?"

Likewise, such Beat Generation poets and novelists as Jack Kerouac, Allen Ginsberg, Lawrence Ferlinghetti, and William Burroughs express an anarchic freedom, laced with Zen Buddhism, alcohol, drugs, and jazz music, that defies conventional social norms.

The threat of nuclear war, the memory of the Nazi concentration camps, and the stifling society of the 1950s led novelist Norman Mailer to an existentialist focus on the self. In his 1957 essay "The White Negro," Mailer sees the hipster as the new American hero, a bebopping, reefer-smoking subversive. Anyone seeking to be authentic, Mailer says, has "to divorce oneself from society, to exist without roots, to set out on that uncharted journey into the rebellious imperatives of the self." The person who doesn't become what Mailer called "a frontiersman in the Wild West of American night life" is consigned to the "Square cell, trapped in the totalitarian tissues of American society, doomed willy-nilly to conform if one is to succeed."

By the mid-1960s, the trust in government, the "faith in faith," and the social constancy that typified the 1950s had surrendered to existentialist philosophy, humanistic psychology, the counter-cultural lifestyle, and the activism of the civil rights and anti-war movements. As millions of baby boomers entered college, it became the antiauthoritarian era of "do your own thing," psychedelic tripping, sexual liberation, and political radicalism.

The pendulum of American character had again swung a full 180 degrees, from locked-tight conformity to unlatched individuality—so much so that by the late 1970s, some writers claimed that Americans had gone too far and had become excessively self-obsessed.

In his 1979 book *The Culture of Narcissism*, Christopher Lasch argues that many Americans, especially the educated classes, have substituted warm emotions and creature comforts for a sense of purpose and a search for truth. "Having no hope of improving their lives in any of the ways that matter, people have convinced themselves that what matters is psychic self-improvement: getting in touch with their feelings, eating health foods, taking lessons in ballet or belly dancing, immersing themselves in the wisdom of the East, jogging, learning how to 'relate,' overcoming the 'fear of pleasure,' " he wrote.

President Jimmy Carter was so taken with Lasch's book that it was the basis of his 1979 "malaise" speech that criticized the American penchant to "worship self-indulgence and consumption" and warned that "piling up material goods cannot fill the emptiness of lives."

That was not the message most Americans wanted to hear. Ronald Reagan won the 1980 presidential election largely on his promises to reaffirm the nation's global supremacy and to launch a new era of economic prosperity through turbocharged capitalism. The words of Gordon Gekko, the conniving financier in Oliver Stone's 1987 movie, *Wall Street,* became the motto of the 1980s: "Greed is good." Fueled by a huge national debt and a yuppie lust for designer labels, Americans went on a buying spree unmatched since the 1920s—conspicuously consuming everything from imported French cheeses to high-tech military hardware—and merging and leveraging corporations at a pace not seen since the giant trusts in the late nineteenth century.

Lasch again provided the jeremiad. In his 1984 book *The Minimal Self,* he describes a nihilistic culture in which all frames of reference have disintegrated, except for a preoccupation with "lifestyle."

"The idea that 'you can be anything you want,' though it preserves something of the older idea of the career open to talents, has come to mean that identities can be adopted and discarded like a change of costumes," Lasch wrote.

That means choice has no real consequences and freedom is merely the liberty to choose values, principles, or religions as you would select detergents, toothpaste, or breakfast cereals. Even mental health and education are just forms of social management. Everything can be mediated by therapy; traditional notions of character and virtue do not matter. "The combined influences of advertising and the 'helping professions' had liberated people from old constraints only to subject them to more subtle forms of control," Lasch wrote. "These agencies freed personal life from the repressive scrutiny of church and state only to subject it to medical and psychological scrutiny."

Lacking the possibility of making a real difference, the self is simply another commodity in the marketplace, "where ostensibly competing products become increasingly indistinguishable and have to be promoted, therefore, by means of advertising that seeks to create the illusion of variety and to present these products as revolutionary breakthroughs," Lasch argues.

Like the market in goods, the market in the self always generates a new need for every want that it momentarily satisfies, and the chasm between the two is never bridged. Personal growth becomes an ever receding target because identity has been divorced from tradition, community, and morality. All those character-forming forces are replaced by a fashionable appearance — a public-relations self.

"Since it is no longer possible to base any claim on one's own experience, there is nothing for it but to perform an appearing act without concerning oneself with being — or even with being seen. So it is not: I exist, I am here! but rather: I am visible, I am an image — look! look!" wrote Jean Baudrillard.

Identity in the 1990s is determined largely by consumer choices: clothing, music, television shows, and even political ideas become props to display personality. Success hinges on repackaging ourselves to meet the ever changing demands of the cultural marketplace. The irony is that the baby boomers, who profess individuality, have become mere expressions of the products that incorporate their lifestyle.

Americans in the 1990s don't even have the communal security of the crabgrass, barbecue-pit, picture-window suburban conformity of the 1950s. The late twentieth century fosters a society disconnected from true community, a society in which communication thrives in the anonymity of the Internet, the Walkman, and telephone sex, a society in which the inanities of pop psychology pass for intellectual depth.

In 1985 a team of sociologists led by Robert Bellah of the University of California warned that Americans were losing their feeling of national purpose that binds political life to personal identity.

In their bestselling book *Habits of the Heart,* Bellah and his group use case studies of individual Americans to show the near disappearance of shared national values—the lack of civic awareness, the dismissal of religion from public life, the self-serving handling of personal relationships.

That attitude emerges in an interview with Sheila Larson, a young nurse. Ms. Larson, who had undergone psychotherapy, describes her religion as "Sheilaism."

"I believe in God. I'm not a religious fanatic. I can't remember the last time I went to church. My faith has carried me a long way. It's Sheilaism. Just my own little voice," Ms. Larson told Bellah's team. "It's just to love yourself and be gentle with yourself."

By thousands of names, Sheilaism is the dominant religion of the Age of Melancholy. It is an undemanding faith in the ego, a sacrament of the self, a liturgy that asks people only to be happy with themselves.

Many of the themes raised by *Habits of the Heart* also concerned one of the most influential political scientists of the 1990s, Harvard professor Robert Putnam. In his much-discussed 1995 essay, "Bowling Alone," which uses falling membership in bowling leagues as a metaphor for the decline in community activism, Putnam says that America has squandered its social capital—the communal networks, mutual dependencies, and civic organizations that promote the common good—by a sweeping retreat from public life.

"The social fabric is becoming visibly thinner, our connections among one another are becoming visibly thinner," Putnam says. "We don't trust one another as much, and we don't know one another as much. And, of course, that is behind the deterioration of the political dialogue, the deterioration of the political debate."

The late-twentieth-century America that I have covered as a career journalist is a nation of fragmented individuals in a fragmented culture. I perceive the Age of Melancholy as the massive psychic and social rejection of the postmodernist claim that life has no ultimate truth and purpose. Rather than simply seeking to please ourselves, melancholics learn to distrust our egos and become highly attuned to the clever tactics that we have used—and that society condones—to evade disturbing realities about ourselves and American culture.

As I stared at myself through the cold prism of melancholic self-doubt, I often lacerated my mind with memories of past mistakes, and my pain pried open troubling truths. I was appalled at how puffed up I was with pride in my own power, my own learning, and my self-confirmed perfection. I finally realized that melancholy often comes from a God-implanted conscience that has been neglected by a society that emphasizes human freedom without moral accountability.

But the postmodern ego is a cagey enemy, and the Age of Melancholy is a third millennial battleground in the war for the human soul.

5

FALSE

CONSCIOUSNESS

Happily Dazed

In Aldous Huxley's futuristic cautionary fable *Brave New World*, whenever people feel something unpleasant, they take the drug *soma,* which relieves anxiety and enables them to remain blissfully unaware of old age, death, or anything else that might disrupt their carefully programmed lives.

Published in 1932, Huxley's novel depicts a grim world in which technology and tyranny govern every facet of life. People are conceived in bottles, hatched in incubators, reared in communal nurseries, and conditioned to collectivism and passivity. A scientific caste system decides which people will be manual workers, mid-level functionaries, or intellectuals.

The book's action centers on a character named Bernard Marx, whose prenatal care apparently went haywire, because he is unhappy with life. Marx visits a reservation in New Mexico and brings a "savage" back to London. The Savage is initially fascinated by the new world, but he soon revolts because he has educated himself by reading Shakespeare and believes in moral choice.

Faced with the conflict between individual freedom and a scientifically regulated, trouble-free society, the Savage goes berserk and
kills himself.

Another central character in the book is Mustapha Mond, the
World Controller who bears a striking resemblance to Fyodor
Dostoyevsky's Grand Inquisitor. Both men realize that a personal
belief in God poses the greatest threat to their societies. Just as the
Grand Inquisitor chases Jesus from Spain, the World Controller
suppresses religious books and any ideas that might give people a
"conception of purpose" toward life.

As the World Controller tells the Savage, "Once you began admitting explanations in terms of purpose—well, you don't know
what the result might be. It . . . might make [intelligent people]
lose their faith in happiness as the Sovereign Good and take to believing, instead, that the goal was somewhere beyond, somewhere
outside the present human sphere; that the purpose of life was not
the maintenance of well-being, but some intensification and refin-
ing of consciousness, some enlargement of knowledge."

Mond understands that questions of purpose inevitably raise
religious issues, such as the meaning of life and the reality of death,
that underscore the tragic nature of existence. For a society built
on human pleasure, acknowledgment of pain would be fatal.

At the time of publication, *Brave New World* was usually cri-
tiqued as an allegorical warning against fascism and communism,
which were sweeping across Europe. Huxley's larger target, however, is modern society in general, which he felt substitutes humanity's spiritual instincts with a managerial efficiency and a
sensual hedonism that continually generates new desires that have
to be satisfied.

A shrewd analyst of technology, self-centeredness, and the
weakening of religion in contemporary life, Huxley anticipated
the Age of Melancholy. His concerns are among the central

themes of this book: that Western civilization has forsaken self-transcendence for selfishness; that freedom has turned into untempered self-gratification; that science has replaced morality as the overseer of human nature; that people believe happiness comes from pleasure-seeking and avoiding suffering rather than from searching our souls, loving God, and building community.

Late-twentieth-century America has ignored Huxley's warnings and relies largely on secular explanations for how the world works, creating a false consciousness that condemns people to a shallow, passionless lifestyle. To illustrate what's happening today and to update Huxley's point, I split postmodern America into what I call Mandarins and Melancholics, in the same way that Huxley separated his society into Alpha Plus Intellectuals and Epsilon Minus Morons.

The Mandarins operate the bureaucratic state, don't question society's corporate priorities, believe in technology, and devote most of their energy to promoting their careers, protecting the existing order, and pursuing their own pleasures. Melancholics are people who question society's direction, recognize that wealth and status don't ensure a meaningful life, find their mind increasingly shrouded in doubt, and while often trapped in mid-belief, are at least tentatively exploring the spiritual realm.

The Mandarins think that human knowledge, as expressed in the social sciences, medicine, and technology, will solve most of society's problems. They are big on method and process, not so keen on meaning and purpose. The Mandarins' consuming quest is for the appropriate technique, whether administrative, psychological, or scientific, to keep society and individuals functioning smoothly.

The Melancholics are skeptical toward the Mandarins' promises of human and political perfection. They are disenchanted with the postmodernists' drive for total human power over the universe. Melancholics tend to agree with Percy Shelley that "poets are the unacknowledged legislators of the world," and they would rather probe their soul than run a corporate human-resources department.

The late-twentieth-century culture war between Mandarins and Melancholics shows that Huxley's alarms are more appropriate today than when first issued. The past sixty years have witnessed a steady movement toward a soul-denying existence that justifies Huxley's pessimism. America's Mandarins have dehumanizing powers greater than those wielded by Huxley's new-world Alphas. Late-twentieth-century Mandarins can offer Americans not only a pharmaceutical cornucopia to anesthetize their worries but a host of distractions to obscure any disturbing thoughts. Today's *somas* include television, videotapes, sports, movies, and celebrity journalism that cocoon Americans in trivia and fluff that shove out substantive, thoughtful reporting.

In a world of machinery, medication, and merriment, the traditional Judeo-Christian God, with his party-pooper insistence on self-sacrifice and spiritual redemption, is something of a celestial Luddite gumming up the gears of aggressive acquisition. Nothing threatens prosperity more than an anticonsumption ascetic. "Industrial civilization is only possible when there is no self-denial," Mond tells the Savage. "Self-indulgence up to the very limits imposed by hygiene and economics. Otherwise the wheels stop turning."

So much for simplicity, spiritual struggle, morality, or intellectual integrity as ingredients in a meaningful life. Above all, be happy. And to be happy, just be happy. If you don't know how to be happy, government propaganda and corporate advertising will tell you. If you encounter trouble in life, a therapeutic hug, a prescription drug, or a shopping spree will make it better. Don't bum yourself out by thinking that the world might not exist solely for your sake; don't tolerate the mental or spiritual pains that could grind the Mandarin society's motors to a halt. After all, what's the actual market value of a human soul?

It shows how far the late twentieth century has come from the view of nineteenth-century English philosopher John Stuart Mill that it is "better to be a human being dissatisfied than a pig satisfied; better to be Socrates dissatisfied than a fool satisfied."

Yet nature has a great antidote to human happiness—death. The inescapable fact of our bodily disintegration forces a choice: Does an honorable life result from piling up consumer goods and indulgently pampering ourselves, or does it come from an earnest effort to confront the big issues of existence and seek to end our days as a better person? That is the most important question facing every man and woman.

A meaningful life includes joy and suffering. The two are inextricably twined in a yin-yang circle of ecstasy and misery that speeds individuals toward moral growth, which is the uniquely human experience of deepening awareness of ourselves and exceeding our earthly limitations. In suffering, people cry out for divine help and break the confines of their own world. In joy, people expand their sense of well-being beyond their own narrow universe. The result is what moral philosophers call "the good life." It's not an easy life, not a pleasure-soaked life, but a life that joins the individual soul to the larger community and to God. As philosopher Craig Clifford noted, "Aristotle said that happiness is the activity of the soul in accord with virtue. In other words, what you aim at is living in such a way as to have a good soul." In the same vein, Thomas Jefferson's statement in the Declaration of Independence that humanity's God-given inalienable rights include "the pursuit of happiness" ties political and personal freedom to divine providence.

In the late twentieth century, in contrast, material affluence, self-esteem, and feeling good in body and mind have become the primary criteria for happiness. Of course, those amoral satisfactions pose no threat to Mandarin control. And suffering is to be avoided or medicated, lest the individual encounter a melancholic need for a more purposeful life.

The World Controller couldn't have planned it better.

The Mind-Managing Mandarins

The smooth-running, postmodern bureaucratic-corporate society of the late twentieth century needs mentally disciplined and highly cooperative worker bees who thrive in a ruthlessly competitive marketplace. Ideally, these individuals define happiness as getting lots of things, trusting technology to create a better future, and not worrying much about such abstract concepts as tradition, truth, and spirituality.

But sometimes even the finest-honed minds crash, their mental pistons mushing up. They need skilled mechanics to lift up the hood, clean the cultural filters, blow out the psychic carburetors, and put the machinery back on the road. These attitude-fixers are the psychiatrists, psychologists, and other mental-health Mandarins who are responsible for maintaining the productive habits that keep American society humming along the economic superhighway. As James Hillman, an iconoclastic psychologist and best-selling author, put it: "Therapy is collaborating with what the state wants: docile plebes."

That's a harsh indictment. To be fair, many psychotherapists are well intentioned and want the best for their patients. They recognize that life involves tough challenges and seek to guide patients through the choppy currents of depression and other mental traumas. They don't exaggerate their professional capabilities and concede that the most they can do is help patients manage and comprehend life's unavoidable shocks.

For example, cognitive therapy, widely used in depression, tries to help patients overcome what Albert Ellis, a psychologist who pioneered the treatment, called "illogical, unrealistic, irrational, inflexible, and childish thinking" that distorts patients' perceptions of themselves and their situation. Directed by an artful therapist, cognitive methods can dispel hopelessness, obsession with death, social disconnection, and similar emotions as damaging misconceptions. That is a great accomplishment for most patients. But not all therapists have the compassion and insight to realize that many of their patients' complaints are primarily moral and spiritual rather than medical or circumstantial. Sometimes an individual's world truly is crazy and alienating; the patient is right to reject it and not merely adjust to it. Despair, anxiety, and similar feelings might reflect a realistic appraisal of personal and cultural problems that demand drastic action.

Nonetheless, many despondent individuals want fast relief and aren't particularly interested in acquiring critical-thinking skills or in hunting the deeper, often spiritual sources of melancholy. Pressured by employers and insurance companies that pay the bill, they want medical and mental-health professionals to return them to the playing field quickly. Whether that's done by psychological jargon or attitude-adjusting drugs makes no difference. Like a quarterback with a shoulder injury, they take a mental-painkilling cortisone shot and rush back into action; otherwise, they are out of the lineup, their career over.

Since Mandarin experts claim to know best, and have behind them the prestige of academic degrees and professional credentials, most Americans meekly accept their dictates on everything from child rearing to death-bed counseling. This has been called "the therapeutic culture"—a society constructed not on religious teachings or personal virtues but on psychological and medical techniques and theories that reinforce the dominant social regime.

In their book *Habits of the Heart,* Robert N. Bellah and his coauthors compare the psychotherapist to the modern corporate manager in that neither expert is especially concerned with remaking society and that both see their job as helping the employee/patient "to achieve some combination of occupation and 'lifestyle' that is economically possible and psychically tolerable, that 'works.' "

Bellah and his colleagues also assert that psychotherapy separates the self from a nurturing environment by accelerating the collapse of the family, neighborhoods, religion, and civic life. In its incessant concentration on the detached individual, Bellah and associates argue, psychotherapy helps people lose "those common understandings that enable us to recognize the virtues of the other."

In more clinical language, Joseph Veroff, Richard A. Kulka, and Elizabeth Douvan make the same argument in their book *Mental Health in America: Patterns of Help-Seeking from 1957 to 1976:* "Modern psychiatry isolates the troubled individual from the currents of emotional interdependence and deals with the trouble by distancing from it and manipulating it through intellectual/verbal discussion, interpretation, and analysis."

The upshot of such self-centered psychology and dollar-denominated happiness, according to Don Eberly, editor of the book *Building a Community of Citizens,* is that many people disregard traditional ethical virtues and spiritual principles: "The twentieth century has traded in moral man for economic and psychological man, subjecting him at every turn to either economic inducements or therapeutic treatments. If we are to recover as a society, the 21st century will have to recover a vision of man bearing inherent moral value and moral agency."

From such scholarly analyses, I argue that psychotherapy has helped fashion a familiar postmodern hybrid: supposedly free-agent individuals who lack feasible options other than to pour themselves into a corporate mold and to internalize its reward system of money, material status, and career advancement. Millions of Americans demand unfettered freedom of choice, but God, community, and other self-affirming humanistic and spiritual values that don't equate the good life with egoistic consumerism have been removed from their menu of choices by sociopsychological surgery.

A catchy phrase to sum up what Bellah and other academic commentators are getting at comes from Philip Rieff, a professor of sociology at the University of Pennsylvania: "Religious man was born to be saved; psychological man is born to be pleased."

Through his books *Freud: The Mind of the Moralist* and *The Triumph of the Therapeutic,* Rieff has emerged as an astute critic of psychotherapy. Among Rieff's complaints is that psychotherapy has substituted the traditional human role as part of a divinely written drama with a monologue as a self-scripted actor. Instead of priests guiding people toward salvation, spirituality, and moral righteousness, psychotherapists lead individuals toward self-help, self-indulgence, and self-actualization. And because the therapeutic culture labels almost any aberrant behavior as an illness, moral judgment and personal accountability are eased. "It lightens the heavier burdens of guilt and responsibility, for many offenses can be made to appear smaller if perceived in sufficient depth," Rieff wrote.

According to Rieff, the primary mark of psychological man is an "analytic attitude" in which the individual develops the unruffled temperament of a scientist, looking impartially at himself and practicing a "cultivated detachment and calm." Personal psychological competency, not eternal salvation, community cohesiveness, or universal truth, becomes humanity's most important quest. That means psychological man should not accept religious doctrines or social philosophies that demand commitment to something other than the self. "It is characteristic of our culture that there is no longer an effective sense of communion, driving the individual out of himself, rendering the inner life serviceable to the outer," Rieff wrote.

With no need for traditional religion and without acknowledging any standard of truth other than self-knowledge, psychological man is a self-contained, complacent member of society who is not morally obligated to other people or bound by any ethical code other than selfishness. In Rieff's term, the therapeutic society is composed of "virtuosi of the self."

The therapeutic society has its own mystical language and liturgy that make psychology a surrogate religion for many people. In fact, the psychologist or psychiatrist often serves the same role as the shaman in primitive tribes. Like an African witch doctor or Native American medicine man, the mental-health professional possesses an arcane intelligence that connects him to a deeper world—in this case, the patient's neuroses. The shaman/shrink's first duty is to exorcise his patient's evil spirits (negative attitudes). But he is also supposed to maintain good relations between the tribe (the consumer society) and natural (biomedical) and supernatural (psychic) forces, and to render the destructive power of these spirits harmless.

Just as the shaman embodies the community, physically and symbolically, the phenomenon of transference occurs when patients identify their well-being with the mental-health professional. The patient often becomes heavily dependent on the expert, who takes on the aura of a guru/teacher. Watch any of the popular psychologists on television or in lectures when they flash their beatific smiles, talk about their life-enhancing powers, and lay out their belief systems, and the comparison with the shaman sitting before the communal fire initiating his followers into the mysteries of the universe is compelling.

Today many Americans, especially in the upper-income and high-education brackets, are more conversant with the language of psychology than that of traditional religion. Few of these people understand such concepts as *atonement, redemption,* or *original sin,* but most of them are well-versed in *sibling rivalry, Oedipal complex,* and *attention-deficit disorder.* They perceive life not as a hard, disciplined struggle to connect humanity with divinity but as a quest for the "self," an almost mythological creature defined according to the latest therapeutic model of mental health or trendy psychological theory of consciousness that promises control over life while brushing aside the moral anxieties that have burdened people for countless generations.

In an ironic critique of his own work, Sigmund Freud said that he cured the miseries of his neurotic patients only to open them up to the normal woes of life. His point is that psychotherapy can't refute the existential truth that despair and the fear of death are part of the human psyche and that only the deeply disturbed person believes that life can be endlessly joyful. Being human is the problem of humanity. If mental-health Mandarins were strictly candid with their patients, they would warn them that if they truly discovered their "real self," they would encounter the dreadful horror of the human condition.

Elie Wiesel, who learned much about humanity and God while imprisoned in a Nazi concentration camp during World War II, tells the following story from Hasidic literature.

In the Eastern European village of Lublin during the Napoleonic Wars, Rebbe Yaakov-Yitzhak Horowitz saw the upheaval across Europe as cause to pressure God to fulfill his messianic promise to the Jewish people. Known as the holy Seer of Lublin, the rebbe conspired with other Jewish leaders to promote the French emperor's cause and try to influence the outcome on the battlefield. Working to precipitate events that only God could control, the Seer put himself in cosmic peril.

Napoleon's defeat in Russia proved that he was not part of God's plan for the Jews, and the Seer's hopes for redemption were dashed. Russian and Polish Jew-haters resumed their atrocities.

To fight melancholy among the oppressed Jews, the Seer's religious services stressed fervent singing and enthusiastic clapping rather than quiet meditation. "I prefer a simple Jew who prays with joy to a sage who studies with sadness," he said, a scandalous remark to many other Jewish teachers. The Seer also associated with a local clown who would make him laugh to ease his depression.

To observe an important Jewish holiday in 1814, the Seer told his followers: "Drink and celebrate—it's an order. And if your ecstasy is pure enough, contagious enough, it will last forever—I promise you that." The crowd obeyed and let go in festive exuberance.

Unnoticed, the Seer left the gathering and went to his private upstairs study. No one knows what happened there, but the people soon heard a scream and ran into the street. A short distance from the house, they found the Seer lying on the ground, twisting in pain, moaning, "And the abyss calls for another abyss." He never recovered.

The event became known as the Great Fall. No one ever figured out how the Seer could tumble from his second-floor room; the window was too small for a man of his size to go through. Although the meaning was unclear, the tragedy definitely had spiritual significance. "Could it be that, having tried to bring the Messiah through joy, he thought of trying . . . despair?" asked some of the Seer's followers.

Few contemporary Americans want to hear such provocative messages: that God has his own priorities, that individuals court catastrophe if they put their interests ahead of God's, and that melancholy could be a means to comprehend the divine.

Certainly, acceptance of the idea that humanity is accountable to God and that physical pleasures and psychic comforts aren't the prime goals of life would have severe repercussions on American society. No shopping-mall economy wants people to stop satisfying themselves, to start pondering the timeless questions of life, and to struggle with their personal share of an often shameful, sinful human nature. No way. Sin supplies much of the U.S. gross domestic product and suffuses popular culture. The country would be bankrupt without it. Avarice alone accounts for billions of consumer dollars. Imagine restaurants or liquor stores without gluttony; the fashion and movie industries without lust; television sports without couch-bound, remote-control sloth; celebrity tabloids without envy; law firms and car-repair shops without anger; politics, universities, the arts, and journalism without pride.

The widespread disenchantment of the Age of Melancholy suggests that millions of Americans like me suspect that Mandarin psychology has elements of a false religion. We wonder why bountiful material possessions, "self-actualization," and unrestrained hedonism have not made us happy. We understand the dire situation of being the only earthly creatures who seek immortality but are conscious of mortality. We yearn for higher meaning in life but think that our own lives are absurd. We want certainty but realize that finding the truth about human existence requires agonizing suffering. And we desire a heightened sense of community but are vulnerable to the sterile, deadly indifference of the corporate economy and bureaucratic state.

The Prozac Personality

In his bestselling book *Care of the Soul,* Thomas Moore says that he would like to put what he calls "psychological modernism" into the American Psychiatric Association's catalog of adjustment disorders, known as DSM-IV, which doctors and insurance companies use to diagnose and classify emotional and behavioral problems.

To Moore, psychological modernism is "an uncritical acceptance of the values of the modern world. It includes blind faith in technology, inordinate attachment to material gadgets and conveniences, uncritical acceptance of the march of scientific progress."

The almost total trust that many Americans have in science is another symptom of the Age of Melancholy. If we could be disabused of our excessive confidence in science—which is yet another manifestation of postmodern humanity's insatiable will for mastery—we might be more open to a reflective, contemplative understanding of life that could enhance the end-of-the-millennium search for meaning and purpose. Most important, we should not be intimidated by science, and we should agree with British philosopher Bertrand Russell that "all our progress is but improved means to unimproved ends."

In the late twentieth century, science is the most powerful system of thought to explain the workings of the world. It charts the conceptual maps, designs the imaginative patterns, and provides the organizing principles that establish order and structure in life. Science, at this time in Western history, has largely won its centuries-long battle against religion to write the narratives that shape society and personality.

Like medieval lepers and cripples seeking miracle cures at a martyred saint's shrine, many Americans today think that there is a scientific answer for every mental, physical, and social ailment.

And with good reason.

Thanks largely to science, Americans enjoy technological marvels and experiences that were science-fiction fantasies a short while ago. My grandmother, for example, rode to school on a horse; today, I could take a college literature class on television. She was the second woman in Kansas to hold a motor vehicle driver's license; I could buy a car that has a satellite tracking system. Machines and medicines heal diseases that were death sentences to my grandmother's contemporaries. Exotic and ethnic foods she never tasted are now on Wichita grocery shelves. And though my grandmother never ventured overseas until late in life, I have hopscotched the globe.

Over the past several decades science has generated an explosion of knowledge ranging from tracing the course of subatomic particles to attending the birth of new stars in distant galaxies. Medical science has diagrammed the wiring of the human brain and documented the mechanical workings of the human body. Modern communication systems have created history's first truly global civilization, binding together in a common destiny cultures that a short time ago were virtually ignorant of one another.

Given such accomplishments, it's no wonder that many Americans believe that technological progress is the same as human progress—that, given enough latitude and resources, science will find a solution to every human problem.

Today's technological society is close to culminating the eighteenth-century Enlightenment vision—first sought by Adam and Eve—of a completely autonomous humanity. Substituting

146

the theory of evolution for God as the ordering mechanism of the universe, the Mandarins of science have fashioned a closed world that encases humanity within natural and biological facts. Humanity is in a box. In its extreme form, the argument is that everything that can't be proved by scientific inquiry, perceived by the senses, or kicked across the street is excluded from reality. Because the "invisible," metaphysical truths of beauty, justice, and God's presence can't be weighed, dissected, or calibrated, humanity is reduced to blood types and neural circuits, distinguishable only by bodily size, shape, and color.

"Man is part of nature, in the same sense that a stone is, or a cactus, or a camel," said historian of science Jacob Bronowski.

Having the power to make deserts bloom, create life in test tubes, and even vaporize the world, humans are tempted to promote their own reasons for existence. "We no longer have to resort to superstition when faced with the deep problems: Is there a meaning to life? What are we for? What is man?" wrote biologist Richard Dawkins.

In his book *The Selfish Gene,* Dawkins describes human life as basically a conveyor belt for DNA, the fundamental genetic building block that some scientists believe determines everything from hair texture to mate selection.

Dawkins and like-minded scientists argue that humanity has no function greater than procreation. Instead of a loving creator who made humanity in his image, God is an imperialistic genetic code. Immortality isn't a celestial city in the hereafter, but the continued migration of DNA through the biological chain. The mission of life isn't to develop virtuous character but to mate and reproduce.

The ideas of Dawkins and others have pushed one of the most influential scientific trends of the late twentieth century, sociobiology and evolutionary psychology, which apply genetics and the dynamics of evolution to human emotions, social actions, and sexual behavior. Continuing work begun by Charles Darwin in the mid-nineteenth century, these scientists say humanity can't escape its primeval past or its basic biological imperatives. For example, choices in mates are supposedly determined mainly by which potential partner offers the most security for the female or the most offspring for the male. Love is a lust to propagate. Beauty is a lure for procreation. Morality and community are parts of a self-defensive system of reciprocity among people to help ensure that their genes survive a nasty, merciless environment.

As Steven Pinker insists in his 1997 book, *How the Mind Works:* "The mind is a system of organs of computation, designed by natural selection to solve the kinds of problems our ancestors faced in their foraging way of life, in particular, understanding and outmaneuvering objects, animals, plants and other people." That means human behavior is heavily determined by brain wiring, and the mind is not the "blank slate" that such philosophers as John Locke said was filled by the life experiences that make each person unique.

Although conceding that morality, free will, and a sense of the self remain mysteries (though ones that might eventually be solved), Pinker, a psychology professor at the Massachusetts Institute of Technology, argues that religion doesn't come from divine revelation but from humanity's ability to analyze other people's behavior. From the capacity to impute minds to others, Pinker says, "it's a short step to think of minds that just don't happen to have bodies. And minds without bodies are what we call souls, ghosts, gods, devils, genies."

Like a personal computer, the mind needs software. This mental operating system "could be patterns of information, not a magical substance or a divine essence, just an information-processing device where patterns of matter cause changes in other patterns of matter," Pinker says.

Personality also could be a genetic inheritance. According to a study reported in the journal *Science* in December 1996, researchers found a significant correlation between the length of a certain gene and psychological neuroses and other emotional and mental disorders. Some scientists further contend that the brain has a set point, similar to a preprogrammed tendency toward weight, that determines whether a person has a happy or grumpy outlook on life.

Not every scientist accepts all the tenets of evolutionary psychology. In the October 5, 1997, issue of the *New York Times Book Review*, Mark Ridley, a biologist and editor of *The Darwin Reader*, notes that the theory of natural selection pushed by Pinker and others doesn't explain humanity's appreciation of art or skill in calculus. Harvard professor and science writer Stephen Jay Gould discounts Pinker's evolutionary psychology as "unproven and unprovable."

Additionally, as seen in Chapter 7, some physicists exploring the farthest reaches of the cosmos, the smallest elements of matter, and the evanescence of energy find in their research what they describe as evidence of divine order, an intelligent design to the universe that links the mind of God with creation.

Yet the intellectual momentum seems to be on the side of genetic and evolutionary interpretations that displace spiritual understandings of existence. Increasingly within the social and biological sciences, humanity's physical and moral natures are described without reference to metaphysical forces. Rather than the traditional religious concept that something is rotten in the human soul, Mandarin scientists think that most of life's miseries and imperfections are caused by faulty genetic architecture, malfunctioning brain chemistry, or poor social engineering. The Mandarin program for the next millennium: once its technical and therapeutic tools are sophisticated enough, humanity can abandon its infantile illusions about God and master its own fate.

Yes! Finally! Adam and Eve vindicated! Faust rules!

But some people rebel against the Mandarin agenda. They reject the notion that humanity is merely a natural occurrence, that we are only sexually aggressive primates with an unusually high level of curiosity about ourselves and our surroundings. They fight the monopoly sought by the medical and therapeutic professions to define and direct the human condition. They won't trade a morally demanding God for an amoral marketplace.

Why did I resist? Why didn't I accede to my evolutionary heritage, my inner Cro-Magnon? Why did I refuse standard treatments for depression? Why didn't I rely solely on doctors and therapists?

The most important decision melancholy presented me was whether to use drugs to ease my mental pain. On recommendation from my doctor, I took Prozac, the popular antidepressant. It worked, if "working" is defined as flattening my mood and keeping me on task at work. And for months, that was enough. Any relief was welcome. I sensed, however, that chemically induced mellowness let me avoid rooting out my troubles, by freezing my emotions and robbing me of creative intensity. Prozac became my means to deaden pain; then, emboldened by my experiences during my summer sabbatical at the University of Kansas, I wanted to take possession of my melancholy, to jump on it and ride like hell—or into hell.

Exploring the issue of depression, I learned how dependent the medical establishment has become on the laboratory to manage mental complaints. In fact, in 1995, with sales rising 24 percent from the previous year, Prozac became the world's first mental-health drug to reach $2 billion in annual sales. Eli Lilly and Company, which manufactures Prozac, said that more than 20.7 million Americans took the drug in 1996. To push the idea of curing ills with pills, in 1997 Lilly budgeted $20 million for a massive magazine advertising campaign. The pitch included weather imagery with dark clouds clearing to a 1970s-style "happy face" sun, suggesting that the bright side of life is just a dose away. All told, Prozac and its medicinal cousins, Zoloft and Paxil, ranked among the seven top-selling drugs in the United States in the one-year period ended August 1997, with sales totaling more than $3.8 billion, according to I.M.S. America, a market research company.

A couple of qualifying notes: Prozac and similar antidepressants regulate brain chemicals, notably serotonin, thought to affect a person's moods. But the drugs are no sure thing. A study reported in the September/October 1995 issue of *Psychology Today* found that one-third of patients showed a positive response to the medication, one-third did not improve, and one-third improved with placebos. And some physicians question the Prozac protocol: "No causal relationship has ever been established between a specific biochemical state of the brain and any specific behavior, and it is simplistic to assume it is possible," says Peter R. Breggin, M.D., in his book *Toxic Psychiatry*.

As advertised, Prozac seemed to calm me. I want to be clear, *very clear*. Antidepressants can be miraculous. They can save lives. And no one should stop using them without serious thought, a sober assessment of the potential dangers, and close consultation with a doctor to maintain a medical safety net.

My hesitancy toward the treatment was not medical, but moral: that psychotropic drugs threaten to reduce character and self-identity to biotechnology. Pour a certain drug into a particular cerebral lobe and get a predictable reaction. The classic religious and philosophical distinctions between soul and body, mind and brain, God and humanity, burble away within the chemical stew inside our skulls. Hopes and fears that people feel as profoundly personal expressions can be distilled to organic or evolutionary processes. To me, this idea is an unacceptable denial of human dignity. I wanted my life to have moral consequence, even if it was only a melancholic refusal to cooperate. Defiantly flushing thirty capsules containing 20 milligrams of Prozac down the toilet climactically reasserted my human integrity and freedom, however deluded that act might appear to the medical and social sciences and however much additional pain I might encounter.

While the effectiveness of Prozac and its kin is hit-or-miss today, researchers will no doubt improve results with their upcoming product lines. In a quantum leap in humanity's long history of grasping for godlike powers, science eventually could have the technological skill to cast individuals into whatever image society prefers. In the near future the Mandarins might even chart the course of evolution by chemically tinkering with supposedly innate drives, a postmillennial predestination that would enable experts to shape everything from the mental habits to the muscle mass to the politics of future generations.

It's the highest alchemy: rather than medieval sorcery changing base metals into gold, third-millennium science could transform cantankerous human beings into obedient drones. Free will could become a choice of whether you want your personality delivered by tablet or capsule, leaving religion and philosophy as relics of a less technologically complex era. The purpose of life could become a properly balanced bodily chemistry; such virtues as honesty, loyalty, spirituality, and trust would be nothing more than variable doses of different drugs. No longer would people be independent moral agents responsible for their own actions, but medicinally programmed clones. The only sin would be to forget to take your "be happy, behave" pill.

An extreme example of what is at stake is found in Anthony Burgess's futuristic novel *A Clockwork Orange,* which seems to prophesy the therapeutic culture of the late twentieth century.

Best known in its film adaptation by Stanley Kubrick, *A Clockwork Orange* floated out of the caverns of memory while I was struggling with the issue of free choice. I had reviewed the movie when it was released in the early 1970s and later read the novel, though the book's Russian-derived slang made it tough sledding.

The story is set in a Britain of the future in which roaming gangs of young men brutalize anyone who gets in their way. In the key scene, Alex, a vicious teenager and head of the band of droogs, beats a woman to death with a giant phallic sculpture. Imprisoned for murder, Alex becomes a guinea pig in a rehabilitation program based on aversion therapy. He is temporarily transformed and appears ready for a peaceful life. But something deep inside rejects the therapy and erupts in violence.

To me, *A Clockwork Orange* exhibits the logical extension of the therapeutic culture. Motivated by a sincere desire to "cure" a killer, the scientists in *A Clockwork Orange* seek the same divine power as Adam and Eve to determine human nature. They are willing to sacrifice liberty—humanity's unique attribute—because it inevitably leads to suffering and social deviancy. It's a great temptation: political and personal tranquillity in exchange for shelving free will. Sure, a few snakelike Alexes might break out, but they can be rounded up and reprogrammed; besides, is moral freedom really worth the price of the evil it unfailingly produces? God might have permitted sin to ensure maximum human freedom, but why not let the therapeutic culture improve the product by eliminating emotional maladjustments, divisive conflicts, cognitive/ego distortions, and other imperfections?

Those points shouldn't be rejected as a technophobic opposition to scientific advancement or as a literary fantasy of dystopia.

Similar concerns, though not as dramatized, underlie one of the surprise bestselling books of the 1990s, *Listening to Prozac,* by Peter D. Kramer, a Rhode Island psychiatrist who noted that some of his patients became "better than well" after taking the antidepressant. Their memories improved. They had more energy. Their minds were calmer. And they appeared to have greater self-confidence.

Those responses led Kramer to wonder whether Prozac is "a medication or a medical steroid. Are we using it cosmetically to make people more attractive?"

Although many people would prefer a placid, smiley-faced disposition to the misery of depression, the question arises whether the medications mean that people can avoid the pain and challenges that lead to moral development. Will people, Kramer asks, settle for a drug-addled version of happiness rather than explore "the morally beneficial effects of melancholy and angst?"

Yet, historically, many people have refused to take ownership of their psychic sorrow and have sought chemical relief. Is it coincidental that opium was popular among melancholics in the Romantic era, cocaine and heroin were used by some melancholics in the late nineteenth century, and Prozac is the drug of choice in the late twentieth century?

As discussed previously, ages of melancholy are partly counter-reactions against the arrogance of science and technology. The Romantics were appalled by the destructive excesses of the Industrial Revolution. Many sensitive late Victorians worried that Darwinian theories — sometimes used to justify racism and capitalist excesses — undermined human freedom and dignity. And many melancholics in the late twentieth century want to restore the primacy of ethical and spiritual sensibilities and overthrow the amoral tyranny of modern technology.

The philosopher of science Paul Feyerabend described the struggle for the heart and soul of humanity this way: "Scientists are not content with running their own playpens in accordance with what they regard as the rules of the scientific method; they want to universalize those rules, they want them to become part of society, and they use every means at their disposal—argument, propaganda, pressure tactics, intimidation, lobbying—to achieve those ends."

The result is scientism: the uncritical use of scientific principles to define reality and the shunting aside, as mental phantasm or fictional whimsy invalid in describing the world, of any moral or philosophical claim to truth not susceptible to empirical verification.

The late twentieth century finds many Americans in a quandary. We enjoy the benefits of technology—a longer life span, mass communications, creature comforts—but we intuit that humans are more than animals stumbling through a nonsensical universe. We don't want to be standardized, rationalized, tranquilized, and computerized. Something deep inside me and many melancholics rejects that life is merely atoms colliding, DNA multiplying, and brains processing.

Instead, we yearn to get out of ourselves, to find a freedom outside technology, to transcend prosaic human existence. We seek truths greater than those of human-fixated scientism. We want to heed the warning of the prophet Isaiah: "They shall be turned back and utterly put to shame, who trust in graven images, who say to molten images, 'You are our gods.'"

The Rebellious Soul

Although written almost one hundred years ago, Mark Twain's tale *The Mysterious Stranger* presages the Age of Melancholy of the late twentieth century. In the short story and in contemporary American society, human happiness is the highest value and scientific principles are triumphant; but rather than the promised utopia, people are isolated from one another and truth is an illusion.

Set in Austria in 1590, *The Mysterious Stranger* opens with a boy sitting with two friends when Satan appears, disguised as a well-dressed and amiable stranger named Philip Traum. Using his unlimited mental powers, Satan takes the boys on fantastic voyages around the world, showing them the wretchedness of humanity. He also persuades them of the falseness of morality, of the kindness of killing a cripple, and of the nonexistence of heaven.

There is a way to be happy on earth. When Father Peter, the village priest, is unjustly accused of theft and acquitted, Satan makes him think he is in fact guilty of the crime. The old man's reason is shattered by this false belief. He plunges into insanity, fancying himself emperor of Austria, and is "the one utterly happy person in the empire."

When the boys argue that the priest's contentment comes at a terrible cost, Satan responds: "Are you so unobservant as not to have found out that sanity and happiness are an impossible combination?"

Satan further suggests that, by relying on its own visions of truth and breaking the connection between the transcendent and the self, humanity has condemned itself to a meaningless existence of its own creation. "There is no God, no universe, no human race, no earthly life, no heaven, no hell. It is all a dream, a grotesque and foolish dream. Nothing exists but you. And you are but a *thought* —a vagrant thought, a useless thought, a homeless thought, wandering forlorn among the empty eternities," Satan says.

As allegory, *The Mysterious Stranger* underscores many of my points. Scientism-debased scientists have tried to erase the divine origins of humanity. Evolutionary psychologists define twentieth-century individuals as hunter-gatherers in well-tailored suits, living in leafy suburbs instead of on grassy savannas. Some physicians treat people as chemically dependent animals differing mainly according to physical size and prescriptive dosage. Sociobiologists claim that philosophical ideas and moral virtues are genuine only as they serve the domineering impulses of DNA molecules.

At best, science offers a provisional understanding of existence that only temporarily satisfies humanity's need to comprehend the universe. Indeed, science has not been an especially reliable authority, because it is constantly revising its description of fundamental reality. Recall the scientific paradigm shifts discussed in Chapter 3: Copernicus's repositioning of the sun and earth redrafted the ancient maps of the heavens; Einstein's theory that time and space vary according to the perspective of the observer refuted Newton's mechanical natural laws. While it's doubtful that any future scientist will repeal the law of gravity or rearrange the solar system, some of today's most secure scientific "facts" will surely be discarded by the progress of science itself.

For many of the issues raised in this book, cracks are apparent in the edifice erected by biochemistry and evolutionary psychology. If humanity is an evolutionary product, why are we the only earthly creatures capable of moral awareness? What genetic impulse sparked human imagination? Where does hope come from? What neurotransmitter first carried the message of death? Why is melancholy rampant in the era when science has never been more triumphant?

"We live in mystery, yet believe everything is known," British playwright Christopher Fry said sardonically of the twentieth-century mind.

For all its explorations of the psyche, science never discovered the soul—that turbulent self-consciousness that allows humanity to touch the sacred. The soul is also the energy that inspires art and philosophy and lifts humanity to a higher level. But the soul can't be weighed on an atomic scale or subjected to a variable-regression analysis of statistical data. Furthermore, the concept of the soul implies that humanity has access to a dimension of reality that science can't catalog and that threatens scientism's monopoly on truth.

As regards the soul, many of today's scientists are like Frederick II, the thirteenth-century Holy Roman emperor. A religious skeptic, Frederick executed a convict by suffocating him inside a barrel. He then opened the barrel's cork a bit and asked members of his court if they observed the man's soul rise to heaven. No one did. Frederick concluded that he had refuted the belief that the soul survives death.

The soul has devastating weapons to annihilate such human arrogance: fear, misery, and hope. While the Mandarins in the biological and social sciences hang truth solely on human and natural forces, the soul seeks a fuller explanation for existence because it can never shake the horror of death and it wants to believe that life has ultimate meaning.

Earthbound humanity might never really know the purpose of its own creation, but it can feel something straining inside, a driving force that can't be neatly categorized by science and that transcends reason. From the time humans began burying their ancestors with weapons, coins, and food needed in an afterlife, they have sought to crawl out of the biological swamp, to rise above their animal nature and attain some sort of spiritual immortality. All individuals want a special place in the universe; most of them refuse to accept that they have endured decades of life's travails just to end up as organic debris.

The soul, stirring in the Age of Melancholy, revolts. Despair infuses society with seemingly unbearable pain that reminds people of the existential human condition. It is a fear and trembling that shakes down the defenses — status seeking, wealth, soulless pleasures — that society and its therapist acolytes have constructed against suffering. The laws scientism claims as truths are refuted by a melancholic sob.

The soul does not see life as exercises in self-indulgence or reproduction. It interprets life as an inner conflict between human pride and spiritual virtues. The soul realizes the fragility of human knowledge and how easily humanly derived truths can be discredited. The soul understands that security in life depends on something more powerful than humanity. And to teach humanity such truths, the soul wields suffering as a learning stick. As the seventeenth-century French essayist Blaise Pascal put it: "Man's greatness comes from knowing he is wretched; a tree does not know it is wretched."

At the end of the most technically oriented century in history, the claim that scientifically adept, psychologically savvy individuals could create societies so perfect that, in the satirical observation of poet T. S. Eliot, "no one need ever be good" has collapsed amid the moral chaos and cultural grimness of the late twentieth century.

But the new consciousness offered by the Age of Melancholy won't emerge unless humanity surrenders its vanity to its soul.

"This is the salvation through self-despair," William James wrote. "To get to it, a critical point must be passed, a corner turned within one. Something must give way, a native hardness must break down and liquefy."

And that could be the fundamental choice for American society at the end of the twentieth century: therapy or transcendence?

6

CHOOSING TRAGEDY

Terror of Inner Life

Like many young newspaper journalists, I began my career as a police reporter. The thinking of editors is that a year or two covering the "cop shop" teaches cub reporters a thing or two about real life. No better way to harden naive, middle-class college graduates than to have them interview rape victims or listen to a streetwise homicide detective graphically describe the size of the bullet wound that killed a convenience-store clerk the previous night.

In the fall of 1972 I had just turned twenty-four years old and was hired for my first newspaper job. It was with the *Hawk Eye* in Burlington, Iowa, a blue-collar, Rust Belt Mississippi River town of 32,000 noted for beautiful river-view parks and mini-mansions built during the city's nineteenth-century heyday as a steamboat and railroad center. Burlington's main employers are the J. I. Case Co., a farm-implement and heavy-machinery manufacturer, and the Iowa Army Ammunition Plant, which in the early 1970s was working three shifts around the clock to make hand grenades and mortar shells for the Vietnam War.

After a couple of days trailing around a veteran police reporter to get to know the routine, I was working as the *Hawk Eye*'s lone Saturday reporter. About 8:30 A.M. a call came over the police squawk box of a shooting in a barking-dog-in-the-yard, pickup-truck, working-class neighborhood. The city editor told me to check it out.

I arrived at the address and entered the squat, yellow-brick bungalow with an officer about my age. A rookie like me, he hadn't yet learned to keep reporters away from a probable crime site.

Three young children were huddled on the living-room couch. The eldest, a girl about six years old, was sobbing but also trying to protect her little sister and baby brother by holding them close to her.

The officer and I were drawn to the bedroom. A woman's body was sprawled on the bed. Her clothes were ripped. Her blood had soaked a dark burgundy stain into the tangled royal blue quilt and sky blue sheets.

A man lay crumpled on the floor. A shotgun angled beside him. His face had been blown off. The wall nearest his body dripped with human gore, oozing a grisly Jackson Pollock–style abstract expressionist collage of hair, blood, and brain tissue.

As I reported in the Sunday morning paper, a police investigation concluded that the couple had gone to a popular country-and-western bar Friday night. The wife had apparently flirted with another man, throwing her husband into a jealous rage. They argued at the bar, and the fight escalated when they got home. It ended after the man took out his double-barreled shotgun, blasted his wife in the chest, and turned the weapon on himself. The noise awakened the children; the six-year-old daughter discovered the carnage and ran next door to a neighbor, who dialed the police emergency number.

That brutal event, so contrary to my upbringing, taught me

how quickly normal family life can explode into violent destruction, how thin the line is between civilization and barbarism. From there, intrigued by how some people sink instantly into savagery, I turned crime into a career specialty. I have covered dozens of criminal trials. I know that victims bleed much more profusely when shot at short range than when hit from a distance. I have visited some of the nation's toughest prisons, including the federal penitentiary in Marion, Illinois, where the U.S. government houses its hardest cases. I have hung out with local cops and FBI officers to get the lowdown on crime stories that didn't get fully detailed in court. I have heard heartrending laments from crime victims. I have attended academic seminars, listened to the experts, and read voluminous reports on crime.

For years I accepted the view of the National Crime Commission, which reported in the mid-1960s that "America can control crime if it will." That meant crime was amenable to social engineering. By eradicating poverty, improving education, broadening health care, expanding job opportunities, and undertaking other worthwhile projects, Americans could remedy the crime problem, the experts said. The philosophical assumptions were that there is no such thing as indelible human nature and that criminals were primarily products of their social circumstances. By changing that environment through appropriate public policies and mental-health programs, social workers, psychiatrists, and government bureaucrats could reduce crime.

But I began noticing analytical gaps. Many of the vicious criminals I interviewed didn't come from underprivileged backgrounds. Most people who grow up in poverty don't become outlaws. Crime rates were much lower during the Great Depression of the 1930s, when millions of Americans were destitute, than in the comparatively robust economy of the 1970s and 1980s.

Moreover, the crimes that disgusted me the most—such as child molestation and domestic violence—have no economic motivation and occur within all classes and races. Those abuses seem to spring from sinister psyches that get pleasure from controlling and humiliating weaker individuals. Perhaps, I thought, crime had less to do with sociology than with morality. In laying crime largely to class and social position, the experts might have ignored some deeply seated corruption within human nature. I saw too many "normal" middle-class individuals—doctors, lawyers, fathers, mothers—commit dastardly crimes for me to buy the socioeconomic argument wholesale. Instead, something truly vile had exploded within them.

A secular, academy-trained society, however, rejects the notion of existential evil and has abandoned the biblical concept of human depravity. Trusting their own abilities to comprehend, categorize, and correct human actions, the experts refuse to admit that a congenital darkness might lurk within each individual.

Among the most radical cultural changes of the past few decades has been the redefining of deviancy. The new mind-set is examined by psychiatrist Karl Menninger in his 1973 book *Whatever Became of Sin?* According to Menninger, one of the most respected members in his field, the "new psychology" of the post–World War II era has substituted the traditional concept of sin for a new idea on child rearing: no matter how nasty the action, the inner child is blameless.

"A greatly increased emphasis was put on love and tenderness toward the child," Menninger wrote. "Words like 'bad,' 'wicked,' and 'immoral,' while still employed, began to sound old-fashioned. 'Sin' began to be questioned."

Meanwhile, behavior once labeled sinful was reclassified as criminal, and then reclassified again as symptomatic of deep social or mental stress. "Whereas the police and judges had taken over from the clergy, the doctors and psychologists were now taking over from the police and judges," Menninger observed.

In other words, the therapeutic culture had arrived on the crime scene. Scientism filled the void left by the decline of religion over the past few decades. Medical and psychological regimens replaced ethical instruction. Sin became sickness. Guilt and shame became unhealthy responses to harmful personal decisions because they weakened the individual's self-esteem. Antisocial behavior became a mental disorder rather than a moral wrong.

But shifting the terminology for human actions and reinterpreting individual motives don't explain why people capable of free choice often do horrible things. For me, resolving that issue required an encounter with one of history's most horrendous crimes.

In the mid-1980s, a time of heightened Cold War tension, a German-based foundation worried that U.S. support was lagging for the defense of Europe. It decided to bring American journalists to West Germany to help buttress U.S. backing for the Atlantic alliance. I was among the journalists selected for a two-week junket in 1984.

While most of the tour focused on NATO's military preparedness, economic cooperation, and common democratic values, we also visited the Nazi concentration camp at Dachau, a small village outside Munich. There I encountered the ghostly remnants of absolute evil: a rifle range where innumerable Russian prisoners were shot; the rusted crematorium where the bodies of thousands of innocent victims were incinerated, along with a letter from a camp official noting that coke was as efficient as the more expensive coal gas in burning corpses; the gray concrete room where hundreds of inmates were subjected to cruel medical experiments, including being submerged in freezing water to test the body's tolerance for cold.

For me, the most important discussion on the trip focused on what Germans call the "historians' debate," which tries to fathom why Hitler and the Holocaust happened in Germany. The scholarly consensus laid Hitler's rise to unique economic and political factors in post–World War I Germany. The Holocaust was primarily due to Nazi fanaticism. The debate was renewed in the mid-1990s when Harvard government professor Daniel Goldhagen, in his book *Hitler's Willing Executioners,* claimed that the Holocaust was a "national project" motivated by virulent anti-Semitism among the German people.

Those explanations don't totally satisfy me. Stalin killed more people than did Hitler. Mao slaughtered more people than Stalin and Hitler combined. And Pol Pot murdered millions of Cambodians after the world had promised that such atrocities would never happen again.

Does this century—among the bloodiest in human history—need more proof that something is perversely twisted in the human soul, a level of depravity that can't be dismissed as a cultural or psychological malfunction? But didn't twentieth-century scientism and progressive thinking promise that humanity could control its own destiny and create an enlightened, prosperous, and harmonious society?

If the therapeutic culture and the social sciences could really modify basic human behavior, evil would have disappeared years ago and the world would be a religionless nirvana. Yet the presence of evil is as strong in the 1990s as at any time in history. It's the decade of serial killers in California, a cannibal in Wisconsin, ethnic cleansing in Bosnia, genocide in Rwanda, a bombing in Oklahoma City, children murdering a baby in England, and terrorist incidents around the globe: Algerian fanatics, armed with automatic weapons, axes, swords, and knives, slaughtering thousands of people; Egyptian zealots gunning down tourists at the ancient monuments at Luxor.

Furthermore, as evidenced by the media frenzy around sensational murders, mass suicides, and other outrageous human actions, evil dominates popular culture. Books by frightmaster Stephen King top bestseller lists and true-crime narratives rush off the printing presses; slasher movies splatter blood across suburban-mall screens, and Darth Vader and the dark force made a boffo box-office return in 1997. Good might triumph in the final reel or chapter, but the contemporary imagination is transfixed by evil characters. In today's cultural climate Judas wouldn't have hanged himself in shame; he would be a talk-show celebrity with a million-dollar book contract.

It's enough to make anyone depressed.

And for me, through depression came understanding.

A product of the civil rights and antiwar movements of the 1960s, I have been quick to condemn in my newspaper commentaries the sins of violence and injustice committed by society. I understand that racism isn't perpetuated solely by ignorance and hatred, but also by institutions that support prejudice. Militarism isn't simply testosterone-fueled patriotism, but part of an economic system that thrives on large defense budgets. As individuals, people could lead highly moral lives, but as members of society they are implicated in collective evil. Personally, however, I largely exonerated myself of sin because I was trying to eradicate the worst examples of evil through political advocacy on newspaper editorial pages. I was a good guy; a bit self-righteous, perhaps, but on the side of the angels.

My midlife melancholy proved, metaphorically, that my personal character was red in tooth and claw. The precipitating cause was my contemptible behavior toward my mentor, George Neav-oll, whose career I was willing to wreck to advance my own. It didn't help that George later told me that he loved his new job in Maine and was glad that I took over for him in Wichita. George's best wishes were eclipsed by a ferocious introspection. The deeper that melancholy dropped me into the inner sanctum of my psyche, the greater the horror of self-recognition. Forced to be ruthlessly candid with myself, I conceded that most of my life decisions were based on naked self-interest and that anyone who got in my way was just so much collateral damage, like civilians dispassionately wiped out in a military air attack.

This confession of personal sin, coming after years of trauma, insomnia, self-doubt, self-deceit, and emotional abasement, was a tremendous relief. While the initial shock was intense and repel-lent, the reality was compelling and irrefutable. Melancholy having deflated my ego, I could perceive my operational sin — self-absorbed pride.

And I had the full complement of hubris: pride of status, from my career and stature in the community; pride of intellect, from my educational accomplishments and rhetorical abilities; pride of power, from my influence in local and state politics; and — the most damaging of all — pride of spirit, the sanctimonious confi-dence that, until melancholy hit, my life had gone so well because destiny favored me.

Indeed, pride is so insidious that even in professing my errors, I detect the taint of sin. I felt like the Carthusian monk explaining to a visitor the distinctive feature of his religious order: "When it comes to good works, we don't match the Benedictines; as to preaching, we are not in a class with the Dominicans; the Jesuits are way ahead of us in learning; but in the matter of humility, we're tops."

My life had become a whinefest. I felt indignantly insulted that life was no longer interesting, that my ambitions had been spent, that I was being carried through middle age on a current of ennui. Yet even as I laughingly mocked myself, I detected arrogance in my tedium—how noble was my sorrow, how well earned was my cynicism.

My condition couldn't be treated solely by antidepressant drugs or psychological counseling because those therapies are impotent against my real disease: the prideful sin of putting myself at the center of the world. In doing so, I separated myself from other people and the spiritual values that could have helped restrain my excessive self-love.

Self-loathing from stubborn wickedness showed me that "sin-inclined" is the most intellectually honest description of human nature. Although often derided by many mental-health professionals as a mean-spirited offense to human dignity, sin is the only explanation for the human condition that is empirically verified by history—slavery, barbarism, racism—and subjectively proved by personal conduct—indifference, narcissism, hatred.

It has been identified by novelists: "The human race is implicated in some terrible aboriginal calamity," said Graham Greene.

It has been pondered by philosophers: How is it that "men know what is good, but do what is bad?" asked Socrates.

It has been diagnosed by psychologists: "Illness is to a large extent rooted in eternal causes. The Christian doctrine of original sin and the Buddhist Four Noble Truths teach that human life is wounded in its essence, and that suffering is in the nature of things," remarked Thomas Moore.

It has been affirmed by poets: "In all the actions and desires of the purely natural man, you will find nothing that is not ghastly," noted Charles Baudelaire.

Paradoxically, sin is both wholly human and horribly antihumane. It differentiates humanity from dumb animals, yet it leads people to attempt to snatch power that God has reserved for himself. Sin turns people into sorcerer's apprentices, usurping divine authority and flooding the world with guilt-inducing calamities that are beyond our control. Yet imagine life without sin: English literature without Iago, heroes without malevolent enemies, and humanity without choice. Literary critic George Steiner put it well: "To have neither Heaven nor Hell is to be intolerably deprived and alone in a world gone flat."

Melancholy acknowledges sin-prone human nature and recognizes the fraudulence of a self-idolizing faith in humanity. It teaches that individuals are severely flawed but have the potential for spiritual redemption. Melancholy is the repressed memory of the divine presence, a subconscious aching to return to the good graces of the creator, a mysterious compulsion to seek meaning in life. By shattering illusion and pretense, and laying bare humanity's deepest terrors, melancholy makes God more apprehensible because we feel a desperate need of divine intervention to forgive our sins.

Further, by admitting the ugly—but necessary, if humanity is to have free will—fact of evil, humanity advances personal responsibility. To deny sin means that the great criminals of the twentieth century—Stalin, Hitler, Mao, Pol Pot—were "abnormal," which relieves them of accountability and makes them merely victims of cultural, historical, and psychological deformities, rather than free agents who could have sincerely submitted to God or at the very least not committed atrocities.

Sin-aware melancholy could become a central element in forming a new spiritual consciousness in the Age of Melancholy. Even in the skeptical twentieth century, when many people doubt the existence of God, no one can dispute the reality of evil. Because of sin, the human drama can't be analyzed by therapy and must be staged as tragedy.

Twice-Born Tragedians

The unusual thing about the 1973 flooding of the Mississippi River in the upper Midwest was that the highest water came in the fall rather than in the spring.

In September 1973 I was still on the police beat at the *Hawk Eye* and was covering the flood.

Most of the damage in the Burlington area was in the lowlands on the Illinois side of the river. The small community of Gulfport was submerged, and thousands of acres of prime farmland were deluged.

As in any flood, the danger of disease from contaminated water was high. The men, women, and children shoring up the levees were also susceptible to accidents and sheer exhaustion from hours spent standing in mud, filling and throwing sandbags against the rising water. It all put a considerable strain on local medical services.

Four Catholic nuns who were nurses in the central Iowa town of Ottumwa volunteered to drive out and help. A few miles from Burlington, their small compact car collided with a pickup truck that had crossed the median strip. The four women were killed; the driver of the truck, who had been drinking a six-pack or more of beer, survived with just a scratch or two on his forehead and a sore shoulder.

When I arrived at the scene, Iowa State Police officers already had lined the four sisters' bodies along the roadside and covered them with blankets, but I could see blood on the highway and in their car. The greater horror, however, was visceral rather than visual. Four women of God on a mission of mercy had been slaughtered by a drunken driver who under the laws at the time would probably not spend much time in prison because he was "mentally impaired" at the time of the crash.

A few days later I attended a memorial service for the nuns at St. John's Catholic Church in Burlington. Although few of the mourners knew the sisters personally, everyone felt a strong sense of loss. And many of them had come to the church wondering why something so terrible could happen to such good people.

It's an eternal question, and the priest presiding at the service responded with a verse from the New Testament Book of Luke, in which Jesus deals with a similar tragedy.

"Those eighteen upon whom the tower of Silo'am fell and killed them, do you think that they were worse offenders than all the others who dwelt in Jerusalem? I tell you, No; but unless you repent you will all likewise perish," Jesus said.

The daily newspaper is filled with inexplicable tragedies — earthquakes, fires, freak accidents, killer diseases — that leave people groping to understand suffering. But such things didn't really bother me until the sisters' death.

When discussing the nuns' death with my city editor, who also had spent several years on the police beat, he said that a big part of a reporter's job was to write about "other people's tragedies."

That phrase became a mantra that gave me the psychological distance that firefighters, emergency-room doctors, and others who deal with grim situations must have to do their job. Don't take it personally. Don't let it affect you. Don't get intimately involved. Just do your job as well as possible. But don't linger over the larger issues, because they can be so debilitating that you can't work.

Protected by that emotional shield, I spent parts of the next twenty years reporting "other people's tragedies"—a three-year-old girl raped by her father, a young man fascinated by Japanese samurai disemboweled himself hara-kiri style, a factory worker scalded to death after falling into a cauldron of boiling cleaning solvent, a four-member family en route to a summer church camp wiped out when a seventy-five-mile-an-hour freight train crumpled their car at an unmarked railroad crossing.

And I was good at it. I could tell from the police dispatcher's tone of voice whether a traffic accident was likely to produce enough mayhem to justify the time to cover it. I could assess a crime scene with clinical coolness and lay odds of the victim's chances for survival according to the caliber and location that the bullet, or the angle and depth that the knife blade, entered the body. I encouraged victims' families to cry over their loss, wanting those tears for descriptive images—grabber sensations for maximum reader impact.

Death—the higher the toll the better—advanced my career. While working for United Press International in Maryland, I covered a commuter plane crash. The initial body count was fourteen people, with several others injured. To beat my rival from the Associated Press, I asked an emergency-room nurse whether the survivors would make it. She said two were in doubt. It was 1 A.M., about the time that news editors along the East Coast would slot either my UPI story or the AP version in their papers. I reported, knowing it was erroneous, that sixteen people had perished; AP had fourteen dead, which told the editors that I was on top of the story, so they carried my account on the biggest event of the week. At worst, I could blame the hospital for the wrong information if the victims held on, but my bosses would already have the UPI vs. AP story count from the morning papers, and I would have won the crucial numbers game. In fact, two more people did expire overnight. To me, those were good deaths; they boosted my professional reputation.

Indifference is a subsidiary of self-centered pride. Rather than sensitize me, the suffering of others isolated me within my ambitions. For me, hurt people were objective means toward my goals, not subjective ends to be cared for. I sought self-sufficiency to avoid messy, career-damaging compassion. I was above it all, absolving myself of responsibility for an apparently capricious universe.

For personal theology, I deduced that either a God who allowed the terrible acts I reported almost daily was a sadist or that the cosmos was organized around random cruelty. To me, people who couldn't endure the senselessness of life were foolish, sentimental weaklings. I had seen it many times: all the world's teachings about love and goodness could be refuted by a drunk in a gravel truck.

Because of that detachment from other people and my haughty contempt for religious ideals, I was especially vulnerable when melancholy hit at midlife. I was emotionally naked once my solipsistic barriers were broken by my betrayal of George Neavoll. Sin-infused guilt filled the breach, guilt aggravated by my professional exploitation of the distress of people caught in natural or human-made disasters. As melancholy led me to review my life, I was appalled by my callousness toward others and my almost sneering dismissal of spiritual values. For the first time in my life, I felt shameful self-loathing.

I then recalled the Catholic priest in Burlington citing Jesus' words that tragedy was a call to repentance because we never know when the end might come and catch us short. Perhaps melancholy is a price we pay for the guilty knowledge that we could do more for others, yet usually refuse to do so. Could melancholic misery be a subconscious plea to reconsider our lives, change direction, and exert our power, however limited, to relieve pain in ourselves and society?

I recalled various reactions to tragedy. Some people ranted against the apparent wantonness of fate and fell into inconsolable gloom or bitter self-pity. Others gained strength and a certain nobility from a mortal illness or potentially fatal injury. To them, tragedy was not a chance event but a transforming experience. They accepted suffering as the largest mystery—but the central reality—of existence.

Society usually defines tragedy by its mass-media use as something bad that just happens. Death or disaster—anything labeled as news—is merely the same old event affecting different people. Fill in the new names, seek a different lead on a story that has been told millions of times before, get a gush of emotion from victim or survivor, and put it into print. Repeat the process the next day, every day.

Reason and science can't explain tragedy. Confined to our own powers of comprehension, we humans could conclude only that life is unintelligible. I realized through melancholy, however, that something is out there, some force with a special interest in the human predicament. It ambushes people through tragedy, forcing them to expand their spiritual horizon if their lives are to have meaning.

British journalist Malcolm Muggeridge told the following story to explain why there is pain in the world.

A woman offended by the suffering of King Lear met William Shakespeare in heaven and upbraided him for the hideous treatment that his character received.

Shakespeare shook his head in apparent sympathy with the woman's complaint and acknowledged that he could have arranged for Lear to take a sedative at the end of Act I.

"But then there would have been no play," Shakespeare added.

As that fanciful anecdote suggests, it is through tragedy that humanity recognizes itself. Tragedy is ultimately life-affirming because it exposes the true nature of the human condition and, according to American playwright Arthur Miller, demonstrates the "indestructible will of man to achieve his humanity."

Dramatic tragedy in the late twentieth century lacks heroism on an ancient Greek or Shakespearean scale, partly because many sophisticated theatergoers lack belief in the fates or God, who were central actors in earlier dramas. For instance, the emblematic tragic figure of the modern American stage is Willy Loman, the pathetic lead character in Miller's 1949 play, *The Death of a Salesman*.

Hardly the aristocrat presence of a Greek king or Danish prince, Loman is an everyman of the post–World War II era. He tries to live by the rules and honors the boosterism values of the middle-class go-getter. He doesn't wallow in Hamlet's doubt or endure Agamemnon's agony. All Willy wants is a measure of success and respect from family and community. "He's only a little boat looking for a harbor," Willy's wife says.

In the end Willy's suicide isn't a defiant challenge to inexorable fate but the self-destruction of an unremarkable man whose personal heroism is significant only because he would not passively accept society's assault on his dignity. Willy finally realizes that the American dream is a fantasy. The harder he tries, the more he wants to fit in, the rougher life becomes. Society offers Willy no ideals other than material security and career status; midlife despair is his reward for doing what he was told. His tragedy is that of millions of Americans in the late twentieth century who refuse to embrace suffering as a godsend to plumb their souls, conquer their fears, and find significance in life.

The Age of Melancholy, however, is open to the paradox of tragedy—that through suffering, humans can be liberated from despair. That paradox explains why Jesus kissed Judas after he was betrayed to the authorities. Jesus understood that Judas's treachery was a necessary prelude to his divinely ordained destiny of crucifixion and resurrection.

Likewise, the Buddha outlined the essentials for enlightenment through his Noble Truths. Near the end of his life, speaking to friends in the Deer Park in Benares, Buddha summed up the First Noble Truth: "Existence itself is painful." He meant that efforts to alleviate pain are counterproductive because they cause more pain—which leads to the Second Noble Truth: "The cause of suffering is found in desire. It is craving, accompanied by delight and greed, pleasure and lust. It is the search for pleasure and the avoidance of pain."

The Buddha and Jesus gave trenchant critiques of why the therapeutic culture of the late twentieth century can't eradicate melancholy, a pain ingrained in the human condition. They understood that suffering is woven into the human fabric. They both taught that tragic suffering points to a reality greater than anything constructed solely by humanity.

That reality seems incomprehensible to the twentieth-century Western intellect, but it is the subject of the greatest tragedies in Western civilization. Why was Oedipus destined to incest and death? Why should Hamlet avenge his father's murder? Why must Haemon kill himself in grief over Antigone's death? Why did Macbeth and his wife accede to their murderous ambitions? Each of those dramas confounds the therapeutic culture. After all, a DNA test could have stopped Oedipus' lust for his mother; some cognitive therapy might have made Hamlet more resolute; antidepressants could have enabled Antigone and Haemon to spare themselves; and marital counseling might have made the Macbeths an amiable couple.

The philosopher William James said that the deepest religious faith rises out of despair. This is the "twice-born" believer who overcomes resentment toward a God who permits sin to exist and subjects humanity to tragedy. What James called the "iron law of melancholy" toughens twice-born individuals so they recognize that "life and its negation are beaten up inextricably together" and that "all natural happiness thus seems infected with a contradiction."

Unlike the familiar "born-again" Christian who often sees God as a benevolent father concerned primarily with human affairs and mitigating the effects of sin, the "twice-born" believer sees God as a creator with his own plan. This is the God who used his loyal servant Job as a poker chip in a bet with the devil; it is not for Job to reason why he is being tormented but to reaffirm his trust in God.

Just as Job came out of his ordeal with his spiritual faith intact and his prosperity restored, melancholic sorrow can lead to a redemptive faith in God, humanity, and community.

Free will requires sin. Without choice, human actions would be purely instinctual. Sin creates the opportunity for moral decision. The guilt and tragedy that inevitably follow destructive human actions become a black market of hope because suffering can unite people in a community of mutual despair and lead them to God. From sin, guilt, and tragedy come virtues that lift humans above their animal nature and their own egos, creating a democracy of wounded, but healing, people.

A sense of tragedy also counteracts humanity's striving for personal perfection and the obsession to create a heaven on earth that hinders the development of soul-fullness. When individuals accept the necessity to live with imperfect knowledge and anxiety, the soul opens itself to a profound spiritual life. Rather than join the therapeutic culture and chase evil from consciousness, humanity should feel that the pain and suffering caused by sin are integral to a complete life.

In his letter *De Profundis* (Latin for "from the depths of despair"), written while he was imprisoned on charges stemming from a homosexual scandal, British wit and playwright Oscar Wilde movingly testifies to sin's central role for God and humanity: "The world has always loved the saint as being the nearest possible approach to the perfection of God. Christ, through some divine instinct in him, seems to have always loved the sinner as being the nearest possible approach to the perfection of man. . . . In a manner not yet understood of the world he regarded sin and suffering as being in themselves beautiful and holy things and modes of perfection."

Tragedy is the dynamic element in wisdom. It shreds the emotional and philosophical umbrellas that shelter people from the darker aspects of life. It also gives individuals strength — the awareness that tragedy is a divine plot — to cope with imperfection. And out of sin and suffering, not biotechnology or psychotherapy, comes salvation.

Soul Heir

For thirteen years my father, Stuart Awbrey, battled multiple forms of cancer before the disease killed him in October 1985.

A newspaper reporter, editor, and publisher in Kansas and Iowa for forty-seven of his sixty-seven years, with time out to serve as a U.S. Army infantry lieutenant in World War II, he wrote some of his most poignant columns from the cancer ward at the M. D. Anderson Hospital in Houston. He had a special sympathy toward the individual tragedies he observed as cancer ravaged its victims and left many of them physically and emotionally deformed.

He also wrote about the almost welcome feeling of joy that

some people displayed when faced with imminent death and believed that they were embarking on a new adventure in existence.

But most important, cancer led my father to explore the great questions of life. His vocal speech impaired by cancer of the larynx, he expressed himself most eloquently in newspaper columns that chronicled his personal quest for truth.

"Sometimes in the grip of morphine or some prescribed drug, I see pale light in the dark, but it is a false light as many faiths are false lights," he wrote. "In these searches into the abyss, our restless souls give rise to most of our religions, and all our great agnosticisms. Christianity offers a whole inventory of whys and wherefores and predictions. Nietzsche, who feared the negation of life through death, went back to Pythagoras for a vain concept of man's eternity."

My father felt closest to God during his bleakest hours, the periods when radiation necrosis tortured him with intense pain that he knew would end only in death.

But his God wasn't a sugar-daddy deity with a Santa Claus beard; his was a God who revealed himself most fully in tragedy and sorrow. Misery was my father's most reliable proof of God's existence.

"The confusion is in the belief that God tolerates human suffering. You can argue that through the years, but what comes out inescapably is the conviction that God is certainly involved in that suffering—one way or another," he wrote.

Toward the end, my father concluded that life is not a matter of victory or defeat, that wisdom lay in the acceptance of uncertainty and that love-inspired seeking holds people together. All we can ever know, he said, is that life is a continuum, a brief spark of light, a flutter of movement between birth and death. "We go from dark to dark, but in between, we live. We share, others share with us. We are part of a whole, not an onlooking visitor on our own endless mysterious journey from unknown to unknown," he wrote in one of his final columns.

For me, my father's death was more than the loss of a loving parent. He was also my professional role model, advising me on journalistic issues and ethics, and teaching me writing skills. Moreover, his passing marked a personal milestone. I was no longer the kid/protégé. A family and journalistic mantle descended on me. My father's biography merged into my self-awareness. His story wasn't over, summed up in funeral eulogies and obituaries in journalism publications. I began to measure myself by his professional and personal integrity.

He also became my most inspiring guide through melancholy. Shortly after my father's death, his newspaper colleagues published a collection of his columns, ranging from musings about cats to his chats with the specter of death. Several years later, under the shadow of melancholy, I reread his writings in hopes of finding the perspective that would lead me to a similar joy toward life.

My still ongoing relationship with my father reflects a larger American family narrative. He was a member of the World War II generation; I am a quintessential baby boomer. My favorite picture shows my father dressed in his khaki military uniform, shortly before he was shipped overseas, smiling proudly as he holds my eldest sister in his arms. To me, that photograph captures the dramatically different stories of our two generations: the older one off to face death to safeguard Western civilization for the younger one.

Landing in Europe shortly after the D-Day invasion, my father endured some of the war's most hellish combat on the front lines in the Battle of the Bulge. He seldom commented on that nightmare, except to say that it was bitterly cold in Belgium the winter of 1944–45 and that he was lucky to survive the last-gasp German attack to win the war.

After the defeat of Germany and Japan, my father returned to civilian life and joined other veterans to realize "the American Century," a vision laid out in a 1944 editorial by *Time* magazine publisher Henry Luce that a U.S.-led postwar world "has within it the possibilities of such enormous human progress as to stagger the imagination." That mastery, and the belief that the United States was in a deadly contest with communism to shape the future of humanity, energized Americans to transform their country and leave behind the hard memories of economic depression and wartime sacrifice.

And did they ever change America. Almost every indicator of material and economic progress—home ownership, steel production, highway construction, college degrees, technological innovation—soared in the quarter century after World War II. The vets' success meant that the baby boomers, twirling hula hoops and wearing Davy Crockett coonskin caps, grew up during a time of unprecedented American prosperity and confidence.

Going through my father's effects after his death, I realized that his passing was part of a large historic transition. My most important discovery was a faded, hardbound copy of a book published in 1963 by the Associated Press to commemorate the inauguration of President John F. Kennedy. *The Torch is Passed* consists primarily of news accounts and photos of the youthful president. The title refers to the accession of a new generation into power—the junior officers of World War II taking command from President Dwight Eisenhower and the other top leaders of America's victory over fascism. My father identified strongly with Kennedy; it was their time to lead. One of his proudest moments was at the 1960 Democratic convention in Los Angeles when he was in the press pool that escorted Kennedy to his nomination-acceptance speech. During the campaign his newspaper had endorsed Kennedy, a sharp departure from its Republican heritage.

Looking through the book, I could feel my father's excitement as he heard Kennedy's clarion call in his inaugural address: "In the long history of the world, only a few generations have been granted the role of defending freedom in its hour of maximum danger. I do not shrink from this responsibility—I welcome it."

As they entered midlife, my father and other World War II vets had a clear duty—defeating tyranny and guarding the ramparts of liberty—that gave their public lives a distinct purpose. Despite some horrible mistakes, notably Vietnam, members of my father's generation achieved their historic mission. Their lofty place in Western civilization is secure. From Pearl Harbor in 1941 to the opening of the Brandenburg Gate in 1989, they whipped fascism and communism and preserved the paramount Western political and cultural values.

The collapse of the Berlin Wall not only signaled the end of Soviet-style Marxism, it opened a new historical era that presents baby boomers with challenges far different from those of their World War II parents. This momentous change was succinctly outlined in one of the most controversial essays of the post–Cold War period, Francis Fukuyama's "The End of History?" published in 1989.

Citing philosopher G. W. F. Hegel's theory that history evolves toward the civilization that best satisfies humanity's deepest needs, Fukuyama says that the disintegration of the Soviet Union left market capitalism and liberal democracy without serious rivals to organize society. Although the fragmented post–Cold War era is more disorderly and in some areas more violent than the old bi-polar world, Fukuyama is right that core American ideals won the centuries-old intellectual and military struggle against monar-chy, aristocracy, fascism, and communism to dominate Western culture.

Contrary to postmodern nihilism—and whether it's through Hegel's abstract "universal spirit" or an activist Judeo-Christian

God—the late twentieth century appears to confirm that history unfolds according to design. Cultural trench warfare breaks out between visions of the future when the existing worldview cracks under the weight of its own contradictions or fails to absorb new technological or intellectual developments. As seen in the discussions of the Renaissance/Reformation, the Romantic era, and the late-Victorian period, those transitions often are suffused with a melancholy that moves people toward life's spiritual aspects because they sense that forces larger than themselves are in the driver's seat.

Through the vehicle of generational change, that same dialectic is revving up in the late twentieth century as the baby boomers replace the World War II generation in running society. With the wisdom of hindsight, Americans today understand that history's wheel can grind very painfully. Indeed, the turnover from the vets to the boomers embodies the nation's move from innocence to disillusionment.

My father's generation's war was a noble crusade against despotism; my generation's war was the napalming of Southeast Asia. His generation broadened civil rights protections and pulled millions of once-disenfranchised Americans into the middle class; my generation watches the country split along racial and class lines. The vets believed a government that won World War II could defeat poverty and maintain political morality; we baby boomers reached political maturity during Vietnam and Watergate and witnessed the dehumanization and dependency caused by the welfare state. My father's generation brought economic prosperity; my generation worries about filthy air, poisoned water, and ecological destruction from financial greed.

True, post–World War II optimism often deteriorated into smugness and swagger. The best intentions sometimes produced disastrous results. The more Americans manipulated nature and their own psyches, the more anxiety they stirred up. The closer people got to "having it all," the unhappier they became. For all the nation's military power, financial wealth, and technological complexity, the American Century became the Age of Melancholy.

None of this is to disparage members of the World War II generation. They met their challenges and leave a long, impressive chapter in the history books. All Americans should be grateful that the country is not threatened by foreign dictatorships and that the United States has the world's premier economy.

In the late twentieth century, as the torch of leadership passes to baby boomers, my generation has no coherent focus, no overarching mission that gives purpose to life. At middle age, many boomers—some of them disillusioned idealists from the antiwar and civil rights activism of the 1960s—give primacy to their individual egos and lack a religious or philosophical consensus that puts life in a larger context.

What it comes down to is that while the World War II vets saved human freedom, my generation needs to salvage the human soul.

Through the epidemic of melancholy of the late twentieth century, some higher power is seizing many people's lives and demanding a transformation in human awareness. If we baby boomers demonstrate the same courage as did the World War II vets, the next churn of history's dialectic could re-establish the realm of the sacred in human life. But it won't be easy. America's fascination with technology and the therapeutic culture's ability to engineer mental and emotional impulses limit spirituality to an increasingly smaller dimension of life.

The World War II generation, however, might have one more heirloom for its baby-boom offspring: an understanding of suffering. Through the hardship of the Great Depression and the terrors of global warfare, many vets felt they were always at the mercy of harsh forces. They saw it happen. In the 1930s today's rich man could live under a bridge tomorrow. In the 1940s today's newly minted second lieutenant was tomorrow's battle-scarred cynic. The test of character wasn't in the quality of your cards, but in how you played them.

My father displayed that attitude toward the end of his life. Rather than complain that he was dying at a relatively young age, he used his final years for spiritual enlightenment. He let the world touch him deeply, and from the cancer ward he wrote of the bravery it takes to accept life as a whole—that all things born must die. On my last visit two months before his death, I kissed him for the first time since childhood and could feel the compassion and forgiveness that come from laying bare our common human frailties, fears, and griefs.

At death, my father was fully human. He had a sense of tragedy. He knew that suffering unites creation. He felt connected to the divine spirit that is the source of true selfhood. He died with the only thing that extends beyond the grave: the hope that life has ultimate meaning.

I often thought of my father when my melancholy was particularly severe. He knew life as a real fight with real issues. He sought no sanctuary from hardship and instead saw life as a small window of opportunity to perceive at least partial truth.

Even when doped with morphine, my father recognized that medical science couldn't cope with humanity's most serious problems. It couldn't cure sin, or help people break through self-importance and fuse with a reality greater than their ego.

The same point was made by novelist Madeleine L'Engle: "We're afraid to be human because if we're human we might get hurt. We live in a society that tells us to 'Take Aspirin, Anacin'— so there's no pain, whatever we do. We don't grow if we're not open to hurt."

Or as the Apostle Paul said in his letter to the Romans: "We rejoice in our sufferings, knowing that suffering produces endurance, and endurance produces character, and character produces hope, and hope does not disappoint us."

As my father, L'Engle, and Paul suggest, melancholy can be a truth serum. It shows that humanity needs something more than physical existence and that suffering can mystically enlarge life. If people turn a deaf ear to the sirens of the therapeutic culture, they can liberate their human potential. "You must first be nailed on the cross of natural despair and agony, and then in the twinkling of an eye be miraculously released," wrote William James.

From the hollowness of our lives and undeniable mortality, millions of baby boomers have broken down and are ready to break out of despair and accept the spark of divinity that makes real individuality. Out of the world's unceasing tension, anxiety, and ambiguity, those souls could help create meaning in the next millennium.

But to undertake that mission, only volunteers need apply.

Free-Will Metaphysician

While hardly a Paul-on-the-road-to-Damascus encounter, my midlife epiphany included a quotation by nineteenth-century German philosopher Arthur Schopenhauer: "The first forty years of life give us the text: the next thirty supply the commentary." Having entered my forties, having written truckloads of text, I nonetheless comprehended little of what I had observed during a quarter century in journalism. I might have had a front row seat to history, but my personal story suffocated under a colossal pile of yellowing newspapers.

At midlife I recognized how alone I was in the world, how little the professional awards, career accomplishments, and opinions of others matter when I needed an inner sense of who I am. Instead of a soul-centered self, I had a well-honed persona capable of morphing to meet any immediate occasion.

A term coined by psychiatrist Carl Jung from the name of the mask worn by actors in ancient Rome, the *persona* is the functional image that people present to the public. It is the ego's packaging, its public-relations agent, the window dressing that advertises the individual to the larger society. The problem arises when individuals identify themselves with their persona and go about their lives projecting impressions and performing little ego melodramas that dissolve when hit by an existential crisis.

Midlife melancholy unmasked my persona. The character I observed going about his daily activities wasn't really me. My persona was a competent, responsible journalist who confidently commented on daily events and managed an editorial page staff. My internal self, however, was racked by doubt, self-loathing, and meaninglessness. I was a duplicitous masquerade—a Jekyll and Hyde, a Dorian Gray with disguised, conflicting identities.

As briefly discussed previously, Buddhism, Christianity, and most other major religions and philosophies teach that true living requires the death of the ego. Hakuin Ekaku, an eighteenth-century Japanese Zen Buddhist master, urged his followers to starve the ego by not feeding its need for constant attention. That attention includes the desire for self-improvement and the endless monitoring of how life is progressing. Similarly, Paul taught that attachment to the physical body and the ego blocks the expression of the soul and spirit that are the lasting elements of human nature.

"Give up yourself, and you will find your real self," said C. S. Lewis. "Lose your life and you will save it."

Added American fiction writer Flannery O'Connor, "The first product of self-knowledge is humility."

I gravely wounded my ego by confession of sin. The despair, guilt, and isolation brought by melancholy lasted until I willingly humbled myself to a wisdom greater than myself, a wisdom expressed in the great religions of the world. I took to heart these penitential words in the Anglican Book of Common Prayer: "We have left undone those things which we ought to have done; And we have done those things which we ought not to have done."

The ecumenical lesson of melancholy is that humanity is not the sole author of truth. There is an overwhelming force that works from within but is clearly distinct from ourselves, that can crush our egos and turn us, in the words of William James, into "melancholy metaphysicians."

For a journalist, metaphysics is a heavy load. I had spent my adult life in the practical world of observable deeds and confirmable facts. I was skeptical of fuzzy phrases and abstract ideas that couldn't be grounded in concrete events. I agreed with nineteenth-century American essayist Ralph Waldo Emerson that "truth lies on the highway."

The issue was, How could I maintain my pragmatic journalistic training—which had served me well as a detector of fakery, hypocrisy, and dishonesty—and yet embrace spiritual truths that I sensed were valid but that couldn't be verified beyond dispute? At the least, I wanted the same certainty from the transcendent that I expected from a coroner's autopsy of a murder victim.

A breakthrough came when I remembered a concept I learned in a college philosophy course. Named after a medieval theologian, "Ockham's razor" held that the simplest explanation for something is usually the most reliable. Wielding that principle, I peeled my psyche like an onion—stripping away the layers of arrogance, hubris, and self-deceit that had become encrusted over the years—and was left with the one essential human trait: the free will that Adam and Eve took from the Garden of Eden. That meant I didn't have to be a victim of my feelings or an expression of my ego. I could choose. I had God-given freedom of thought. And the first decision to emerge from my midlife crisis was to believe in my own free will.

That might seem trivial; after all, people make hundreds of decisions every day. But to me the mere fact of choice was a "eureka" revelation. I knew that I had some power to shape my destiny and, by extension, that I had some say in the universe. I mattered. Through a desperation driven by self-doubt and melancholy, I was brought to the truth of my own uniqueness. I was partly a product of impersonal causes and effects, but I had some liberty to respond to life's traumas.

My decision: to believe in God.

No, I never found a legalistic, irrefutable proof of God's existence. Always in the back of my mind were the words of William James: "We may be in the universe as dogs and cats are in our libraries, seeing the books and hearing the conversation, but having no inkling of the meaning of it all."

The human soul doesn't weigh evidence like a federal judge. Neither petri dishes nor telescopes can conclusively demonstrate God's presence. It's not faith unless there is some doubt. In my final, pragmatic, what-works analysis, faith came down to a throw of the dice. If free will is the essence of humanity, life is a casino.

I would appoint Blaise Pascal as the theologian of the Age of Melancholy. A brilliant seventeenth-century French mathematician, Pascal invented one of the first computers and is considered a father of modern physics. But he also was a deeply troubled man who wanted to reconcile his scientific mind-set with his belief in

God. From probability theory, which he helped develop, and his experiences as a gambler in his wayward youth, he devised what's known as Pascal's wager.

Simply and elegantly, Pascal said that humanity has two choices: to believe in God or not. The scientific method offers little help because its conclusions are always provisional, subject to further research and the inherent limits of humanity investigating its own consciousness. "Man is altogether incomprehensible by man," he wrote. Thus, based on purely practical reasons, the best bet is that God exists. If God is real, the gamble pays off; if he doesn't exist, the bettor loses nothing, Pascal decided.

Doubt is an integral part of faith-seeking because it tests human intelligence, torments the soul, and complicates the mystery of life. The task is to find a true faith that honors human dignity and provides a sturdy ladder for people to climb out of the abyss of despair—one that isn't merely a golden calf offering therapeutic comforts without fundamentally changing an individual's character. True faith stands up to severe emotional and intellectual scrutiny, presents credible answers to life's most urgent questions, and touches the furthest reaches of the soul. "True faith comes after it has been challenged," said Rebbe Barukh of Medzebozh, an early-nineteenth-century Hasidic master.

Unlike earlier eras, when most people accepted the dictates of popes, pastors, and philosophers, the late twentieth century has little confidence in inherited religious or ideological systems. That's why Americans must learn from Pascal that truth sometimes hangs on a desperate bet. People who gamble on belief often find that faith is an alternative way to think. It doesn't refute reason; it transcends reason to help people understand the most critical matters in life. Unlike postmodernist theories that deny objectivity and absolutes, faith expands humanity's knowledge base through a God who reveals ultimate truth. While secular culture degenerates into nihilism, faith opens a vast territory of moral and intellectual wisdom to explore. Rather than confining people within themselves, faith asks individuals to read themselves into the divine narrative of sin and salvation, to follow the human story from innocence to fallenness to redemption.

"The heart has its reasons that reason knows not," Pascal said. The evidence of faith is established supernaturally; it is a separate authority that supplants rationality and empirical science when dealing with issues of the soul. As Augustine said, "Seek not to understand in order to believe, but believe in order to understand."

From my midlife crisis I learned that the most reliable anodyne to melancholy isn't antidepressant medication or anguished soliloquies to a psychologist but a free-will commitment to God. In making what Søren Kierkegaard called a "leap of faith" across the chasm from human to divine truth, people land on another level of consciousness. From that jump, a new self is created, one that participates actively in the world but that brings an eternal dimension to everyday affairs.

7

THE GOD-CREATED
SELF

Faithful Decision

If Jimmy Carter was going to be shot, I wanted to be there.

In May 1976 I was covering the Maryland state government and politics for United Press International. The biggest political event that month was the Maryland Democratic presidential primary contest between Carter and California governor Jerry Brown. While most of the attention focused on the candidates, we journalists also remembered the Maryland presidential primary four years earlier, when former Alabama governor George Wallace was severely wounded in an assassination attempt at a suburban Washington shopping center.

A similar attempt in the Carter-Brown race could be a career-maker for an ambitious young wire-service reporter who got the news out first. And I was determined not to repeat the mistake of the reporter who was responding to nature's call at the moment that Wallace was shot and had to explain to his editors why he missed one of the largest news stories of the decade.

The Maryland primary was critical because Carter had just

scored a smashing victory over several rivals in Pennsylvania and Brown was perceived as his last credible opponent for the Democratic nomination. Brown's unconventional personality and Carter's outsider status piqued the curiosity of the Washington journalistic corps, and some of the heaviest-hitting reporters and columnists from the *Washington Post,* the *New York Times,* the *Los Angeles Times,* the major TV networks, and other news organizations were day-tripping into Maryland. Everyone wanted to get close to the candidates to get insight into their character or snag a revealing comment.

Because of the media crush in the late stages of a presidential nomination fight, a press pool usually is formed to stay in constant contact with the candidates and notify the journalistic pack of anything unexpected in the supposedly quiet moments of the campaign. Given the recent history in Maryland, we called it "the death watch."

One night, after Carter spoke at a Baltimore union hall, his press secretary, Jody Powell, had to pick among the media sharks for the press pool to accompany the candidate to his hotel and put him to bed. No one envied Powell. Any favoritism could lead to vengeance against Carter by the highly competitive journalists stranded on the press bus.

Powell finessed the problem with a quiz. The journalist who answered a specific question would be the first person in the pool.

The question, which perhaps was partly intended as Powell's subtle rebuke to big-city media attacks on Carter's rural Southern Baptist origins: What did Jesus use to heal the blind man?

Total silence. Several dozen of the nation's premier journalists—some of the most influential people in the country—did not know a simple Sunday school story.

Recalling my Episcopal Church confirmation class, I yelled from the back of the bus, "He used his own spit."

Two minutes later I was in Carter's campaign van, asking about his strategy to win the important primary and getting some good quotes for my in-depth profile of the eventual president that was featured in dozens of newspapers nationwide.

That anecdote epitomizes the lack of religious education among the nation's ruling establishment. Time and again, I have watched journalists, professors, business executives, and other movers and shakers display total ignorance of the Judeo-Christian narratives and concepts that laid the foundation of Western civilization. Even among politicians demanding a return to "family values," few are steeped in biblical thought. As a newspaper commentator whose writing is geared to political insiders and government leaders, I seldom mention religious history or ideals, because few readers would catch the references.

As they enter the next millennium, Americans should ask themselves whether God exists and, if so, how that belief affects their lives. That sounds like an amazing statement, given that polls show the vast majority of Americans profess religious faith. But, as reflected by the journalists on Carter's bus, the depth of theological learning among Americans is extremely shallow. Gallup polls taken in the mid-1990s, for example, found that fewer than half of adult Americans could name the four Christian gospels and only three in ten teenagers knew the Easter story. Such results led Gallup pollsters to observe that the United States is "a nation of biblical illiterates." In the February 15, 1996, edition of his newsletter, *Context,* historian of religion Martin Marty, a Lutheran minister and professor at the University of Chicago, labels it the knowledge gap—"the often vast difference between Americans' stated faith and their lack of the most basic knowledge about that faith." In the January 1996 issue of *Emerging Trends,* a publication of the Princeton Religion Research Center, George Gallup, Jr., noting the "low level of Bible knowledge" among Americans and that "people's stated opinions don't always translate into behavior," concludes: "People want the fruits of faith but not the obligations."

For the first time in U.S. history, it is no longer presumed that Americans inherit a belief in the biblical Judeo-Christian God. The country honors a civil religion of flag, democracy, equality, and liberty, but spiritual faith is mostly a private concern and not a formative trait of the contemporary American character. Especially among educated, affluent, and career-centered Americans, such as the political journalists in Maryland, religion is at most a cultural nicety that gives a ritualistic gloss to weddings, funerals, and similar life passages.

Postmodern secularism is the leading ideology among today's artistic and intellectual fashion setters. Critical skepticism is the proper attitude; truth, if it exists at all, varies according to individual experience—notably racial, gender, class—and has no valid claim to universality. An all-encompassing God who created a common human nature and sustains a common human destiny doesn't suit that mind-set.

Open to everything, except a sincere commitment to anything other than advancing their own self-interests, many of the nation's most talented and powerful individuals have turned U.S. society into a cultural badlands.

I want to persuade my fellow members of the knowledge class to reconsider God. I know, that's a stretch for people who see religion through the media stereotype of the religious right or rigid fundamentalism. But I ask them to put aside their prejudices and realize that for more than three thousand years Western civilization has upheld some concept of divinity. The choice between sacred and secular that we face today will affect the future of Western civilization in much the same way that the Emperor Constantine did in establishing Christianity as the official religion of the Roman Empire in the fourth century. Premillennial Americans should decide whether God fits into the new consciousness to emerge from the Cold War and the cybertech revolution, or whether the future will be totally a self-regarding, self-absorbed, secular-scientistic world.

Simply asserting God's presence won't overcome the cultural elite's suspicions toward faith. And although I will outline my own spiritual memoir, I don't expect people to make salient decisions about their essential being and personal philosophy based on my say-so. Educated high-achievers who acutely feel the hollowness of postmodernism require solid arguments for God, or at least pragmatic indications that their lives would feel more significant and less trivial if they believed in God than if they didn't.

Purpose in life depends on choice, but nothing is harder than making a fully satisfying decision. I intend to help give people the courage to choose to believe — to find themselves in God and to create a new commitment to spirituality that could renew society.

The intellectual irony of faith is that the harder that individuals mull issues of meaning, the more they realize how much they already know. Often sparked by the anxiety endemic to the human condition, an internal pilot light flares up and eternal truths are illuminated. In his allegory of the cave, Plato describes it as the sun that people encounter when they break the chains of the shadow world distorted by "their own passions and prejudices." It is the Buddha-nature that is the birthright of all human beings. It is the divine presence that lifts the soul above the ego. It is the continuity of the spirit, the principle of unity within creation, the connection between individuals and God that enables humans to be conscious of themselves.

As T. S. Eliot put it in his poem "Little Gidding":

We shall not cease from exploration
And the end of all our exploring
Will be to arrive where we started
And know the place for the first time.

While Plato's prisoners had to crawl out of their cave to perceive the timeless Idea of the Good, I had to trek thousands of feet up the Himalaya Mountains to revive a subliminal spiritual memory.

In 1986 I wrote an editorial in *The Wichita Eagle* advocating American support for international family-planning programs. The Population Institute named my piece as the editorial of the year on the subject. The best part was that the award would be presented in Nepal, where the winning journalists could see birth-control programs at work.

We stayed one night at a lakeside resort 20,000-plus feet above sea level in the Annapurna range of the Himalayas in western Nepal. I awoke early in the morning and wandered along the lake. The sun glared pink off the mountain snow. Wisps of fog steamed from the lake. Shoreline trees stood like calligraphic brushstrokes. A heron, an Asian symbol of longevity, fished among the reeds in the water.

Halfway around the world, in a place as mountainous as my native Kansas is flat, I felt at home. The beauty of Asia disclosed a spiritual dimension that enlarged my Western-centric self. My old religious and intellectual categories couldn't contain the new insight. For the briefest, most infinitesimal moment, I felt the wholeness of existence, the sacredness of creation, the unity of humanity.

Several journalistic colleagues caught up with me, and the spell was broken. Back to the politics of global population programs in the U.S. Congress and the problems of economic development in the Third World.

Years later, in the throes of midlife melancholy, I recalled my awakening at Annapurna. I had touched some mystical core that has always been inside me, that anxiously struggles for release, that desperately seeks reunion with the transcendent reality that gave it birth and implanted it within me.

Aldous Huxley named it "the Perennial Philosophy," the nexus where all the world's great religions contact truth. It is the wisdom and spiritual power that, although varying in expression and carrying numerous labels, both seeks humanity and is sought by individuals. Indeed, the variety of means by which humanity pursues the divine is further evidence of the truths of faith. "Why else were individuals created, but that God, loving all infinitely, should love each differently," wrote C. S. Lewis. "If all experienced God in the same way and returned him an identical worship, the sound of the church triumphant would have no symphony; it would be like an orchestra in which all the instruments played the same note."

Writing several decades ago, Lewis was referring to the many Christian communions, but his ecumenical point is equally applicable to the late twentieth century. As the world becomes more integrated economically and technologically, it could develop a new religious awareness among people now exposed to what they once thought were exotic religious traditions. Potentially, the next century could be a remarkable period of spiritual syncretism comparable to the emergence of Christian theology out of Greek philosophy and biblical scripture early in the first millennium, or the coalescence of imported Buddhism and native Taoism in ancient China.

For numerous cultural, political, and dogmatic reasons, a universal religion won't happen in our lifetime, but spiritual inquirers have long recognized a paradox common to most religious traditions: that despair often leads to faith. Zen Buddhism calls it "the great doubt." Islam describes it as the "state of self-accusing." Christian mysticism says it is the "dark night of the soul."

Religious faith is not simply agreement with a set of theological tenets or the end result of pragmatic calculations. Those factors can bring people to the edge of belief, but the most profound spiritual transformation occurs within the abyss of despair. The individual has to be broken down, emotionally gutted, mentally purged, intellectually humbled to give God space to work. "Herein God secretly teaches the soul and instructs it in perfection of love, without its doing anything, or understanding of what manner is this infused contemplation," wrote the medieval mystic Saint John of the Cross.

Faith in God came to me out of a melancholic sense of abandonment, an emptiness that could not be filled by worldly goods or egoistic goals, a yearning for something that seemed impossible. Faith didn't come during a specific event—no stupendous opening of the heavens to the fanfare of angelic trumpets, no nirvana in the blooming of a flower, only a gradual awareness that something "other" was participating in my life. And, yes, I still have depressive episodes and I have no sure idea where my life will lead. But the anguish is gone. Having felt his absence, I want God to exist. I recognize that my life has meaning only as part of some eternal scheme. I don't know exactly what that design is, except that it connects me to the heart of creation.

Language is inadequate to define this state; Buddhists characterize it as "bliss" and Christians use the term *holiness*. It is God's invitation to love him and his creation. It is divine grace through which God supplies some of the love that sinning, imperfect individuals, in due course, humbly return to him. It is a consciousness—an overwhelming will—within ourselves that is not solely our own.

And, most important, it is the power that allows humanity to join in the ultimate act of divine creation.

A Beautiful Proof

In August most Kansans would book a cruise through hell to escape the heat back home. In the scorching-hot Great Plains, late summer isn't the humid Midwestern steam or the dry Southwestern sauna. It's the worst of both. Sticky, drippy sweat and blast-furnace wind.

It was that kind of day when I sought escape inside the Spencer Art Museum at the University of Kansas during my sabbatical from my newspaper in the summer of 1993. One of the nation's finest collegiate art museums, the Spencer is known for its outstanding collection of Japanese prints and Chinese landscape scrolls. I had just finished a summer-school course in Asian art and, in addition to taking refuge in the museum's air-conditioning and cool tile floors, wanted a last look at some of my favorite works.

Although I had passed by it numerous times, I never really noticed the museum's replica of a Japanese teahouse set up just outside the room containing the Asian art displays. The boxlike exhibit included a wall-hanging calligraphy of a Japanese poem, a ceramic teapot with a bamboo tea whisk and ladle, and a rectangular, brown straw tatami mat on the floor. But my eye centered on the "dry landscape" Zen garden that completed the exhibit.

Except for a student guard meandering aimlessly through the galleries, the museum was empty. I sat on the floor and stared at the garden, which on the surface was nothing more than two black oblong rocks set among raked, brownish-gray-colored gravel.

No, it wasn't a true Zen moment. I haven't undergone the years of disciplined meditation and instruction to justify that claim. But it was a feeling of serenity and refinement, simplicity and complexity, that I had not previously encountered. Earth and metaphysics; rock-hard physicality and mind-crunching abstraction. One glance captured a couple of boulders on a blanket of pebbles; the next look flashed basic truths. *Yes! Yes! That's it! It's symbolic! The small stones are the ocean surrounding the big stones as the islands. It's the interconnection of all existence. Stones and ideas. It means . . . It means . . . No! I lost it. . . . Something's there, but thinking about it makes it disappear. . . . Just accept . . . Let go! . . . Let go! . . . Can't . . . Gone.*

Because I was still suffering with my midlife melancholy, the hint of Zen enlightenment at the museum garden was incredibly transforming. Unlike Judaism and Christianity, Zen Buddhism lacks belief in a single, distinct God and seeks a divine nature that is within each person and encompasses all existence. Maybe it's just a matter of definition, interpretation, and perspective: aren't the Judeo-Christian soul and the Buddha-nature different terms for the faith-seeking enterprise common to all human cultures? Regardless, I had a new source of spiritual meaning: the art of Zen Buddhism. I encountered the same mysterious religious force in the Zen garden that some of my mystically inclined friends have described feeling inside a medieval French cathedral, in the Blue Mosque in Istanbul, or at the Temple Wall in Jerusalem.

For me, art is a reliable proof of God. Beautiful art, provocative art, even repellent art, can evoke a sense of transcendence not dependent on religious dogma or philosophical doctrine. Art communicates without words. It creates form out of chaos; coherence out of impulses; consciousness out of marble, paint, and metal.

In the late twentieth century, however, some of the most-talked-about artists have abandoned art's traditional mission to depict the sacred, and when they do approach religion, it is usually to make a blasphemous comment calculated to outrage believers or amuse secularists. Change and novelty are the principal postmodern deities, with proper homage paid to the demigods of commercial sales, political correctness, and government arts grants.

From the Zen garden, I learned that humanity's highest aesthetic achievements are intimately connected to a spiritual vision. As Irish poet William B. Yeats noted, "No man can create as did Shakespeare, Homer, Sophocles, who does not believe with all his blood and nerve, that man's soul is immortal." Recapturing that inspiration could help bring Americans out of the contagion of spiritual despair that has brought the Age of Melancholy. But first, Americans need to take art not as interior decoration, a speculative investment, or a gesture of with-it trendiness, but as evidence of God's existence.

My initial exposure to the spiritual in art was as a "tapestry Christian." While some kids are gym rats, I was a church mouse. I loved the historic ritual, the richly embroidered vestments, the stained-glass windows, the dark wooden pews, the deep burgundy carpeting, the intricately carved railings, and the Elizabethan-accented English of the Book of Common Prayer of the Episcopal Church that I grew up in during the 1950s. The best experience was serving as an acolyte, particularly when I poured red wine into the silver chalice and watched the priest offer it as the blood of Christ to the congregation. I also loved wearing the red-and-white acolyte robes and carrying the brass processional cross to open the Sunday worship service.

Rather than based on theological argument or a "born-again" infusion of the Holy Ghost, my Christianity was mainly habitual. Like most Beaver Cleaver–type children in the 1950s, I automatically went to church each week. Religion was an integral part of community life in the Midwest, and only a few village cranks questioned the link between God and country. Christianity presented indubitable truths that were the basis of our moral lives. It was an enclosed world reinforced by prayer in the public schools, patriotic anthems in church, and a tablet of the Ten Commandments in front of the civic auditorium.

My great disillusionment came during the civil rights crusade and the anti–Vietnam War movement of the 1960s. In college at the time, I watched respected church leaders fail to condemn racism, and support the U.S. policy in Southeast Asia. True, at least an equal number of religious figures sought peace and racial harmony, but that only convinced me that Christianity in America was more about political power than spiritual salvation. Too often, the gospel was presented either as a right-wing talisman against America's Marxist enemies or as a divine manifesto for a leftist welfare state.

My apostasy was total after two years as a police reporter in Iowa. What kind of God, I wondered during my unsentimental education covering murder and mayhem, could permit the horribly evil acts occurring daily in every major and medium-sized U.S. city? Further, in the midst of Watergate and the final calamities of the Vietnam War, I was thoroughly disgusted with American politics.

Like earlier generations of Americans in similar circumstances, I went to Paris. In the summer of 1974 I had the pose perfected: the young, alienated, Left Bank, café-revolutionary, black-trench-coat-and-horn-rimmed-glasses, existentialist, expatriate American. I lived in a small student hotel near the Sorbonne. I took French language classes at the Alliance Française. I toured every major museum listed in the *Michelin Guide.* I knew where Gertrude Stein and Alice B. Toklas had lived. And I attended Galloise-smoke-filled literary nights at the Shakespeare & Co. bookstore just off the Boulevard Saint-Michel.

One day, sitting in the Luxembourg Gardens, I was reading

Albert Camus's essay "The Myth of Sisyphus." Inspired by an ancient Greek legend, Camus wrote of the king of Corinth who offended Zeus and was condemned to the eternal punishment of pushing a rock up a hill only to have it roll back just before he reached the top. Camus argued that "one must imagine Sisyphus happy" because he was aware of his fate and that the struggle toward a goal, not its achievement, gave purpose to life.

An editor and writer for *Combat*, an underground newspaper supporting the French Resistance against the Nazis in World War II, Camus became my role model of the engaged journalist. Life might be unfair or it might be nonsensical, God might be a fantasy, but I could be an ethically committed reporter of the comedy of the absurd. My resolution: return to the United States, shove against the rock of journalism, and interpret any setbacks as confirming the inanity of life.

Anyway, that self-awarded heroism swiftly turned into raw careerism. After I reached my professional peak, my existentialist ego was no help when I tumbled into midlife depression. I wanted more than a philosophy that sees life as a void that individuals fill with their actions, attitudes, and ideologies. Rather than Sartrean dramas, Kafkaesque novels, or Brechtian theatrics, I was drawn to the great themes of Western religious art: sin, guilt, sacrifice, and divine redemption. Can humanity express more joy than Handel's "Hallelujah Chorus" or more sadness than Bach's *St. Matthew Passion*?

In the postmodern 1990s, when ambiguity, irony, money, and media hype seem to be necessary parts of the aesthetic experience, it's easy to forget that most of humanity's greatest art is God-haunted. It's art that points to the mysteries beyond language, to a logic other than reason, to intuitions that can't be analyzed. Holy art includes the sexuality of an Incan fertility idol, the solemnity of an Islamic funeral dirge, and the mental knots of a Zen Buddhist koan. Painting, sculpture, literature, music, and other arts inform civilizations, which ultimately are constructions of a religious and moral worldview. Greek kings are forgotten, but Homer survives. The Renaissance popes are dead, but Michelangelo lives. And only scholars care about British politics in the early nineteenth century, but almost everyone admires Romantic poetry.

Art that expresses the deepest human feelings connects the personal with the public, the microcosm with the macrocosm, the temporal with the eternal, the self with the soul. It is where the unconscious flows through the conscious to touch the transcendent. Regardless of religious tradition or doctrine, great art can speak to all people. A Vedic Hindu statue, an Orthodox Christian ikon, and a Tibetan Buddhist silk *thanka* can reveal the spiritual, as well as reflect the highest standards of human craftsmanship and open people to truths and values not encompassed by their own cultural heritage. If only for an instant, the reveries induced by a great lyric, painting, or poem overcome our fear of mortality. We are enveloped by the absolute.

Artistic sensibility is strong evidence for God. In the Middle Ages, Saint Thomas Aquinas argued that humanity has an innate sense of beauty. People are aware that some things are more attractive than others, which implies varying degrees of beauty. It follows that there must be absolute beauty, or people could not make aesthetic comparisons among art objects. At the top of the hierarchy of beauty must be perfection itself. That perfection, Thomas said, was God.

And the subject matter need not be specifically religious to reflect the transcendent, as I learned from one of my best friends, Jim Brothers, a sculptor who often portrays Indian warriors, mountain men, pioneer women, and other personalities from the American West.

I met Jim when we were students at the University of Kansas in the late 1960s. One day early in our acquaintance, I was at his house and needed an ice cube for a soft drink. I looked inside his refrigerator freezer, expecting to find the usual graduate-student sustenance—ice cream, frozen margarita mix, and fuzzy-frost-covered packages of peas and carrots. Instead, I found two dead roosters, fully feathered.

The chickens weren't for eating, Jim explained. They were models for a cockfighting piece he was planning. He would spend the next few weeks studying the birds' anatomies, getting the exact structure of their bones, the texture of their muscles, and how sinews and tendons tied the animals together. Several months later, the result was a bronzed flurry of clawing and pecking of two proud, vain roosters in a death match.

I often visited Jim during my 1993 summer in Lawrence. At the time he was working on a larger-than-life sculpture of Mark Twain that had been commissioned by Hannibal, Missouri, the hometown of Samuel Clemens. As Twain's image emerged clay bit by clay bit in Jim's studio, I thought of God's creating Adam. A flick of Jim's thumb made Twain's eyes come alive; the sweep of his trowel smoothed Twain's riverboat captain's coat. Although I had lived along the Mississippi River and had read most of Twain's works, I never knew him as a real person—something other than one of his self-inventions—until I saw Jim's completed statue. The boy rascal, the riverman, the miner, the journalist, the humorist, the literary lion, the moralist, the religious agnostic, the failed entrepreneur, the brilliant lecturer, were all there.

Jim isn't an especially introspective artist and has no idea where his talent comes from. Much of it, of course, is natural skill, meticulous research of a subject's biography and physique, a large aptitude for hard work, and a concentrated attention to detail. But with a chunk of clay or a welding torch in his hand, Jim is a different person from the joking, cursing, antique-rifle-shooting, beer-drinking ex-hippie that he is away from his studio.

The ancient Greeks called it the *daimon,* the transcendent, magical "otherness" that guides the artist into the creative dimension. Captured by the *daimon,* the artist becomes the instrument of a higher presence. Indeed, the twentieth century's preeminent artist, Pablo Picasso, thought that the supernatural gave art authority: "We ought to be able to say that such and such a painting is as it is, with its capacity for power, because it is 'touched by God.' But people would put a wrong interpretation on it. And yet it's the nearest we can get to the truth."

Artists might be the least credible authorities on their own work. Jim Brothers was only trying to give the best possible representation of Mark Twain; that the piece contributed to my religious conversion was an added bonus. But the reception of art is as important as its making. Although composed of clay and bronze and forged through fire, Jim's statue stood partly outside its material elements. To me, the statue was beyond human artifice and was almost musiclike because its emotional impact defied verbal expression.

Perhaps when Jim and other artists deny responsibility for the meanings people get from their work, they testify to the *daimonic* in the aesthetic experience. Sculptors, poets, musicians, and other artists might even be unintentional conduits for their audience's dialogue with God. Through paper and ink, stone, and steel, artists might offer access to a reality undetectable empirically, but even they can't determine the relationship between their art, their audience, and spiritual truth.

In the postmodern, after-Warhol era that defines some graffiti, pornography, and fashion advertising as art, it's hard to see painting, music, and sculpture as spiritual disciplines. But that's a comment more on contemporary culture than on the spiritual potential of art.

The word *beautiful* seldom appears in late-twentieth-century art criticism. Instead, the highest accolades go to works described as "challenging," "disturbing," or "tough." In fact, so despiritualized, blasé, and secular are most postmodern cognoscenti that anyone really wanting to irritate much of the arts community today should claim that the finest art stirs rumblings in the human soul, that art should lift culture to a higher plane rather than mark descent toward dissolution.

Postmodernism's rejection of religious faith has deafened many people to the music of the spheres and blinded them to the beauty of the cosmos. But God won't be closed within an art-history textbook or embalmed in an art-museum retrospective. When humanity can't see divine truth in art, God reveals himself elsewhere. And, perhaps surprisingly, from the labs of cell biology and the calculations of astrophysics a new understanding of God's handiwork, a new version of scientific truth, and a new vision of reality are emerging that could open many skeptical late-twentieth-century American minds to spirituality.

Faith Through Science

From the east came the Osage. From the west, the Cheyenne and the Arapaho. From the north, the Pawnee. From the south, the Comanche and the Kiowa Apache. They pursued the migrating buffalo herds and hunted elk and antelope in what is now Kansas. Along the shallow, broad rivers of the Great Plains, the tribes converged at the center of North America to trade, forge alliances, and make war.

They found gods in nature: the buffalo that fed them, clothed them, and surrendered its hide to cover their winter tepees; the hawk, whose freedom and fierceness they sought to emulate; and the wolf, whose deadly stealth proved the model of the prairie hunter. Superior to all was the Great Spirit, called Wakanda, the master creator.

Around the campfires at night, in the shelter of a riverside grove of cottonwood trees, the tribal shamans passed the ceremonial pipe and sought the gods' help in the next day's hunt. The rhythmic chanting and hypnotic drumbeats echoed across the vast openness, perhaps drawing near a curious coyote—an ancestral cousin of the tribe—also eager for tomorrow's adventure. The stars formed celestial animals, a reverse image of the life-teeming prairie; the moon took the nighttime place of its brother, the sun: the universe vibrated in harmony.

Although golden wheat has replaced bluestem tallgrass and farm machinery has plowed the buffalo wallows, the Kansas plains can still conjure up the spirit of the Native Americans. At the horizon, where land and sky join, the mingled elements suggest the unity of existence, a merger among the gods of earth and air, the union of mother and father.

Where vision is limited only by strength of human sight, where an individual is dwarfed by the endless expanse of space, and where nature seems indifferent to a person's ego and ambitions, the prairie is a humbling place. Humanity is not the sole center of concern but exists within the meaningful, if fearfully mysterious, pattern of the ever changing but always recurring cycle of life and the seasons.

Gazing across this land, it's easy to understand why the supposedly barren places—the deserts, the mountains—gave rise to many of the world's greatest religions. Time stops. Pride dissipates. Humanity looks outward on the majesty of nature, turns inward to feel a personal connection to creation, and is enveloped in the sacred.

American Indians and other early peoples looked at the universe in awe. They retreated to caves to scratch symbols of the sun and earth and water, or to arrange great stone slabs to mark the course of the stars, which they felt held their fate. In rainstorms, they received messages from the gods, either a life-restoring blessing for the parched land or a punishing thunderbolt for a moral transgression. In animals, they found a kinship so close that they believed souls passed back and forth between humans and birds, bears, and other critters.

For most late-twentieth-century Americans, the rational, scientific mind-set has edged out the sacred to explain physical reality. No longer imbued with supernatural force, the world is mainly inanimate "stuff."

Although humanity has gained much through the triumph of the scientific method, it has lost something in natural wonder. A violent thunderstorm might be a collision between warm and cold air masses instead of an expression of Zeus's anger, but didn't many of the ancient myths offer great insight into the meaning of life? With chilling elegance, science can autopsy the workings of the world—but at the cost of some of the transcendence that has stimulated the human imagination, including the ultimate question, "Why do I exist?"

But in the late twentieth century the mystery of the spirit, perhaps even part of the magical wisdom of primitive humanity, might be returning—and from the most unexpected source: brilliant, highly trained scientists using today's most cutting-edge technology. It's not the Mandarin scientism described in Chapter 5, but an intellectually open awareness that the mystical might also be an aspect of reality.

Although decades of strife have led science and religion to de-clare an uneasy truce, each respecting the other's territory—science as demonstrable fact subject to constant review, religion as revealed faith reinforced by dogmatic claims—compelling evidence for God comes from some of today's vanguard scientific research. For Americans needing scientific imprimatur to accept religious truths, the new science, emerging from areas as diverse as cellular biology and interstellar cosmology, could provide additional assurance.

Possibilities for a reconciliation of the material and the mystical were heightened in 1996 when Pope John Paul II stated that evolution is "more than a hypothesis." That pronouncement abandoned the Catholic Church's long-standing position that Darwinian ideas were still open questions, and represented a new attitude toward science by the same church that persecuted the seventeenth-century astronomer Galileo.

The pope's remark underscores that the relationship between science and faith is changing radically in the late twentieth century. No longer are science and religion perceived as wholly separate spheres, with each using different standards of proof in search of different versions of truth. Instead of antagonists, science and religion could become complementary means to comprehend material and spiritual existence. Or as Albert Einstein observed decades ago, "Science without religion is lame; religion without science is blind."

What's happened is that science has answered most of the big questions of how the universe works. Darwinian theory is widely accepted, at least as a general process, for how plants and animals came to be. Science has also established beyond reasonable doubt the existence of DNA, atoms, gravity, and the expansion of the galaxies.

But, according to architect Ludwig Mies van der Rohe, "God is in the details." The deeper that science explores physical matter, the more it encounters the metaphysical. For example, from his research into the structure of the cell, Michael J. Behe, a professor of biochemistry at Lehigh University and author of *Darwin's Black Box,* detects a pattern in the building blocks of life that could not result from chance. "I think that the complex systems were designed—purposely arranged by an intelligent agent," Behe says. "Intelligent design may mean that the ultimate explanation for life is beyond scientific explanation."

Over the past few years several writers have used science to amplify the spiritual. Fritjof Capra, in his bestselling book *The Tao of Physics,* finds similarities between nuclear physics and Eastern religions. John Polkinghorne, a professor of mathematical physics and president of Queen's College at Cambridge University, argues in his book *The Faith of a Physicist* that science can't evaluate unique acts of God, such as the resurrection of Christ. Frank Tipler, author of *The Physics of Immortality* and a professor at the California Institute of Technology, contends that mathematics can provide a model of how to think about God.

For me, the most persuasive of these spirit-justifying scientists is Paul Davies, author of *God and the New Physics* and its sequel, *The Mind of God.*

A professor of mathematical physics at the University of Adelaide in Australia, Davies says that some recent scientific discoveries could validate traditional religious doctrines. For instance, quantum cosmology and refinements in the big bang theory indicate how the universe might have appeared from nothing—ex nihilo—as written in Genesis: "The world was without form and void."

Davies concedes that many scientists have been surprised by what they don't know, and probably will never discover, about the universe. Whether in biology, physics, or mathematics, the question comes back to, Where did scientific laws and principles come from in the first place? "Thus 'ultimate' questions will always lie beyond the scope of empirical science as usually defined," Davies has decided.

Nonreligious, secular scientism is like a cat chasing its tail—it ends up grabbing itself from behind. Logically, a rational exposition of the world is limited to rational assumptions about the world. "If we wish to progress beyond, we have to embrace a different concept of 'understanding' from that of rational explanation," Davies says.

Reflecting on the amazing intricacy of the physical universe, Davies doubts that such a creation is possible without a cosmic architect. The world can't be a mere happenstance or accident. There must be a better interpretation. "Whether one wishes to call that deeper level 'God' is a matter of taste and definition," he says.

Only now, at the end of the millennium, are people starting to comprehend fully the new vision of God, humanity, and creation brought by high-energy twentieth-century physics, notably the quantum theory and the uncertainty principle. Together, they have helped rearrange humanity's ideas of matter, motion, and energy; by extension, they have opened a new spiritual dimension.

Briefly, the quantum theory says that a small packet of energy, called a quantum, can behave either as a wave or as a particle, depending on the situation. That's contrary to the previous idea that energy is solely a wave. The upshot is that the universe is much more vital and fluid than conceived by earlier science. It also means that two mutually exclusive ideas could both be true: if a wave can be a particle and a particle a wave, couldn't humanity be body and spirit?

An offshoot of the quantum theory is the uncertainty principle. First enunciated by German physicist Werner Heisenberg in 1927, the uncertainty principle holds that it is impossible to accurately gauge the time, speed, energy, and position of an elementary particle because any measurement requires an outside observer whose very presence could affect the research. The principle means that scientists can't be totally sure that they are analyzing nature correctly and impartially. It also undermines human confidence in tracing cause and effect, making narrowly rational, scientific descriptions of the universe problematic.

The Age of Melancholy is the end of certitude for human-crafted knowledge, the collapse of Western civilization's effort since the Age of Reason of the seventeenth century to establish truth on purely objective grounds. The universe turns out to be too complicated—too chaotic—to be fathomed solely by conventional scientific methods. Change and disturbance, not order and stability, appear to be the universe's functional principles. From black holes at the boundary of time and space to subatomic particles bouncing randomly, the universe is a volatile system that can't be comprehended fully by the human intellect.

This is where God reappears in the machinery, where nature becomes a spiritual resource.

Through the new physics, God exposes himself to the late twentieth century. That may seem to be a strange means of divine revelation. Why not a burning bush or other dramatic apparition that would get great coverage on the evening news? Yet advanced physics is the most powerful paragon for truth to reach a secular-minded, technology-driven, postmodern society.

God may be eternal, but he discloses himself in specific cultural and historical circumstances. He unveils truth in ways that people can grasp and that fit their unique condition; that's why an incredibly diverse human race has always had a spiritual ideal in multiple manifestations. This generation accepts a dynamic universe, so God in the late twentieth century can't be the unmoved prime mover of Aristotelian philosophy who sets the world in motion and then retreats. He can't be a distant deity upholding a rigid medieval hierarchy of angels, humans, and animals that parallels a frozen social order of monarchs, aristocrats, and peasants. He can't be an Enlightenment tinkerer setting the world spinning like a top and leaving it alone. He can't be a Victorian family patriarch or a flag-waving partisan ideologue with a political agenda.

Instead, God invites contemporary humanity to help develop the universe. Having recognized as scientific fact that consciousness partly shapes physical reality, humanity has evolved far enough to become God's junior partner. This is the fulfillment of God's plan that began in the Garden of Eden when Adam and Eve were exiled from a static paradise so creation could continue. It is why God incarnated himself in Jesus and gave Western history a divine impetus. It is why Buddhists teach that enlightenment is a progressive search. It is why Hindus endure karmic rebirths toward reunion with Brahma.

At this point in history, when many envelope-pushing scientists and millions of despairing individuals are opening themselves to the spiritual dimension of truth, humanity can respond to the question that has stumped generations of scientists and philosophers: Why is there something—sun, moon, emotions, intelligence—rather than nothing? The answer is that God affirms his creative power through humanity. "Through conscious beings the universe has generated self-awareness," Davies says. "This can be no trivial detail, no minor byproduct of mindless, purposeless forces. We are truly meant to be here."

This is what humanity was made for, what the painstaking process of creation is all about, the culmination of eon after eon of putting together a solar system, centuries upon centuries of changing life-forms: to believe in God, to grow as moral individuals, and to embrace existence and help direct its evolution.

In the twenty-first century, if humanity is to capitalize on the historic opportunity to forge a new consciousness in concert with God, people must reenchant the world by recapturing some of the spirit-fed imagination of their primordial ancestors. Like the Native Americans on the buffalo-trampled Great Plains of Kansas, contemporary people need to connect themselves to nature rather than stand at a critical distance on the periphery. They need to participate in the cosmos rather than act as disinterested observers of physical phenomena.

Most important, contemporary humanity should resurrect the sacred and readmit wonder into life. Reality is not just the mineral composition of a stone or the molecular structure of water; it is also the feeling of majesty when approaching a mountain and the sense of amazement when watching the ocean. Through those experiences, humanity realizes that God is neither scientifically objective nor emotionally subjective, but the creative spark at our deepest selves.

And that self is the conclusive evidence of God's presence.

"A Beyond Within"

The last moments in the life of Dietrich Bonhoeffer, a Lutheran minister, theologian, and member of the anti-Nazi resistance inside Germany, were recorded by a physician at the Flossenbürg concentration camp. The date was April 9, 1945. In less than a month Adolf Hitler would commit suicide, the Soviet army would occupy Berlin, and the Third Reich would capitulate to the Allies.

"On the morning of the day, some time between five and six o'clock, the prisoners, among them Admiral Canaris, General

Oster and Sack, the judge advocate general, were led out of their cells and the verdicts read to them. Through the half-open door of a room in one of the huts, I saw Pastor Bonhoeffer, still in his prison clothes, kneeling in fervent prayer to the Lord his God. The devotion and evident conviction of being heard that I saw in the prayer of this intensely captivating man moved me to the depths," Dr. Wolf Dieter Zimmerman recalled.

A few minutes later, the prisoners were ordered to strip. They were led down the steps of the prison to the place of execution. Naked under the scaffold, Bonhoeffer knelt to pray for the last time. Five minutes later he was dead.

Bonhoeffer was part of a small group of German intellectuals, aristocrats, and military officers who schemed to kill Hitler. The plot miscarried in July 1944 when a bomb poorly placed in Hitler's bunker exploded without taking the führer's life. The leader of the conspiracy, Count Claus von Stauffenberg, and hundreds of other dissidents were rounded up and executed.

At the time of the bombing, Bonhoeffer was already in Tegel Prison in Berlin for his anti-Nazi activities. While incarcerated, he smuggled out his most popular book, *Letters and Papers from Prison,* a last testament of his ideas on religion, society, and human nature.

One of the last, most courageous victims of Nazi tyranny, Bonhoeffer was an especially poignant loss. Only thirty-nine years old at his death, he became one of the most influential Christian theologians of the post–World War II period. His writings challenging the religious practices and attitudes of the early twentieth century have dramatically affected contemporary spiritual life. His martyrdom and dignity in the face of unmitigated evil made him a modern saint.

Bonhoeffer's words are particularly relevant to the Age of

Melancholy because he realized that the challenge of the twentieth century was to liberate humanity from its own dungeons of despair. His example shows the power of religious faith to find hope in the worst imaginable circumstance. For me, Bonhoeffer's sacrificial blood is stronger evidence of God's existence than are scriptural scholarship, philosophical speculation, artistic imagination, or scientific data. I cite him as my best proof that God is always present in the human situation.

As Bonhoeffer wrote in a letter shortly after the July plot had failed and he knew that his chances for survival were virtually nil: "I am still discovering, right up to this moment, that it is only by living completely in this world that one learns to have faith. . . . By this worldliness I mean living unreservedly in life's duties, problems, successes, failures, experiences and perplexities. In doing so we throw ourselves completely into the arms of God."

Through his defiance of a human-made hell on earth more ghastly than Dante's inferno, Bonhoeffer understood that the misery caused by human sin is redeemed partly by bringing people closer to God. And God reciprocates by identifying with human tragedy. "God lets himself be pushed out of the world and on to the cross," Bonhoeffer wrote. "He is weak and powerless in the world, and that is precisely the way, the only way, in which he is with us and helps us."

I am embarrassed to recall Bonhoeffer's suffering and then think of my own problems. How pathetic, if not downright shameful. A middle-age baby boomer wailing that affluence, professional achievement, and social status aren't worthwhile enough. My ego punctured by a midlife crisis, my pride wounded by the guilt from hurting a friend, my arrogance taken down a peg because I am destined to die. Even my honest attempts at self-deprecation echo of special pleading for someone to assure me that, yes, my pain is warranted.

Who better than Bonhoeffer to shake me to the quick? Someone who stared into the eye of absolute evil and didn't blink. Someone who preserved his dignity in one of the darkest hours of the twentieth century. Someone who remained steadfast to God, accepted his historical burden, and offered himself willingly as a model of human decency.

Many nonbelievers died heroically opposing the Nazis, and many people professing religious faith buckled before the horror and even collaborated in Hitler's crimes. Because I suspect that I, too, would have been a coward were I in Germany or the Nazi-occupied areas during World War II, Bonhoeffer's faith is heartening. If I had his spirituality, perhaps I would have acted with equal valor.

It's highly unlikely that I will ever face a Bonhoeffer-like crisis, so any claim that I would respond similarly is moral posturing, and his example is so imposing that it could discourage us lesser persons from seeking a similar religious commitment. Martyrdom, however, is not everyone's fate; and fortunately God doesn't speak to people only in times of extreme duress. Although my midlife anguish might have been barely an emotional pinprick in the larger perspective of human suffering, it was excruciating for me. Yes, I got off lightly. Yet neither health-care professionals nor personal willpower eased my torment.

In the pain of my psychic wounds, I discovered God. My guilt, sorrows, and shortcomings cried out for relief. But not even the most skillful physicians can heal themselves from the human condition. Only divine forgiveness and compassion could soothe my terrors and stop my weeping. Through the dark nights of soul-wrenching despair, I finally realized that mine was a universally shared pain that connected me to the mystery of life. God offered love and self-acceptance, and in return asked only that I give the same to others. Rather than something to medicate or explain away, my melancholy became a wellspring of wisdom, patience, and — as much as possible for a journalist — kindness. In those personal changes, which were inconceivable without divine intervention, I encountered God. He offered me a new way of life, a spiritual awakening, a happiness dependent not on the vagaries of career but on faith in God's grace.

To me, God is revealed most vividly in the narratives, martyrs, and mysticism of Christianity. To make that statement, I have to look beyond the intolerance, the bigotry, the crass political ambitions, the spurious sanctimony, the self-righteousness, and the ignorance of Jesus' basic message of many supposed Christians in late-twentieth-century America. Such people fit Jonathan Swift's remark about individuals who have enough religion to hate but not enough to love.

The Christianity I accept is found in the compassion of Mother Teresa, the intelligence of Reinhold Niebuhr, the artistic rigor of Flannery O'Connor, the social activism of Martin Luther King, Jr., the evangelical fervor of Billy Graham, and the courage of Bonhoeffer. A Jesus Christ who inspired those individuals certainly can help me learn from melancholy. And for anyone seeking confirmation of the spiritual, the example of those people should justify faith in Christianity.

In some respects, I am a Christian in the same way that I am a member of Western civilization. My mental habits and moral values are inextricably connected to Christian history — God and humanity active in the world. Christian concepts are as deeply imbedded within me as bone marrow. I identify with what I understand to be Jesus' fundamental purpose: to reconcile humans to God and to one another.

But I feel no need to deny other religious traditions to reaffirm my own. Salvation is not a lottery in which only people who pick the right faith win God's mercy. No one knows the limits of God's grace.

In chapter 14 of John's Gospel, Jesus says, "In my father's house are many rooms." Likewise, the Buddha taught, "Just as the waters of the great oceans all have one taste, the taste of salt, so too all true teachings have but one taste, the taste of liberation." Those striking phrases from two of the world's great religious figures suggest that heaven has space for all kinds of people. God seems to delight in human variety and doesn't appear to favor any religious personality. It's as if the universe is a vast cathedral with a huge multicolored stained-glass window. Inside stand Jews, Christians, Muslims, Buddhists, and people of other traditions. Each of their faiths is reflected through a singular pane, and all are illuminated by God.

And as I have learned through studying Buddhism and other religious systems, exploring other faiths can enhance spiritual perceptions by seeing God through a different lens. Respecting and understanding another religious heritage can also establish a level of human intimacy and cultural tolerance more than any other endeavor. The mystery of faith is deepened when, for instance, Buddhists explore the Christian Trinity or when Christians meditate on the Buddhist void.

A Buddhist friend said that I should become the best Christian I possibly could; that Muslims should be the best Muslims they could; that Buddhists should be the best Buddhists they could; and that Jews should be the best Jews they could. It is a wise comment. People must commit to their own faith journey. It is best to follow a "name-brand" religion to benefit from centuries of teaching, discipline, and ethical instruction that enable people to bypass time-wasting detours and spiritual dry holes. In spirituality, the roads most traveled usually offer the greatest likelihood of a sanctified arrival, because so much theological surveying, grading, and paving has already been done by sincere, inspired, and intelligent spiritual ancestors. Moreover, by maintaining a sacred "other" that extends through generations and transcends individual egos, people find themselves standing tippytoed on a great mountain of faith built by predecessors.

But while tradition provides valuable guidelines for spirituality, faith must be revived each generation. A religion mummified in churches or temples can't transform people's lives. If the Age of Melancholy is indeed a spiritual crisis, a new religious consciousness must speak to current attitudes. And the new consciousness starts with a new, more intimate relationship between God and humanity.

Bonhoeffer described the twentieth century as "a world come of age." Observing the German prison population of poorly educated, sordid, and generally pathetic humanity, Bonhoeffer concluded that religion wasn't a compelling force in most people's lives. Instead, it is a "religionless time" that gives primacy to wealth, privilege, and power. "Man has learnt to deal with himself in all questions of importance without the 'working hypothesis' called God," Bonhoeffer wrote.

Bonhoeffer's comments show that the late twentieth century needs a new revelation of God. While that might sound scandalous to people practicing old-time religion, God has historically presented himself in new ways. Indeed, Christian scholars have long noticed that God's character evolves in the Bible. He begins as a tribal deity of the nomadic Hebrews. As Yahweh, he defeats such rival deities as Baal and Marduk and emerges as the single god of Israel. In the New Testament he becomes human in the form of Jesus and spreads his message to the Roman world. For the past two thousand years God has been perceived in Western civilization through the culture of the period: a medieval lawgiver, a Reformation judge, an Enlightenment watchmaker, a Romantic nature-spirit, a quantum-sized theory.

Contrary to the traditionally popular view of a God floating in cosmic ether "up there," many people in the late twentieth century respond strongly to a divine presence instilled deep within the soul. Theologian Paul Tillich, a refugee from Nazi Germany, called God "the ground of being," the "deeper layer" that lies within human consciousness. Faith, to Tillich, means "being grasped by an ultimate concern." By seeing God as the source of life, people can subdue the anxiety they feel toward their own existential condition.

God and individuals come together in an amazing way when God is conceived as the "ground" of existence. The creator-creature difference remains, but humanity experiences what Bonhoeffer called "a beyond within" or "a beyond in the midst of our life."

God continually unveils himself. Today, a time when religious institutions and sanctioned theologies no longer command automatic allegiance, he is most active inside individuals, where he is still engaged in his eternal mission to fashion humanity in his own image.

My final proof of God's existence and of humanity's need for him is found in the most powerful psychological drive of the late twentieth century: the search for the individual self, the obsession among many people to "find themselves." Rather than role players wearing the various masks to suit the occasion, people want a distinct self that ties it all together. They desire a unique "I" at the center of their duties as citizen, family member, worker, and the other personas they assume. Amid the ever changing processes of life— aging, learning—people want to weave the strands into whole cloth.

The fragmentation can't be mended by psychological and medical treatments that focus exclusively on the personal. Neither can the selves be integrated by social forces that stamp people by their economic function. Nor can a coherent self be found solely in nature, which itself is constantly dissolving and reassembling physical reality.

A paradox of faith is that the most devout religious people frequently display forceful and original personalities. It seems that individuals who give themselves to God receive in return a robust personal character. The more that people surrender to the "other," the more they develop their own special identity.

The lack of a core self was a primary cause of my midlife melancholy. I defined myself largely by career ambitions and accomplishments. Not even a loving family could overcome the foreboding that my future was lost once professional acclaim no longer gave meaning to my life. Only after I acknowledged the inadequacy of finite, human responses — psychotherapy, drug prescriptions — did I turn, in last-ditch desperation, to the infinite and discover my true self.

Faith-seeking in the late twentieth century includes responding to the creative power embedded within each individual. It is an exploration of consciousness — through meditation, study, contemplation, prayer — that makes us aware of something profound inside of us, something independent of our personalities but that touches our very being and transforms our sense of self. It is the knowledge that I am one with myself, and at peace with God and with the universe.

Spiritual literature speaks often of a "new being" who will help create what the Book of Revelation calls "a new heaven and a new earth." Through my struggle with melancholy, I am trying to be one of these beings, and from that effort I have no doubt of God's existence.

And while constructing a new heaven will have to wait, late-twentieth-century Americans can begin the task of building a new earth.

8

RECONNECTING

Community of Sympathy

Kansas newspaper editor William Allen White was known as "the sage of Emporia" partly because the editorials, columns, magazine articles, and books he wrote in the early part of the twentieth century usually had a heavy dose of what he called "human juices." By putting the mundane events (weddings, business openings, high school sports victories, funerals) and the familiar people (the Rotary Club president, the librarian, the garage mechanic) of small-town Kansas into a larger context of life, White became one of the most popular writers of the increasingly urban America of the 1920s and 1930s.

White said his primary goal as a journalist was to encourage people to recognize their common humanity.

"Passing the office window every moment is someone with a story that should be told," White wrote. "If each man or woman could understand that every other human life is as full of sorrows, of joys, of base temptations, of heartaches and of remorse as his own, which he thinks so peculiarly isolated from the web of life, how much kinder, how much gentler he would be. And how much richer life would be for all of us."

Located along the Walnut River in the grass-and-cattle-covered Flint Hills of eastern Kansas, Emporia was a bit of both Sinclair Lewis's Gopher Prairie and Thornton Wilder's Grover's Corners. It had its share of self-important George Babbitts and frustrated Carol Kennicotts, and it mourned more than a few Emily Webbs who died in childbirth. Emporia was a living community of gossipy but neighborly, prudishly uptight but tolerant people trying to provide for their families, educate their children, and please their God.

The "social sympathy" that White sought is notably lacking in the Age of Melancholy. The late twentieth century is marked by a massive disconnection among people and society. The ties of family, friendship, and neighborliness that bound White's Emporia together have snapped under the pressures of economic, technological, and cultural change. No longer do most Americans chat across the backyard fence or sit on the front porch and keep a disciplinary eye on the mischief-plotting kid down the block. The mom-and-pop grocery, the house-call doctor, the locally owned department store, and the full-service corner gas station have largely disappeared from the nation's social landscape. Instead of gathering for a church supper or high school football game, people huddle within their family entertainment centers and with millions of other similarly isolated individuals simultaneously watch the virtual reality communities of *Frasier, Friends,* and *Melrose Place.* Or they sign on to the Internet and seek human contact that can be turned off immediately and so avoid the often messy complexity of person-to-person communication—the body language, the voice inflections, the irritating personal tics—that are part of the give-and-take of face-to-face communities. For all the miracles of technology, it's hard to squeeze White's "human juices" through a computer modem; a web site is a poor substitute for a coffee shop.

The breakdown in community—the change from Jeffersonian yeoman to television-addicted couch potato—is part of the cultural crisis that has enveloped American society in the late twentieth century. As social critic Allan Bloom notes in his bestselling book, *The Closing of the American Mind,* self-centered people are condemned to loneliness because they have "no common object, no common good, no natural complementarity." Michael J. Sandel, a professor of government at Harvard and one of the nation's premier political scientists, claims in his book *Democracy's Discontent,* "The loss of self-government and the erosion of community . . . together define the anxiety of the age."

By reconnecting with one another, Americans can find greater meaning in their lives. Humans are social animals whose best traits are nourished within community. One of the worst forms of pride is a self-love that denies responsibility for others and blocks commitment to the wider society. If Americans were more charitable toward others—if they realized that no one escapes life without suffering and disappointment—twenty-first-century America could become a more civil and compassionate nation.

This isn't a rose-colored plea to resurrect White's small-town society. Nostalgia and memory are not reliable social history, and many harsh, hateful aspects of the past are well enough gone. For millions of people, Norman Rockwell's America existed only on painted canvas.

Nevertheless, a dispassionate comparison of White's era and today shows that Americans can learn much from the past as we seek new ways to build a more inclusive community in our diverse nation.

White, consistent with the nineteenth-century booster ethic, as-

sumed that the interests of the local business owners were identical
with those of the rest of the community. The local haberdasher, the
banker, and the newspaper publisher felt that their personal fortunes were tied to the prosperity of all. And membership in the
Main Street economic elite carried the clear obligation to be an
active leader in the public schools, town government, county commission, churches, charitable organizations, and other civic institutions. Above all, the practical merchant connected moral virtue
with financial success and insisted that community harmony
hinged on spiritual values. As White noted in analyzing the reasons
for Emporia's economic growth, "The people of this town are honest, hard-working people. They are a church building, school protecting people. . . . That kind of people always prospers."

The geographical distance between White's home of Emporia
and my home of Wichita is about seventy miles straight down the
Kansas Turnpike. But measured by lifestyle and economics, the
distance between White's time and mine is as great as the difference between the old corner general store and a suburban
Wal-Mart.

A demographic spitting image of a typical American city in race,
income, and age, Wichita in the 1990s could be Everyplace, U.S.A.
Like most American cities, Wichita has gradually lost most of its
founding community pillars. Such homegrown companies as Pizza
Hut, Cessna, Learjet, Beech, and Coleman have either left town or
been taken over by outside owners. The city has become another
mass-market branch town. The largest hospital, the newspaper, the
four commercial television stations, the biggest department store,
and most major retail and service businesses are controlled by non-
Wichitans. Knowing that they will be gone in a couple of years,
most local managers care little for the community. They live in suburban real estate developments that cater to corporate nomads

seeking quick-sale housing. They send their kids to private schools. They don't join community groups; corporate résumés aren't built on YMCA or Salvation Army board memberships. They are—if not contemptuous—virtually ignorant of local politics.

Instead of White's Emporia, postmodern American cities are closer to French existentialist writer Albert Camus's Oran, Algeria, as depicted in his book *The Plague,* one of the most important novels of the second half of the twentieth century.

Written in a style called impressionist realism, *The Plague* centers on the reactions of the citizens in a town in Camus's native North Africa while under siege from a pestilence. Although first published in France in 1947, the book works as a mirror for contemporary America in its images of the human condition.

In the opening chapter, the people of Oran are introduced not as members of a community but as individuals fraught with ennui and mindlessly pursuing selfish goals. "The truth is that everyone is bored," notes the narrator, "and devotes himself to cultivating habits. Our citizens work hard, but solely with the object of getting rich." The citizens have little concern for one another or for the quality of public life. While religion is perfunctorily observed, there is no sense of the deeper significance, of the sacredness, in life. Rules are followed, order is maintained, personal pleasure and "doing business" are the main sources of satisfaction. The good life is taken for granted. "In this respect, our townsfolk were like everyone else, wrapped up in themselves," the narrator observes.

For several days the main character, Dr. Bernard Rieux, notices a dramatic increase in the number of dead rats in Oran. The concierge of the young doctor's building grumbles about cleaning up the rodent carcasses and also complains about a high fever and painful swelling. Rieux learns that his medical colleagues have had similar cases.

In a typical example of official denial, the prefect of the city minimizes the problem for fear of alarming the complacent citizenry. But the death toll mounts and the news gets out that Oran is in the grip of the bubonic plague. The city is totally disrupted. At first, the people withdraw into their private lives and cut themselves off as much as possible from their fellow citizens. Civic life virtually disintegrates. The scourge worsens. Gradually, the people recognize that retaining their old self-centeredness means almost certain death. They organize sanitary squads on their own; the government does little because officials have no bureaucratic model to meet such a crisis.

Drawn together under the threat of death, the people of Oran find that mortality links them in a common humanity. Death may win in the end, but the fight to save the city enhances human dignity, and each person's effort contributes to the survival of the community. "There's no question of heroism in all this," Rieux says. "It's a matter of common decency. That's an idea which may make some people smile, but the only means of fighting the plague is—common decency."

As the weather turns colder, the plague lifts. People reappear in cafés, restaurants, and shops. Outwardly, life returns to normal, but the people find themselves strengthened spiritually and socially. They have forged a community out of shared suffering and struggle. In the process, their lives have acquired a metaphysical dimension based on a collective response to the human predicament of unavoidable tragedy.

The Plague is literary art, but its ultimately uplifting message is also found in several places in the United States of the 1990s. Below are three contemporary examples of Americans rallying to improve the quality of life in their communities, and in the process transforming themselves and finding purpose in a common cause.

They are worthwhile case studies of what should happen in thousands of American communities:

- Akron, Ohio, is an industrial city of 223,000 people located fifty miles south of Cleveland. Once known as the rubber capital of the world, Akron has launched a remarkable experiment in race relations called the Coming Together Project. Growing out of a 1993 series in the *Akron Beacon Journal* that explored local racial attitudes, the project sponsors such biracial activities as joint worship services in churches and public forums on race issues. "What we're trying to do is get the races together so they can talk and create a better atmosphere," said Al Fitzpatrick, who works with the project.

    Although the project wasn't intended to promote new public policies in welfare, crime, and other social problems, it has fostered a more cooperative climate to tackle such issues. "I think it has changed individuals," said Pat Selwood, an official at an Akron drug, alcohol, and mental-health center.

- Over the past decade, racists and anti-Semites have designated Montana and surrounding northwestern states as a "white homeland." Skinheads, Klansmen, and other white supremacists have waged a vicious hate war against non-whites and Jews.

    In the early 1990s Billings, Montana, was the scene of numerous hate crimes, including the desecration of a Jewish cemetery, threatening phone calls to Jewish residents, and swastikas appearing on people's homes. On December 2, 1993, a brick was thrown through the bedroom window of five-year-old Isaac Schnitzer, who had stenciled a menorah and other Jewish symbols on the glass to mark the holiday of Hanukkah.

Rather than cower in fear before such an outrage, some members of the community organized against hatred. Led by Christian ministers, hundreds of non-Jewish families put cutout menorahs in their homes in the following weeks. The local newspaper printed a picture of a menorah, and as many as ten thousand residents displayed the symbol in solidarity with their Jewish neighbors. A local sporting-goods store put the slogan "Not in Our Town! No Hate. No Violence. Peace on Earth" on its large billboard.

Although anti-Semitic incidents still occur in Billings, they happen with less frequency than before, and the community has found new strength to resist hatred and promote tolerance.

- Nothing — not millions of welfare dollars or hundreds of trained social workers—reduced poverty in Mississippi. Then state leaders tried a different approach—values and morality in addition to job training and economic-development programs. The Faith and Families Project, launched in 1995 by Governor Kirk Fordice, matches welfare families with churches. The congregations help the welfare clients get jobs and offer them emotional support, as well as help with childcare, household budgeting, and similar tasks. Structured to avoid church-state violations, the project doesn't require welfare families to attend church, and no state money is funneled through the congregations.

The goal is for each of the state's five thousand churches to adopt a welfare family. The hope is that the project will help meet society's pressing need to reduce welfare rolls while encouraging churches to fulfill their spiritual obligation to the poor. Considering the correlation between poverty and illegitimacy and other destructive behaviors, church moral teachings could be the project's most effective weapon. "Stop doing what the government's been doing," said the Reverend Thomas Jenkins, whose church-based foundation offers education and other programs. "Government has been trying to treat the effect, the aftermath. But we've got to go back to the basics and treat the cause."

The Plague, these three American communities, and the melancholic epidemic of the late twentieth century contain an identical message: that sorrow, grief, and crisis create the strongest connections among people. Mutually acknowledged pain helps people develop what German philosopher Wilhelm Dilthey called "empathetic understanding," which lets individuals identify with another person's fears and heartbreaks and broadens sensitivity toward the universal human experience. This contact enables people to appeal to what Abraham Lincoln called the better angels of our nature and form the trusting relationships that are the most gratifying of human pleasures.

The consciousness arising from the Age of Melancholy must heighten community. That doesn't mean society should become a therapy group of sob sisters and brothers wallowing in one another's tales of woe. It means the ego-driven personalities of late-twentieth-century America should recognize the common human condition and learn that selfhood is most fully expressed through community.

As occurred among the citizens of Oran in *The Plague* and in the American communities spotlighted, people can transform society. But first they must renew themselves. As Carl Jung said, "The change does not begin with propaganda and mass meetings, or with violence. It begins with a change in individuals."

History's most significant cultural upheavals arise not after presidents displace kings or governors sign laws, but when people adopt new spiritual and social values. Remarkable things happen when individuals decide they want to be different kinds of persons in a different kind of society. They reconstruct their social institutions and adjust their political ideologies to fit their new moral vision. The civil rights movement, for example, was galvanized when Rosa Parks refused to move to the back of the bus in Montgomery, Alabama, because she was too tired to cooperate with racial segregation and her own degradation. Combining the biblical concepts of sin and redemption with egalitarian values, civil rights activists transformed the United States and pushed the country closer to its religious and political ideals.

The challenge for Americans in the late twentieth century is to liberate themselves from a different kind of oppression—the self-imposed chains of selfishness, consumerism, and social alienation. If Americans are to recapture the democratic virtues that ensure maximum personal freedom within a supportive social network, they need to swing the cultural pendulum away from radical individualism and toward the traditional ideal of American society as a voluntary covenant among citizens.

Democratic Virtue

The wisdom of James Madison, Alexander Hamilton, and other drafters of the U.S. Constitution was confirmed during a debate I witnessed in 1977 while covering the Maryland General Assembly for United Press International.

The floor was held by a state senator who, along with his governmental duties, happened to own a couple of weekly newspapers in a rural, southern part of the state. The senator was sponsoring a bill to require that legal notices in his home county be published in two local newspapers instead of one. The tiny-type announcements of contract bids, sewer bond issues, and other routine governmental matters, legal notices are the bread and butter of small newspapers that don't have much retail advertising. In effect, the legislation would force agencies in the senator's three-newspaper county to put legal notices in at least one of his publications.

Noting that the proposal would financially benefit its sponsor, another senator asked the publisher-legislator to justify his apparent conflict of interest.

"Conflict of interest?" the senator blurted in bewildered exasperation. "Conflict of interest? Absolutely not. This bill is directly within my interests. There's no conflict. There's no conflict at all."

The measure failed, but I'm not sure whether it died because the senator's colleagues were disgusted by the blatant special pleading or because they were punishing him for excessive candor in acknowledging the use of his elected office to line his own pockets.

Having covered state legislatures in Maryland, Pennsylvania, and Illinois, I am thoroughly acquainted with the crude venalities and hypocrisies familiar to American politics. As regards official corruption, I'm like the character played by Claude Rains in *Casablanca* — "shocked" about the goings-on in the legislative back rooms, hotel bars, and lobbyist hotel suites. In Maryland, for example, the weekly legislative session convened early Monday evening and then promptly recessed for "boys' night out," which allowed influential lobbyists to provide prostitutes and parties to entertain the predominantly male lawmakers. In Pennsylvania I watched the House majority leader sent to prison for corruption. In Illinois I spent weeks poring over the divorce proceedings and other financial records of the state attorney general and discovered a pattern of hiding income and diverting campaign funds for personal use; federal prosecutors were also investigating, and one of the state's most powerful politicians went to jail. Even in supposedly squeaky-clean Kansas, several state legislators in 1997 were found on the payroll of a company that had received lucrative state grants. And the repeated financial, moral, and ethical lapses in Washington, D.C., show that money, ego, and power are driving forces in national politics.

In other words, the American political system is working exactly as the founders anticipated. Indeed, no one has had a more realistic appraisal of the human condition than the framers of the Constitution who gathered in Philadelphia in the sweltering summer of 1787. While much of their rhetoric soared in democratic idealism, their actions reflected a sober assessment of their fellow citizens.

Grounded in pessimistic Calvinist theology and the skepticism of the Scottish Enlightenment of the eighteenth century, the framers had no illusions about human perfectibility and thought that government's primary role was to contain destructive human impulses. "If men were angels, no government would be necessary. If angels were to govern men, neither external nor internal controls on government would be necessary," wrote James Madison in the *Federalist Papers* in defense of the Constitution's intricate set of checks and balances.

That brief political-science lesson supports my argument that the melancholy of the late twentieth century is as much social as personal—that the emotional stability of individual Americans is inseparable from the cultural health of American society.

For Americans, democracy is a formative part of our national and self identities. Historically, Americans feel better about themselves when engaged in a visionary national mission. To be an American is to civilize the wilderness, to defeat foreign tyranny, to extend the blessings of liberty, to confront social injustice — in short, to respond aggressively and confidently to the world.

In the 1990s, however, such lofty aspirations are absent. For example, global stability and trade treaties, not universal freedom, have topped the U.S. international agenda in this decade. Meanwhile, the nation's governmental and economic leadership has been embroiled in political, ethical, and financial scandals that usually generate not righteous outrage but debilitating cynicism — which has continually heightened since Vietnam and Watergate — among many Americans.

Furthermore, as analyzed earlier, mass-market capitalism seduces consumers by equating material goods with happiness. Bureaucracies jealously guard their power rather than encourage citizens to pursue democratic principles. The therapeutic culture isolates emotional complaints from larger social issues and tranquilizes people with psychotropic drugs. Postmodernism subverts common standards of truth that could form a coherent philosophical framework. The message in these disintegrative tendencies is that society can't be trusted, so individuals must adapt however they can.

Consequently, we Americans reject the commitments that self-government requires. Bound solely by self-chosen obligations, many of us disregard claims by community, tradition, or morality. Pleas to work for a just society, to acknowledge the needs of future generations, or to do God's will on earth don't resonate with these Americans. In their obsessive quest for "self," many people ignore that full character development includes intense involvement in civic affairs — in what the ancient Greeks called the *polis*. Instead, they are thin, flat individuals whose every reference point is themselves.

But opposition to the manipulative and amoral mechanisms

governing American society is growing among some professors, journalists, and other social commentators. As the United States nears the next millennium, new voices are trying to mend America's frayed political culture, and perhaps lift some fatigued souls in the meantime. Initially conceived in scholarly books and journals, this possible rebirth of community and mutual responsibility is maturing as it enters the larger social arena and could help make the Age of Melancholy an era of historic political transformation.

Intellectual heirs of nineteenth-century French writer Alexis de Tocqueville, whose *Democracy in America* anticipated the atomic individualism of modern society, some of today's foremost political thinkers want to rekindle the American communal spirit. Their ranks include such prominent social scientists and political theorists as Robert N. Bellah, Michael J. Sandel, Wilfred M. McClay, Philip Selznick, Amitai Etzioni, and the late Christopher Lasch. Working within a genre called public philosophy, these academics worry that American politics has focused on protecting selfish interests rather than on forming and implementing shared ideals. In a culture that stresses individual rights, privileges, and entitlements, these scholars want to resurrect communal solidarity, cohesion, and obligation.

This philosophical movement dovetails with the drive to decentralize American government. Under the generic label of New Federalism, presidents from Richard Nixon to Bill Clinton have argued that the Washington establishment has become too strong and that political power should devolve to the states and localities. Thus, over the past few years once largely federal functions such as welfare have become primarily state matters. The goal of the theorists, supported in varying degrees of sincerity by many practicing politicians, is to revitalize democracy at the grass roots. Democracy, the argument goes, is more likely to thrive when nourished in particular communities because people feel little allegiance to remote institutions or support for programs drafted without their input.

A combination of professional self-interest, melancholic lack of enthusiasm for life, and genuine concern for U.S. democracy attracted me to communitarian ideals and New Federalist policies. I realized that the future of newspapers, my own well-being, and the destiny of America were linked to the renewal of the nation's social character.

In the early 1990s corporate leaders at Knight-Ridder, the parent company of *The Wichita Eagle,* noticed an alarming decrease in circulation at most of their newspapers around the country. To find out why, Knight-Ridder executives hired consultants, held focus groups, and compiled reams of market research. Some of the reasons were easily identifiable: competition from television and other media, the time pressures of a hurry-up society, and a younger generation that never acquired a newspaper-reading habit. But one factor stood out: Americans who were not active in their community cared little about the local newspaper. The correlation was clear: community-connected people bought newspapers; community-disconnected people didn't. Common sense and corporate logic concurred: if more people participated in their community, more newspapers would be sold.

Meanwhile, many workaday journalists were plagued by professional self-doubt. The press was under increasing attack for elitism, arrogance, and bias. The public also was turning away from politics, as reflected in lower voter turnouts and antipathy toward government. Although numerous factors contributed to the public's disillusionment with politics, it was obvious that the old methods of journalism were not serving the profession or the American people.

Out of that came public journalism, a concept designed to revive American civic life, replenish the profits of the newspaper industry, and refurbish the craft of journalism. *The Wichita Eagle* helped lead this crusade, largely because editor Buzz Merritt understood as well as anyone in the country the stakes involved.

Although few public journalists had read the public philosophers, their assumptions were the same. Americans needed to reattach themselves to community. To help do so, the *Eagle* redefined the role of journalist. No longer a detached observer of the public scene, the *Eagle* sought answers to the problems it had identified by listing possible remedial actions that individuals could take. Rather than rely on the usual lineup of government officials and community busybodies to comment on local matters, *Eagle* reporters solicited opinions from average citizens. Political coverage was focused not on position papers from candidates but on the issues of importance to readers, as discerned in interviews and surveys. The old journalistic tendency to quote the ideological extremes on any issue — in the name of "balance" — was abandoned for more nuanced, cautionary remarks from well-meaning citizens who often had refreshingly perceptive views toward a particular event or proposal.

Although still in its infancy, and under vicious attack by conventional, we-find-problems-not-solutions journalists, the new approach represents a cultural reformation within newspapers. Most significant, it means that reporters and editors need to develop a sense of place and an appreciation for their community rather than behave like ink-stained gypsies migrating from one job to another. In many respects, public journalism is a return to the small-town newspaper practices of William Allen White, who served as both chief promoter and harshest critic, social tonic and purgative elixir, of Emporia.

Participating in public journalism persuaded me that individuals can reshape U.S. society. Wichita is awash in public commissions, open meetings, community forums, town halls, and other means to encourage citizen involvement. Decisions on arcane matters like trash collection, new water sources, and jail construction that once were left exclusively to bureaucratic experts now must be vetted by the public.

Public journalism, New Federalism, and similar attempts to activate citizens indicate that the cure for the melancholy of the late twentieth century includes a big dose of democracy.

The founders' political genius in erecting the federal system enables Americans constantly to reinvent their democracy. And that is what, though in its early stage, could be going on in Wichita and other U.S. communities where people are relearning the skills of self-government, citizen participation, and democratic deliberation.

Meet Cindy Duckett. A middle-aged woman of moderate financial means, Mrs. Duckett was upset by her stepson's poor academic performance in the Wichita public schools. A few years ago she wrote a long essay to the *Eagle* editorial department claiming that a newly developed reading program and lax classroom discipline were largely responsible for her boy's lagging grades. Normally, we would have chopped up Mrs. Duckett's piece and run it as a letter to the editor, and that would have been the end of it. Instead, sensitized by the values of public journalism, we saw something more—a woman not being served by the community's most important public institution. We published her entire essay. The reaction from readers was amazing. She caught a popular mood of serious misgiving about public education. It was a rising revolt that we at the *Eagle* had not detected because we spent most of our time talking to administrators, teachers, and other members of the local school establishment who claimed that everything was hunky-dory within Wichita classrooms.

From there, Mrs. Duckett helped organize a parents and citizens group called Project Educate that lobbies for tougher academic standards, greater financial accountability, and other reforms. The school administration has responded to public complaints by raising scholastic benchmarks, adopting innovative programs, and setting the schools on track to continued improvement in the future.

For hundreds of Wichitans, the debate over school standards was a graduate degree in citizenship. They no longer felt impotent before the educational bureaucracy but realized that they could make a difference. Rather than brood in isolation, the new activists were drawn out of themselves through immersion in public life. They were empowered, both personally and politically, through contact with their fellow citizens. And in the process they helped reenergize community life in Wichita by showing that everyone has a palatable stake in the schools and by broadening decision making on education.

The founders called it public virtue, the deeds and attitudes that orient people to common goals beyond selfish ends. Although Mrs. Duckett was initially concerned for her own child, she soon recognized that citizenship demanded an interest in all youngsters and the community as a whole. As John Adams wrote, "There must be a positive passion for the public good, the public interest, honor, power and glory, established in the minds of the people, or there can be no republican government, nor any real liberty."

Citizen activism can generate the sympathy and empathy that tie people together. Self-government encourages the character traits of warmth, compassion, tolerance, respect, and responsibility toward others. A nurturing community is made in the soul, in the daily relationships among people, and in the desire of individuals to attain a bit of immortality by leaving a lasting legacy to their town's history.

Public virtues and political participation can help Americans transcend apathetic despair by proving that most of the nation's problems can be solved and that individual lives can be meaningful. Given the sinful and tragic nature of humanity, America will never be Utopia. But there are historical and religious responses that can help turn melancholy into a renewal of democracy.

Under the Rainbow

Is the way out of the Age of Melancholy down the Yellow Brick Road? Can a turn-of-the-century Kansas farm girl lead the United States into the next millennium? Are the Cowardly Lion, the Scarecrow, and the Tin Woodman role models for a wiser, more caring, and closer-knit American society?

Published in 1900, *The Wonderful Wizard of Oz* is a uniquely American fairy tale. Through the 1939 movie version starring Judy Garland, Dorothy's adventures over the rainbow have delighted generations of Americans. Most of those people probably think the story is nothing more than a childish fantasy, complete with evil witches, a plucky girl, and a pompous wizard.

However, as I first encountered in an essay by Henry M. Littlefield published in the *American Quarterly* in 1964 and amplified by political scientist Michael A. Genovese in an op-ed piece published in March 1988 in the *Los Angeles Times, The Wonderful Wizard of Oz* can be interpreted as an imaginative political broadside protesting the radical technological and economic changes that hit Kansas and the rest of the country in the late nineteenth century. Yes, it might seem far-fetched to describe Dorothy in her pigtails and calico dress as an eminent American political philosopher, but fables often hold truths unavailable in academic texts. And a late-twentieth-century reading of the story reveals a sad narrative of political disillusionment, yet it also raises optimism that America in the next few decades could become a society of community, faith, and civility.

Written by L. Frank Baum, *The Wonderful Wizard of Oz* is a parable of the Populist movement that swept across the Midwest and South in the 1890s. Former editor of a weekly newspaper in South Dakota, Baum was sympathetic to the Populist challenge to the banking tycoons, railroad moguls, and Eastern financiers that farmers felt were conspiring to keep them down through low agricultural prices, high interest rates, exorbitant freight charges, and monopolistic business practices. Although written after Populism's political fortunes had faded, the story is a lasting vision of an America that would have been much different from the one that actually evolved in the twentieth century.

The allegory begins with the name *Oz*, which is the abbreviation for *ounce* and refers to the measurement for gold. One of the Populists' major complaints was the gold standard, which they thought allowed bankers to keep money tight and farmers poor; the Populists wanted wider coinage of silver, which they thought would make more capital available to farmers and small merchants.

Dorothy, the naive Kansas girl, is Miss Everyman. A tornado drops her house in a Technicolor world. Her landing squashes the Wicked Witch of the East, who with her sister, the Witch of the West, stand for the bankers and capitalists who keep "the little people," the Munchkins (the average Americans) in bondage. Dorothy sets off down the Yellow Brick Road, another allusion to the gold standard. She encounters the Scarecrow, a Midwestern farmer who didn't have the brains to recognize his political situation. They become a trio with the addition of the Tin Woodman, the industrial worker who has labored so hard that he is incapable of love and whose rusted hulk has been tossed aside by his capitalist bosses. The Cowardly Lion caricatures William Jennings Bryan, the Populists' 1896 presidential candidate whose oratorical roar had no bite against the Republican ticket headed by William McKinley. Toto—is probably a dog.

The Wizard of Oz is the president of the United States, a former ventriloquist who lives in the Emerald City (Washington, D.C.) and rules by smoke and mirrors while in thrall to the witches of capitalism. Like all good politicians, the Wizard appears in whatever form the people want, but he can't deliver what he promises. "You're a humbug," the Scarecrow shouts when the Wizard's deceit is unveiled. Baum's point is that the people must solve their own problems because politicians are controlled by big business. People's ignorance and gullibility allow the special interests to manipulate and rule them.

Dorothy leads her gang to the witch's castle and melts her, reinforcing the argument that the people can defeat their capitalist oppressors. The Wizard flies from Oz in a hot-air balloon after turning power over to the Tin Woodman and the Scarecrow, reflecting Baum's hope for a worker-farmer alliance to govern America. The Lion, now courageous enough to defend small animals, returns to the forest, suggesting that Baum wanted Bryan to retire from politics. Dorothy clicks her heels—the slippers representing the ability Americans have to achieve their dreams—and wakes up home in Kansas, happily nestled within the embrace of family and friends.

How easily the Oz themes translate to the late twentieth century. Like Baum's Populist contemporaries, many Americans today are estranged from politics, isolated from community, deprived of deep feelings of self, and overwhelmed by a capitalist system that is at least as strong and ruthless today as it was in the late nineteenth century.

Above all, Populism was a moral protest against an increasingly industrialized, mechanized, and technology-driven society. The prairie rebels were heirs of the small-town, rural, Jeffersonian, egalitarian ideal. They were the Americans of farmer cooperatives, barn raisings, church buildings, quilting bees, and other communal endeavors. They detested capitalism because it reduced people to anonymous buyers and sellers whose relationships were totally financial, corrupting democratic and religious virtues that linked men and women to community. They sought a more humane, cooperative society at a time of unbridled, social-Darwinist competition. They wanted genuine reform to limit the power of money in American society through antitrust laws and to broaden the democratic horizon through women's suffrage, direct election of senators, the secret ballot, and similar measures. Indeed, in the ensuing Progressive era, much of the Populist political platform was adopted, though Progressives favored a stronger federal government to improve society rather than the local communal alliances sought by Populists.

At the end of the twentieth century, the corporate creed of the Gilded Age, though slightly tamed in practice and refined in rhetoric from the Populist period, largely sets American priorities. Market forces have invaded every sector of society and have become the ultimate measure of political and cultural authority.

An issue for the twenty-first century is whether the seeds of Populism that sprouted briefly a century ago are dead or have merely lain dormant for the past hundred years. Can Americans update the Populist ideals of family, community, and cooperation that were crushed by corporate capitalism and rampant individualism? Can Americans cultivate a national social character that promotes civic, environmental, religious, and similar values and that, in turn, gives purpose and meaning to life? Can Americans sustain the cultural institutions that enhance public life and enable people to resist the fracturing forces of the market economy and the corrosive effects of moral relativism?

As those questions imply, America in the 1990s could be at a turning point like the Populist 1890s. Although the parallel is not precise—the Populists' complaint centered mainly on economic frustration, whereas today's malaise extends to spiritual and existential dimensions—the convergence of potentially revolutionary social and political forces was similar in both eras. The issue is whether discontented Americans of the Age of Melancholy will be more successful than were Populist agitators to restrain capitalist excesses, regenerate democracy, and restore community.

Fortunately, across America in places like Wichita, a new political vision is emerging to rebuild civic life. Taking a phrase from the environmental movement, "small is beautiful," the new consensus combines ideas from the political left and right. It includes conservative efforts to transfer power to states and localities. It updates leftist attempts of the 1960s to empower grass-roots Americans to control their neighborhoods and the government programs that serve them.

If America is to fulfill the values of community and democracy, the next few decades must become a post–Cold War, postpartisan, nonideological, pragmatic period in which people see that government works best when dispersed and based on citizen activism.

It won't be easy. Participatory democracy depends on citizen trust, which is impossible to acquire when the unencumbered, acquisitive self is the dominant cultural and economic model.

Trust is built by close contact among people. A task of the Age of Melancholy is to expand opportunities for individuals to interact personally and, from there, gain the mutual confidence and political skills to confront community problems. Again, history shows the way.

In the 1830s Alexis de Tocqueville noted that Americans had

a genius for what he called "the art of association." The French observer of Jacksonian democracy was struck by how Americans didn't wait for government or an elected official to deal with an issue but instead took the initiative themselves to repair a road, construct a school, or raise a church. Tocqueville warned that extreme individualism undermined this cooperative spirit, which he perceived as essential for democracy.

Additionally, membership in civic, religious, and fraternal organizations helps shift people's focus from themselves to the larger society; it enlarges the sense of self by connecting private interests to the public good; it allows people to practice habits of self-control and self-government. Also through associations, Americans develop the public virtues—respect, tolerance, compromise, integrity, social responsibility—to counter the narrow selfishness that ends in self-absorbed despair.

This isn't touchy-feely, squishy social science. The nation's economic prosperity could depend on stronger community institutions and greater reciprocity among people. That insight comes from one of the most provocative books of the late twentieth century, *Making Democracy Work,* by Harvard professor Robert Putnam.

After twenty years of rigorous, at-the-scene study on regional differences in Italy, Putnam concluded that contrary heritages of civic involvement were the primary reason for the wide economic disparity between Italy's wealthy north and its destitute south. Since medieval times, northern Italians have been active in civic groups ranging from choral societies and chess clubs to artisan guilds and political parties that attracted people across class and social lines. This engagement among neighbors helped account for the region's long history of communal government and its strong local institutions. In contrast, southern Italy historically has been a "feudal, fragmented, alienated and isolated" society centered around family loyalty and patron-client servility, which meant flimsy civic and governmental structures, which in turn contributed to the area's corruption, violence, and poverty.

Putnam's research confirms the communitarian argument that a vibrant, creative society depends on a public-spirited citizenry. Putnam also concluded that northern Italy's economic strength resulted largely from strong civic institutions that generated trust among people, respect for the law, and social stability. Absent such institutions and communal traditions, southern Italy has long been one of Europe's poorest areas.

Although it's a long stretch to compare southern Italy with the United States, Putnam's study raises some salient points. The current American mind-set of unrestrained individualism works against communal involvement. And while the United States in the 1990s is incredibly prosperous, the country also experiences economic dislocation and middle-class anxiety. Moreover, the nation's social infrastructure is deteriorating, as seen in lagging voter turnout and declining membership in some civic organizations that inculcate community values, such as the PTA, labor unions, fraternal clubs, and sports teams. Those trends mean that America is dissipating its social capital of trust, civic participation, public virtue, and democratic habits that Putnam's scholarship shows are critical to economic affluence.

If America is to have its desperately needed renaissance in civic life, the momentum could come from a renewed social activism by religious people. Faced with the failure of the secular experts to solve pressing issues of poverty and moral decay, many Americans are reconnecting community with spirituality. In Wichita, for example, church and civic groups launched a program in 1997 called Wichita Promise to provide at-risk children with adult mentors, educational tutoring, and health care. It's the largest such effort in city history, enlisting thousands of volunteers and dozens of organizations.

Academic studies on similar religiously motivated programs suggest that the Wichita plan will be successful. Historian Marvin Olasky, of the University of Texas, found that spiritual counseling of drug addicts, alcoholics, and other troubled people is more effective than the standard medical and psychological models of treatment. Princeton University sociologist John Di Iulio, an expert in the causes of crime, thinks that churches could be an answer to violence, juvenile delinquency, and cultural deprivation in inner-city neighborhoods. James Q. Wilson, a political scientist at UCLA, wants faith-based programs to play a greater role in job training, education, and welfare. "We've gone down every other road," he said. "This is one road we haven't explored, and the initial indications are that it's very appealing."

Speaking on December 4, 1997, to the American Enterprise Institute in Washington, D.C., Wilson added, "Governments can transfer money; they cannot build character. Our best hope is to transfer the money to private agencies—churches, voluntary associations—that have shown in the past a capacity to change people."

No, it's not a Yellow Brick Road to a wish-fulfilling wizard. The path doesn't have a clear destination; it's a never-ending journey of faith in God and democracy. And its milestones are melancholy, spirituality, and community.

"Only connect," urged British novelist E. M. Forster.

And connection—to one another, to lofty ideals, to moral values—is what millions of Americans seek at the end of the twentieth century.

Melancholy is a symptom of a distorted culture that denies humanity's deepest need for the warmth and security of strong communities, that tries to liberate the self from any obligations other than personal gratification, that exalts humanity for godlike powers.

Spirituality takes people out of themselves by linking them to the timeless truths contained within all great religions, by setting them on an eternal journey toward transcendence, by leading them to the true source of soul and selfhood in what Dietrich Bonhoeffer called "the beyond within" and Paul Tillich described as "the ground of being."

Community overcomes the ego-self through maintaining historic traditions; it extends individual experience across the human continuum; it provides authority to justify the sacrifices and commitments necessary for civilized society and a meaningful life.

"Men are free when they are obeying some deep, inward voice of religious belief. Obeying from within," said British novelist D. H. Lawrence. "Men are free when they belong to a living, organic, believing community, active in fulfilling some unfulfilled, perhaps unrealized purpose."

Midlife in the Balance

Ray E. Dillon had what some of his friends called a "good death." At age ninety-eight, after a lifetime active in business and community affairs, he passed away in a room in the hospital he helped build.

As a young boy in Hutchinson, Kansas, Dillon started working in his father's small grocery store. He was too short to see over the counter, so his father gave him a job tethering the horses of the farmers who brought milk, fruit, vegetables, and other products to trade at the store.

Over the years Dillon built his father's store into one of the largest grocery chains in the Midwest. He became extremely wealthy, but he always recognized that his personal well-being depended on the health of the communities in which his stores were located.

Dillon was as much involved in civic matters as he was in the business that carried his name. He joined the Hutchinson Chamber of Commerce and numerous other organizations. He served on the board of trustees of Wichita State University. He engineered the merger of two Hutchinson hospitals into one facility, which is where he died.

Hundreds of people attended Dillon's funeral services in February 1996. But it wasn't a particularly sad occasion; it was more a celebration of a man who had led a full and worthwhile life. Aside from family, the heaviest hearts were within mourners who recognized that their community had lost a powerful presence.

Ray Dillon is a reminder of how drastically America has changed in the twentieth century. He was born in a time when apples came direct from the family farm, and died at a time when oranges were flown into his stores from Australia. A very close friend and a sometime business associate of my grandparents, Dillon represented to me the stability, vision, and confidence that made my hometown a secure place to grow up in. Things seemed orderly, problems were manageable, because men and women like Dillon were in charge.

Dillon's death was a transition for me. Like many middle-aged baby boomers, I was reluctant to accept full responsibility for society. After all, if Ray Dillon and his type were still around, the city council, the United Way, and the Salvation Army would continue apace. And while as a newspaper editorial writer, I was great at lecturing the governor or browbeating the county commission, I was not so good at the gritty, unglamorous, often unappreciated work of improving my community, of securing the roots of place that connect generations.

Some of the sadness of midlife melancholy is the regret of wisdom learned too late. For me, that wisdom came primarily through a sense of tragedy, in the recognition of my own sinfulness and the inescapability of death. By eliminating all remedial options other than religious faith, melancholic suffering forced me to confront my deepest fears and to seek redemption. "Happiness is good for the body, but it is grief which develops the mind," wrote French novelist Marcel Proust.

Midlife melancholy was my chance to start living again. It demanded a life review that, I hope, will enable me to repackage my memories and abilities for my remaining years. It allowed me to seek a spirituality that put my life in the larger context of religious values, philosophical clarity, and community activism. It let me smash through my own ego's defenses and struggle toward character and integrity.

And from spirituality and community can flow the midlife enlightenment described by the Irish poet William B. Yeats:

> *My fiftieth year had come and gone,*
> *I sat, a solitary man,*
> *In a crowded London shop,*
> *An open book, an empty cup*
> *On the marble tabletop.*
> *While on the shop and street I gazed,*
> *My body of a sudden blazed!*
> *And twenty minutes more or less*
> *It seemed so great, my happiness,*
> *That I was blessed—and could bless.*

In his essay "The Stages of Life," Carl Jung says that the challenge of middle age is to find a mission in life that allows us to overcome our newly discovered limits, to acknowledge our failed expectations, and to accept our mortality. "I have observed that a life directed to an aim is in general better, richer, and healthier than an aimless one," Jung wrote. "As a doctor, I am convinced that it is hygienic . . . to discover in death a goal towards which one can strive, and that shrinking away from it is something unhealthy and abnormal which robs the second half of life of its purpose."

The future of America depends heavily on how the baby boomers react to middle age. We could create a truly golden age with self-aware people in their fifties, sixties, seventies, and eighties who expand human possibilities beyond anything now imaginable. Or we could become, if we don't handle midlife well, a generation of postmenopausal malcontents with senescent bodies and adolescent minds.

Above all, middle-aged Americans must not doubt that we came by our melancholy honestly. As I reached middle age, one of my greatest fears was that my life had been wasted because I had spent most of my adulthood lusting after what William James called "the bitch-goddess SUCCESS." Sure, I had most of the goodies available to a middle-class careerist, but life seemed devoid of great challenges, of opportunities for heroic achievement. The path into old age was a gradually shortening jaunt down a trail lined with pension plans, 401(k) contributions, flabbier muscles, and deteriorating bone mass. What is the point? Where is the idealism that raises the everyday above the mundane? Will I have a "good death" in the fullness of time? Would I have a stone epitaph that said I had left the world better than I found it?

Along with millions of its baby-boomer citizens, America itself is at a crossroads. Although the world's sole superpower, the United States seems to have lost something of its historic confidence. Internationally, the nation's primary goal seems to be making the world safe for rapacious capitalism. Domestically, the hardening of financial disparities in the 1990s has divided Americans along harsh economic class lines, reducing the interactions among people of varying backgrounds that create true community.

In his poem "Ozymandias," Percy Shelley tells of meeting a traveler from an ancient land who talked about a huge broken statue in the desert depicting a "shattered visage" of a long-forgotten monarch. On the pedestal these lines appear: "My name is Ozymandias, king of kings: Look on my works, ye Mighty, and despair!"

If history teaches anything, it is that the reward for Americans who seek only power, wealth, and pleasure is that of Ozymandias — a neglected, crumbling monument in the vast expanse of space and time. What Ozymandias and millions of contemporary Americans never learned is that lasting purpose in life comes through the cultivation of the spiritual, personal, and civic virtues that make civilization possible.

To escape that wasteland, this agenda for the next millennium should be set: to accept the ambiguity and imperfection of human nature; to experience through religious faith and communion with one another the divine love that shines through darkness.

"For us there is only the trying," wrote T. S. Eliot. "The rest is not our business."

SUGGESTIONS

FOR FURTHER READING

Augustine. *Confessions*. Trans. Henry Chadwick. New York: Oxford
University Press, 1991.

Barrett, William. *Death of the Soul: From Descartes to the Computer*.
Garden City, N.Y.: Anchor Books, 1987.

Baudrillard, Jean. *The Transparency of Evil: Essays on Extreme Phenomena*. Trans. James Benedict. London: Verso, 1993.

Becker, Ernest. *The Denial of Death*. New York: Free Press, 1973.

Bellah, Robert et al. *Habits of the Heart: Individualism and Commitment
in American Life*. New York: Harper & Row, 1985.

Bosanquet, Mary. *The Life and Death of Dietrich Bonhoeffer*. New York:
Harper & Row, 1968.

Cotkin, George. *William James, Public Philosopher*. Baltimore: Johns
Hopkins University Press, 1990.

Davies, Paul. *The Mind of God: The Scientific Basis for a Rational World*.
New York: Simon & Schuster, 1992.

Fowler, Robert Booth. *The Dance with Community: The Contemporary
Debate in American Political Thought*. Lawrence, Kans.: University
Press of Kansas, 1991.

Griffith, Sally Foreman. *Home Town News: William Allen White and the Emporia Gazette.* New York: Oxford University Press, 1989.

Hale, John. *The Civilization of Europe in the Renaissance.* New York: Atheneum, 1994.

Hannay, Alastair. *Kierkegaard.* London: Routledge, 1982.

Harvey, David. *The Condition of Postmodernity: An Enquiry into the Origins of Cultural Change.* Cambridge, Mass.: Basil Blackwell, 1989.

Herman, Arthur. *The Idea of Decline in Western History.* New York: Free Press, 1997.

Hillman, James. *A Blue Fire: Selected Writings.* Ed. Thomas Moore. New York: Harper Perennial, 1989.

Hudson, Deal W. *Happiness and the Limits of Satisfaction.* Lanham, Md.: Rowman & Littlefield Publishers, 1996.

Hunt, Morton. *The Story of Psychology.* New York: Doubleday, 1993.

James, William. *The Varieties of Religious Experience: A Study in Human Nature.* New York: Modern Library, 1994.

Johnson, Haynes. *Divided We Fall: Gambling with History in the Nineties.* New York: W. W. Norton, 1994.

Jung, C. G. *Memories, Dreams, Reflections.* Ed. Aniela Jaffé. New York: Vintage, 1989.

Karl, Frederick R. *Modern and Modernism: The Sovereignty of the Artist, 1885–1925.* New York: Atheneum, 1988.

Karp, David A. *Speaking of Sadness: Depression, Disconnection, and the Meanings of Illness.* New York: Oxford University Press, 1996.

Kierkegaard, Søren. *A Kierkegaard Anthology.* Ed. Robert Bretall. New York: Modern Library, 1946.

Klein, Donald F. and Paul H. Wender. *Understanding Depression: A Complete Guide to Its Diagnosis and Treatment.* New York: Oxford University Press, 1993.

Kristeva, Julia. *Black Sun: Depression and Melancholia.* Trans. Leon S. Roudiez. New York: Columbia University Press, 1989.

Lifton, Robert Jay. *The Protean Self: Human Resilience in an Age of Fragmentation.* New York: Basic Books, 1993.

May, Rollo. *Man's Search for Himself.* New York: Delta, 1973.

————. *Freedom and Destiny.* New York: W. W. Norton, 1981.

McClay, Wilfred M. *The Masterless: Self & Society in Modern America.* Chapel Hill: University of North Carolina Press, 1994.

Merton, Thomas. *The Seven Story Mountain.* New York: Harcourt Brace Jovanovich, 1976.

Midgley, Mary. *Science as Salvation: A Modern Myth and Its Meaning.* London: Routledge, 1992.

de Montaigne, Michel. *The Complete Essays of Montaigne.* Trans. Donald M. Frame. Stanford, Calif.: Stanford University Press, 1965.

Moore, Thomas. *Care of the Soul: A Guide for Cultivating Depth and Sacredness in Everyday Life.* New York: HarperCollins, 1992.

Myers, Gerald E. *William James: His Life and Thought.* New Haven, Conn.: Yale University Press, 1986.

Niebuhr, Reinhold. *The Essential Reinhold Niebuhr.* Ed. Robert McAfee Brown. New Haven, Conn.: Yale University Press, 1986.

Pascal, Blaise. *Pensées.* Trans. A. J. Krailsheimer. New York: Penguin, 1995.

Pensky, Max. *Melancholy Dialectics: Walter Benjamin and the Play of Mourning.* Amherst: University of Massachusetts Press, 1993.

Ramsey, Bennett. *Submitting to Freedom: The Religious Vision of William James.* New York: Oxford University Press, 1993.

Rieff, Philip. *The Triumph of the Therapuetic.* Chicago: University of Chicago Press, 1966.

Sandel, Michael J. *Democracy's Discontent: America in Search of a Public Philosophy.* Cambridge: Harvard University Press, 1996.

Scruton, Roger. *Modern Philosophy: An Introduction and Survey.* New York: Penguin, 1995.

Steiner, George. *The Death of Tragedy.* New York: Oxford University Press, 1961.

Stevens, Anthony. *On Jung.* New York: Penguin, 1990.

Stromberg, Roland N. *After Everything: Western Intellectual History Since 1945.* New York: St. Martin's, 1975.

Taylor, Charles. *Sources of the Self: The Making of the Modern Identity.* Cambridge: Harvard University Press, 1989.

————. *The Ethics of Authenticity*. Cambridge: Harvard University Press, 1992.

de Unamuno, Miguel. *The Tragic Sense of Life in Men and Nations*. Trans. Anthony Kerrigan. Bollingen Series LXXXV. Princeton, N.J.: Princeton University Press, 1972.